Lifespan development
Resources, challenges and risks

L ifespan development

Resources, challenges and risks

Leo B. Hendry and Marion Kloep

THOMSON

LEARNING

Australia • Canada • Mexico • Singapore • Spain • United Kingdom • United States

THOMSON

LEARNING

Lifespan development: resources, challenges and risks

Copyright © Leo B. Hendry and Marion Kloep 2002

Thomson Learning™ is a trademark used herein under licence.

For more information, contact Thomson Learning, Berkshire House,
168–173 High Holborn, London, WC1V 7AA or visit us on the World Wide
Web at: http://www.thomsonlearning.co.uk

British Library Cataloguing-in-Publication Data
A catalogue record for this book is available from the British Library

ISBN 1-86152-754-3

First edition published 2002 by Thomson Learning

Typeset by Dexter Haven Associates, London

Printed in Great Britain by The Alden Press, Oxford

C ontents

To all developers across the lifespan –
from little Chloe and Luki to Bob W. and Äti

F igures and tables

Figures

Tables

P reface

This book grew out of a series of planning discussions about university courses for psychology and health science students, and improved through a number of semesters of team teaching and long evening debates, until it was impossible for us to ascertain whose ideas had emerged originally or who eventually proposed any of the theoretical views in any part of the book. So, rather incestuously, we would like to begin by congratulating and thanking each other for the very collaborative way in which the book grew and developed. We would further add a special thanks to the *mellomfag* psychology students at the Norwegian University of Science and Technology, Trondheim, for initially and eagerly discussing the model, and for their useful feedback on the lifespan development courses in which they participated. It is also important to give our thanks to the various people in many different countries who anonymously – and 'in all innocence' – provide the little scenarios that serve as case studies and illustrations of human behaviour and development throughout the book.

Writing a book on lifespan development offered the authors many challenges, including questions like: is the model around which the book is constructed explained sufficiently clearly? Is it over-simplified? Are the supporting empirical studies adequate? Does it have useful insights and explanatory powers? Does it cover the key issues of the life course adequately?

Then, with such challenges come the risks: what will academic colleagues think of the book and the underlying model? Is it a useful book for students in various social-science disciplines? Does it provide any sense of individual empowerment in its central 'message'? Nearly as important, will the book sell anyway?

Fortunately, in meeting these challenges – and trying to avoid too many risks – our resources have been strong and (hopefully) equal to the task, and our support networks have been effective and helpful.

Thus, we would like to thank the Norwegian University of Science and Technology (NTNU) and the Norwegian Centre for Child Research (NOSEB) for giving us sufficient time and space away from teaching commitments in order to write the text, and to Akylina Samara, a doctoral student and part-time assistant at NTNU, for her invaluable help in conducting our literature review.

We are extremely grateful to several international academics who were willing to discuss ideas with us at earlier stages of our thinking and

xii   *Lifespan development*

writing process, and who inspired us to pursue the particular line of argument that we followed throughout the text. These include: Professor Sir Michael Rutter, Professor Glen Elder Jr and Professor Mihaly Csikszentmihalyi, who also kindly agreed to write the foreword. We are also indebted to our friends and colleagues Professor Beatrix Vereijken and Professor Audrey van der Meer (both NTNU) for their insightful suggestions on earlier draft chapters.

Finally, we would like to record our sincere thanks to Anna Faherty (Commissioning Editor at Thomson Learning) for her insightful and timely comments on various drafts of chapters as the book progressed, to the reviewers who sharpened our initial ideas, and to the whole production team at Thomson for converting our ideas into a complete manuscript.

Leo B. Hendry and Marion Kloep, Summer 2001

F oreword   Mihaly Csikszentmihalyi

Most developmental texts are content to summarize previous theories and research, so as to make knowledge about the lifespan easily accessible. Rarely do they provide a novel theoretical perspective of their own. The present volume is a refreshing and ambitious exception. The 'lifespan model of developmental challenge' that informs this volume succeeds in organizing what we know about changes through life in a coherent and meaningful way. Of course, like every good new idea, this one had ancestors: for instance Robert J. Havighurst's concept of 'developmental tasks' is a precursor of the ideas presented here. But nowhere, to my knowledge, has the theme of challenge as a fundamental aspect of development been analyzed so fully and clearly.

Human growth consists in being able to relate to increasingly complex challenges by learning increasingly complex skills. A person whose opportunities for action – or challenges – are restricted will become increasingly apathetic and alienated. One who cannot develop the skills appropriate to handling the opportunities is likely to become stressed, anxious and anomic. Growth is a process of complexification whereby a person is able to relate to more and more subtle aspects of the environment by perfecting his or her inner resources. Not surprisingly, this is also the process that produces the greatest amount of happiness and satisfaction. We are programmed by evolution to enjoy whatever leads to complexity. The subjective side of optimal development is optimal experience.

This was the insight central to Aristotle's concept of *eudaimonia*, the belief that human happiness consists in the fulfilment of one's potentialities. And not only human happiness. As anyone who is a friend to animals knows well, a dog never looks as proud, happy and lively as when it can do what it was bred for: the collie herding, the spaniel retrieving, the kuvasz barking at an intruder. Each organism, each person has capacities that may – or may fail to – engage opportunities in the environment. As life unfolds, new possibilities to use one's skills arise. Those who can take the chances offered at each stage of life and run with them are fortunate indeed.

Using this basically simple framework, Hendry and Kloep have been able to marshal an enormous amount of knowledge about human development into a neatly fitting pattern. What makes this volume special is the systematic review of the various resources that become available to a person as the years go by – in terms of biological maturation, social supports, cognitive and affective resources; as well as the unfolding challenges that physiological changes and social expectations present as a person grows older. As the modernist architect Mies van der Rohe used to say, 'God is in the details' – and it is the vivid, dense and orderly details that make this book not only exciting, but conceptually satisfying.

Perhaps my reading of this book is overly value-laden. If so, I apologize to the authors, who may not have intended the work to be interpreted in this fashion. My view, however, is that it is time for psychology – and especially developmental psychology – to abandon the extreme value-free stance that has characterized the discipline for so long. It seems to me that it is fine to be goaded by 'physics-envy' if that leads us to more rigorous theories and observations. But it is ridiculous to pretend that we need to be neutral as to the substance of our studies. Geologists study the earth's crust with a firm belief that earthquakes are bad and oil deposits are good. Microbiologists are well aware of the difference between normal and cancerous cells. Even physics started in response to the need to use levers to move weights, and to distribute water over cultivated fields. And half a century ago physicists were again rudely reminded that the results of their research could not exist in an abstract vacuum, but had to be somehow reconciled with the priority of survival. Psychology (with the notable exception of its clinical branches) has by-and-large resisted assigning value to the phenomena it studies, and has been impoverished as a result. Of course, the infusion of values in the human sciences is always a dangerous move. If done with prejudice, it can lead to all sorts of mischief. That is why the direction this book takes is so promising – it offers a paradigm securely anchored in objective science, while at the same time suggesting a perspective from which sound and humane values to help interpret the data can be derived. It is the direction psychology should be heading for in this new century.

Mihaly Csikszentmihalyi
Claremont, 2001

Mihaly Csikszentmihalyi is the C.S. and D.J. Davidson Professor of Psychology at the Drucker School of Management of Claremont Graduate University, and Director of the Quality of Life Research Center.

1 Lifespan development

Prologue

Why does the sweet baby of six months turn into a sweet babe of sixteen with many suitors, or into a pimply, unwashed youth painting his bedroom totally black? Later, why does the cherubic, golden-haired young man of twenty-six, driving his MG down the high street, become the boring, bald-headed forty-five-year-old manager of an insurance firm? Or why does the brightest young woman in the psychology class give up her career and have a set of twins between thirty-something and forty? Why did the psychologist and the manager marry anyway? Now that the children have grown up and left home, why do they find life so boring? How would their (separate) lives alter if they were to divorce? Well, she has gone to Mexico and married a much younger national, and is teaching him to speak English in order that he can go to university some day. Her former husband finds his life a mess without her, and drowns his lonely evenings in litres of beer in front of the TV. How could that happen? Further, why does a middle-aged widow suddenly embark on a romantic holiday adventure with a great bear of a man, when she would not even socialize with him if she met him in her home-town? Why do her grown-up children resent this kind of liaison so much at a time in their lives when they themselves have nothing but sex on their minds? What kind of old age might they all experience? Active? Conventional? Adventurous? Boring?

What's your guess?

Then if we consider more traditional cultures, and look at examples of the life course there, we get quite a different set of scenarios from those in Western societies described above. What happens to the sixth child of a Thai woman whose first baby was conceived when she was a teenager of fifteen? Does the baby, as she grows up, become a street child, failing to go to school? Is she adopted by a rich Swedish family, never to meet her biological family again, or does she begin by selling fruit in a local street market, open her own shop from her earnings and become a merchant exporting exotic fruit to Europe? Does an Indian girl look forward to meeting her older husband (arranged by her parents when she was three) now that she is sixteen? What about the Albanian man of thirty, who was in his youth a member of the Communist Party, and is now an entrepreneurial capitalist? Will he comply with the continual requests from his mother to return home to work in Albania and 'marry a nice Albanian girl' after having lived in the West for ten years, sending money home to support his parents? Why does the daughter of a Mexican professor, aged thirty, run away from her patriarchal father and end up pregnant to a married lover in the capital city of her country, knowing he will never marry her? And why has the son of her maid married a much older European divorcee?

Again, what's your guess?

Are the mechanisms of development the same for people in different cultures, or do we need a set of cross-cultural theories to explain different life trajectories in different parts of the world?

Furthermore, what about inter-generational similarities and differences? Imagine for a moment the successful female surgeon, divorced, with two children, talking to her grandmother, who has all her life been a faithful wife and mother of five, about today's ecological concerns, about free sex and serial romantic relationships, abortion, large families, body piercing or cosmetic surgery. What values would they share? Where would they differ? Will the surgeon's children lead a life that is similar to their grandmother's, or even that of their mother's? Or, consider the retired mining worker who started his career when he was fourteen years of age, meeting up with his thirty-year-old grandson, who cannot decide if he should continue his university study for the legal profession or go on a world trip first. Will they share the same values when they discuss women, politics or the state of the world?

More personally, do you know what your grandparents think about the way life is lived today by young people? If so, do you agree with their values? As a pop group, do you prefer Red Hot Chili Peppers or the Beatles? Imagine for a moment that you had been young at the time when your grandparents were in their early twenties: would you have led the same life, held the same values? Or looking into the future: do you think that your grandchildren will have the same values, preferences and lifestyle as you? Would you want them to have these anyway? How is it possible that members of the same family can have such different lives and value systems across time?

Thus, are the mechanisms of development the same across generations, or are they required to follow the broader changes occurring in society and society's changing values? Does a 'post-modern' child develop differently from a 'traditional' one? Do we need different developmental psychologies for every new generation's life transitions?

What do you think?

A rationale for understanding lifespan development

We cannot promise to answer all the specific questions posed above in this book, but we can promise that you will be able to achieve a clearer understanding of these lifespan issues and challenges, and the effects of different cultures on the ways they are resolved by individuals during their life course. In the advanced, rapidly changing, technological societies of the West, an extended lifespan has become a recent phenomenon, against which the more restricted life course of those, for example, living in poverty and malnutrition in the rest of the world form a sharp contrast: about two thirds of the world's population will never reach the last (or even penultimate) age stage discussed by Western lifespan researchers such as Erikson (1959)! Moreover, cultural and material differences between the technological, industrial societies and traditional cultures have stirred an interest in cross-cultural issues of human development. Differences in the life trajectories between, and within, cultures due to a global tendency of de-standardization of the life course, together with the necessity of lifelong learning, has brought about a very real need to understand the whole developmental process from birth to death in a variety of cultural settings. It is no longer regarded as sufficient to consider and explain development in terms of childhood and adolescence, or simply to assume that 'the child is the progenitor of the adult', and leave it at that! There are too many connecting threads that run through the life course from birth to death and, while research has just begun to explore these inter-connections, there are currently sufficient evidence and ideas to offer a framework of interpretation and understanding of the whole life course.

The framework for the book

In order to begin looking at some of these issues, we start by looking at the theories of other scholars in chapter 2. In the past, reviewers have been quick to outline differences among developmental theories. We take an alternative approach, and show that there are, in fact, several commonalities in the views of different important developmentalists and social theorists. These similarities, selected from various authors, become the building blocks for our own holistic model, which we believe can provide a framework for analyzing development across time and place, and also account for individual differences.

We present the developmental challenge model in chapter 3, and examine its key elements. This chapter is followed by one (chapter 4) that introduces the notions of 'normative', 'quasi-normative' and 'non-normative changes' during the lifespan, and explores the different kinds of shifts or 'turning processes' in the individual's life. In chapter 5, two 'non-normative' shifts, namely divorce and economic crisis, are described extensively, together with their implications for individuals and their psycho-social systems, to illustrate the uses of the developmental challenge model in explaining aspects of the life course.

Chronological age as an insufficient marker of life phases

It is difficult to determine, with any clarity, when adolescence really begins. Is it at the onset of puberty? If so, then many young women begin adolescence at eight or nine years of age. Then, does it terminate when all the maturational changes associated with puberty are completed? If so, then many young men and women do not end their adolescent years until their early to mid-twenties. In some societies, puberty marks the transition from childhood to adulthood. Can we use a biological marker such as this to determine adolescence? If so, we could make the mistake of forgetting the 'child in an adult body', someone who could be less mature and may not have the social skills and strategies, or emotional capabilities in tune with their early developed physique. Given the varying social signposts with which young people are presented by adult society on their way to adult status, can we consider as the end of adolescence the time of normative change, at which the individual acquires adult rights and responsibilities? If so, we are left with the task of deciding what are the appropriate rights and responsibilities to choose. In Scotland, one can marry at sixteen, but not ride a motorbike or be tattooed till seventeen; one can leave school at sixteen to start a job or join the military to fight for Queen and country, but not vote till eighteen. Within this problematic categorization of adult status, certain cultures have established different 'rites of passage' to acknowledge the transitions towards adulthood. For example, in Latin American countries, the fifteenth birthday (quinze años) is a significant social event, at which girls wear white 'bridal' gowns, whereas in Scandinavia, and in certain churches in the UK, 'confirmation' is seen as a public marker of approaching adulthood. A similar social ceremony, the so-called Jugendweihe (a civic 'blessing' of mid-adolescents), was carried out in the former German Democratic Republic (and in some regions still exists). In Germany, even the name Reifeprüfung ('maturity exam') suggests that this high school leaving certificate is a public licence to adulthood.

Thus adolescence is a mainly normative transition – though puberty is maturational. If we, on the other hand, consider adolescence to cover transitions through the teenage years – until the young person gains full legal independence from his or her parents – women in some countries, for example Morocco, would never be seen to reach full adulthood. Further, these processes interact so that each and every teenager experiences them differently. If that is obvious for adolescence, it is also true at other points of the life course. Retirement was usually taken at sixty-five in most Western countries, but in the last decade or so the range now often runs from the mid-fifties to seventy years of age. In some more traditional societies there is simply no retirement age: one works as long as one can or wants to, and then hopes to be cared for by the extended family. Equally, becoming pregnant, whilst being most usual in the late twenties, can actually happen from soon after puberty begins till the menopause (or in recent times, with the aid of medical science, even into later phases of the lifespan).

The significant point we are trying to make is that in lifespan development, age definitions are not helpful in understanding the challenges and risks of the life course. Hence, we are aware that there are many overlapping categories of life phases, events and shifts, and so in each chapter we select and analyze shifts that most often occur within a particular age range, but are in no way necessarily restricted to that particular period. For example, parenthood and its various implications could be discussed either under young adulthood or mid-life, while it also has repercussions for late adulthood and old age. Thus definitions are always imprecise, and that is why we do not even try to put chronological age limits on the life phases we outline here.

Thereafter, the book examines a series of life challenges, together with the risks involved, and their effects on the individual's resource 'pool', at various broad life periods from childhood through adolescence to adulthood and old age.

At this point, we want to emphasize that we do not regard chronological age as the transitional marker from one life phase to another, as many books on lifespan development do (see box above). We consider such a division too simplistic by far in modern societies, and choose instead to draw broad categories for the relative shifts common to particular times in the life course.

In chapter 6, we describe childhood development by discussing the developmental tasks of having to learn the variety of psycho-motor skills that are the foundation of further development – including other interactional competencies, such as relating to adults and peers, coping with the transition to school, and learning meta-skills. Adolescence, discussed in chapter 7, is a time of many maturational and social transitions that lead into early adulthood. We chose to exemplify the mechanisms of our model by describing the social implications of becoming an adult and gaining adult status, together with an examination of puberty and first romantic and sexual relationships. Then the discussion moves on to the relatively 'free' situation of early adulthood, in which there are few normative constraints on lifestyle choices because the de-standardization of the life course in Western societies leaves individuals with the possibilities – but also the stresses – of many life options to choose from. By contrast, in more traditional societies the clear-cut set of roles and rules that govern the lives of young adults provides them with a sense of security and conformity, unknown in the West. The following chapter, dealing with middle adulthood, is concerned with such topics as: parenthood, adult children leaving home, work, career and the challenges arising from unemployment, and the role of leisure. Chapter 9 describes the challenges that occur most often in later adulthood. These focus mainly on coping with the signs of ageing, the menopause, retirement and the experiences of becoming a grandparent. The social construction of old age is discussed in chapter 10, along with the challenges that accompany bereavement, changes in one's social network and declining bodily abilities. Finally, in chapter 11, we review the developmental challenge model for its usefulness in understanding cross-culturally the processes of successfully meeting challenges across the lifespan. Development is the major and positive emphasis throughout the book, with a focus on individual resilience and growth.

2 Theories of development

Introduction

From the beginnings of scientific thought, human development and change has always excited the minds of scholars. Earlier theorists have explored aspects of development, and have provoked later commentators and authors to address, emphasize and discuss the differences in these explanations and models. By contrast, this chapter considers the similarities among various theories on development in order to provide a 'framework of commonality' that leads us into the presentation of an integrated model which can offer an inter-cultural and inter-generational understanding of lifespan development.

Hence, the present chapter offers a brief description of the theoretical ideas of such writers as Freud, Piaget, Levinson, Erikson, Vygotsky, Skinner, Bronfenbrenner, Elder and Baltes to highlight the common ideas of 'development in its cultural context' in these apparently different theories. From this distillation of similar elements, the next chapter will develop an explanatory model of lifespan development, the 'model of developmental challenge', emerging from the ideas of these theorists.

Some earlier theoretical perspectives

Obviously we are not the first authors to attempt to explain and interpret human development. In this section we describe how a number of theorists analyze various aspects of development, and we extract and extend the common elements in their writings in order to provide a base-line for our own theoretical framework.

In looking at the ways different theorists describe development, it is fairly obvious that almost all theories include an element of challenge that occurs when the individual attempts to meet the demands of living, and that development occurs when this challenge is successfully met. Equally, most theories suggest that problems appear for the individual if the challenge is not successfully met. The kind of challenge, its origin and how it is described varies between theories, but the mechanisms of challenge appear to be the same in all cases.

Sigmund Freud (1856–1939)

Psychological change is governed by biological maturation and social forces. The child has innate needs ('id') that are sometimes in opposition to the social environment. By confronting the social limits to its needs, the child develops the ability to reason and to find realistic means of gratifying instincts ('ego'). Further, it learns to internalize the social demands and develops a conscience ('super-ego'). To achieve a harmonic balance among these three components of personality, the child goes through five stages of development (i.e. a discontinuous process). Each stage has its own conflicts between the child's needs and the social environment (including its parents). How the child experiences and resolves the conflicts influences its personality growth and its patterns of behaviour in later life. Specifically, these psycho-sexual stages are:

- Oral stage (up to one year of age). The needs are centred around the mouth, as in feeding, sucking, chewing and biting. Conflicts happen around weaning, feeding times and type of food.
- Anal stage (one to three years). The needs are centred around urination and defecation, and conflicts arise during toilet-training.
- Phallic stage (three to six years). Needs develop now in relation to sexual stimulation. Boys develop an incestuous desire for their mother ('Oedipus complex'), and girls for their father ('Electra complex'), which makes them a rival to the same-sex parent and results in a series of conflicts that finally lead to identification with this parent.
- Latency stage (six to eleven years). The sexual urges are now repressed, and the child concentrates on education and concern for others.
- Genital stage (from twelve years onward). Sexual needs, selfish and altruistic love now become balanced, the need for reproduction of the species leads to adult relationships being formed.

Freud (1905, 1938), for example, described how the developing child moves through different psycho-sexual stages, such as 'the oral stage' or 'the genital stage', which have to be resolved and, in doing so, experiences clashes between its own desires and the demands of society (see box above). There is healthy development if the individual succeeds in mastering these stages, otherwise 'fixations' can occur which lead to problems of neuroticism later in life. Throughout the life course, the individual experiences conflicts between personal needs and social constraints, which the 'healthy' individual solves by sublimating them in a productive way, while the 'neurotic' one uses more-or-less effective 'defence mechanisms' to cope.

Similarly, Erikson (1959) postulated a series of 'crises' throughout the lifespan (see box below). These crises involve certain psycho-social demands, like developing trust vs distrust, identity formation vs identity diffusion, or generativity vs stagnation, which the individual has to cope with at different age stages. According to Erikson, successful progress through these life stages from childhood into adulthood is the precondition for a satisfactory old age. Initially studying only men, Levinson (Levinson *et al.* 1978) also made the assumption that lifespan development occurs through the individual having to deal with specific life events within broad age stages, which he called 'eras'. Success in coping with relevant life challenges within one era, such as early adulthood, is seen as the basis for transition to the next life era. Using more concrete examples, Havighurst (1972) describes how various 'developmental tasks' at different periods of life – like orienting to a career, or developing more adult, intimate relationships – are the challenges that guide development.

Erik H. Erikson (1902–94)

During the entire lifespan, individuals develop by meeting a sequence of personal and social tasks that need to be accomplished for further development. Each of them causes a 'crisis' in individuals, until they have learned ways of coping with them. These challenges appear at certain points in the life course, hence development is discontinuous, in stages, but lifelong. These psycho-social stages are as follows:

- Infancy (up to one year of age). The task is to develop trust (in contrast to mistrust) towards others.
- Early childhood (one to three years). The task is to learn self-control and autonomy (in contrast to shame and doubt about one's abilities).
- Play age (three to six years). The task is to develop personal initiative in mastering the environment and to keep a balance between one's own and others' needs (in contrast to feeling guilty about a conflict of interests).
- School age (six to twelve years). The task is to develop industry and self-assurance (in contrast to feelings of inferiority).
- Adolescence (twelve to twenty years). The task is to establish a social, sexual and occupational identity (in contrast to role confusion).
- Young adulthood (twenty to forty years). The task is to achieve intimacy with others and to form mature friendships and love relationships (in contrast to social isolation).
- Middle adulthood (forty to sixty-five years). The task is to express oneself through generativity, that is leaving something of value for the next generation, either by raising children or by making creative work contributions (in contrast to stagnation).
- Old age (over 65 years). The task is to achieve a sense of integrity by evaluating one's life positively (without despair and bitterness).

In their work, these writers are in agreement in describing development as successfully dealing with life demands. However, they all choose typical developmental challenges contained in Western societies as the 'tasks' or 'crises' that stimulate development. Few similar theories describing development in other cultures have made their way into Western textbooks.

One exception to this is Vygotsky (1930). Coming from another culture, he puts emphasis not only on the challenges an individual encounters, but also on the number and kind of resources available to meet them. He particularly stresses the importance of intellectual tools (this is similar to the idea of meta-skills, which we discuss in detail in chapter 11). These could be strategies such as language memory aids, numerical systems or scientific concepts, which are used by different cultures as resources for solving tasks in learning and developing. Hence, Vygotsky lays great emphasis on the interaction between intellectual challenges and personal resources. Crucial to his ideas is the 'distance' between the actual developmental level of an individual and the level of potential development. This he calls the 'zone of proximal development', in which the distance can be reduced by utilizing the resources of others in a teaching–learning relationship. Vygotsky also considers that there is a dynamic interaction between intrinsic developmental and cultural forces that produces new transformations. These are 'critical phases' that mark the transition to more stable periods. Thus, Vygotsky sees development as a dialectic process. Put simply, like the Western theorists, he postulates that there has to be some kind of challenge in order for development to occur.

Focussing mainly on cognitive development, Piaget (1964) also assumes that development is an active, dialectical construction process in which individuals build increasingly differentiated and comprehensive cognitive structures by trying to make sense of their environment (see box below). Experiences that promote cognitive development usually place an individual in a state of conflict. If a task cannot simply be solved with the help of existing cognitive structures, a new structure has to be created in order to recreate cognitive equilibrium. This happens either by 'assimilation' – new objects or information are added into our cognitive structures – or by 'accommodation' – changes in our cognitive structures have to be made in order for new experiences to be fitted in. Piaget called this model of developmental change 'equilibration'.

J. Piaget (1896–80)

Cognitive skills are necessary in adapting to the environment. The vital 'cognitive structures' evolve through assimilation (absorption of new experiences into an already existing cognitive framework or 'schema') and accommodation (modifying existing schemata by incorporating new experiences which do not fit into old schemata – thereby causing a 'disequilibrium'). In this way, children actively construct a new understanding of the world by interacting with it. This understanding becomes increasingly complex as children pass through the four stages of cognitive development:

- Sensorimotor stage (up to two years). Children explore their environment, using their senses and their developing psycho-motor skills. They learn that objects are separate and permanent, and develop a sense of themselves as independent beings.
- Preoperational stage (two to seven years). Children use symbolism (language and images) to understand the environment. Thus they gain a sense of present, past and future. Furthermore, they pre-plan actions. However, their view of the world is still characterized by egocentrism: they consider experiences mainly from their own perspective.
- The stage of concrete operations (seven to eleven years). Children acquire cognitive skills that enable them to understand relationships among objects and other people's views of the world. They also gain the ability to simultaneously co-ordinate two perspectives in making judgements and begin to reason deductively.
- The stage of formal operations (over eleven years). Thought is now systematic, logical and abstract, meta-cognitive skills evolve and multiple problem-solving is possible.

The idea that a crisis is needed to promote development is even more pronounced in the work of Riegel (1979) on dialectical psychology :

> Developmental leaps are brought about by lack of coordination and synchrony. Rather than regarding these critical episodes in a negative manner or from a fatalistic point of view, they provide the fundamental basis for the development of the individual and for the history of society.... A dialectical interpretation of development and aging...does not emphasize the plateaus at which equilibrium or balance is achieved. Development rather consists in continuing changes along several dimensions of progression at the same time. Critical changes occur whenever two sequences are out of step, that is when coordination fails and synchronization breaks down. These contradictions are the basis for developmental progressions. Stable plateaus of balance, stability, and equilibrium occur when a developmental or historical task is completed. But developmental and historical tasks are never completed [p.13].

In other words, the essence of these models could be described as seeing development as the dynamic interaction of various challenges with the individual's existing resources.

One of the common issues in developmental psychology is whether the process of development is determined by maturation, and is innate, or whether the individual chooses actively to seek for challenges to overcome. In this debate, the writings of humanistic psychologists such as Rogers (1961) and Maslow (1970) advocate powerfully the idea of free will. Maslow, for example, describes how the individual actively seeks out a resolution of needs in a progressive manner. For example, once the basic drives of hunger, security and affiliation are met, the individual is capable of moving on towards the ultimate human goal of self-actualization. Thus, only when all basic survival resources are in place is the individual ready to meet further challenges. The idea that a multiplicity of resources is vital in order to progress further in development – though not necessarily the ones Maslow proposes – is an important assumption that we will come back to in the next chapter.

B.F. Skinner (1905–90)

Learning theory assumes that development is the result of learning experiences that are continuous and lifelong. By operant conditioning, actions (that might occur by chance, as a result of trial and error, or through imitation) which lead to favourable outcomes will be repeated, while actions that lead to unfavourable outcomes will be suppressed. Outcomes that produce an augmentation of behaviour are called 'reinforcers'. Reinforcers can be primary, meaning that they have 'natural' reinforcement qualities (such as food, warmth or sex); or they can be 'secondary', meaning that they have acquired their reinforcement qualities through association with other reinforcers (such as money, praise or attention).

The learning of new responses falls into one of two categories:

1. When a situation is recognized as being similar to a previously experienced situation, individuals tend to respond in a way similar to one that has been successful previously ('generalization').
2. When a situation is perceived as being different from a previously experienced one, individuals learn to respond in a way which is more appropriate for this new situation, i.e. responses that have previously been successful in other situations do not work in this one, so a new response has to be implemented ('discrimination').

To illustrate with an example: a little boy has learned that red fruit (like cherries, apples and tomatoes) taste good to eat. One day he finds a red fruit that he has never seen before on the kitchen table. How will he react to it? He might respond with generalization (i.e. objects like this one have tasted nice before), so the appropriate behaviour is to eat it. If he does, and finds it tasty, he has added another 'known' stimulus to his repertoire. Now let us assume that what he gets is the burning taste of eating a chili pepper, which he finds not at all rewarding. He will spit it out and will have learned discrimination: this kind of red 'fruit' is not tasty and should not be eaten. Hence, in the process of meeting these challenges and reacting to them, he has learned something, and thus has 'developed'. Note here how similar the notions of 'discrimination' and 'generalization' are to Piaget's concepts of 'accommodation' and 'assimilation'.

Coming seemingly from a totally different ideological stance, Skinner (1938), as a leading representative of behaviourism, sees development as the same as learning, where learning is defined as a lasting change in behaviour (see box above). The individual meets new situations and new stimuli every day. By various means (e.g. trial and error, imitation and instruction, or by sheer luck and coincidence) individuals find ways of responding to these challenges. If the response turns out to be successful (i.e. is 'reinforced'), that behaviour is added to the individual's behaviour repertoire, and learning (development) has occurred. Skinner's theory is also an 'interactive' one. Already in 1957, as a precursor to modern dialectical and ecological thinking, he stated in the opening sentence of his book *Verbal Behavior*: 'Men act upon the world, and change it, and are changed in turn by the consequences of their action' (p.1).

Thus, the common denominator for all these apparently different developmental theories is that individuals meet (or seek out) some form of task/challenge/crisis/stimulus that 'forces' them to act, and successful solution in interacting with the task leads to strengthened resources, i.e. development.

Some current theories of development

More recent theories have emphasized this interaction to an even higher degree. As one of the foremost ecological theorists of development, Bronfenbrenner (1979) regards the individual's total social environment as 'the contexts of development'. Apart from the immediate contexts in which the individual exists, such as his or her family or peer group (i.e. the micro-systems, see figure 2.1), there are other influences. For example, if members of one micro-system (e.g. parents) interact with members of another micro-system (e.g. schoolteachers), this will have indirect effects on the development of the child (e.g. the child might then be confronted with conflicting values about schooling). Interactions of members of different micro-systems with each other occur in the meso-system. (Analyze, for instance, your own micro-systems: how important is the relationship between your partner and your parents for yourself?)

Furthermore, people within one's micro-systems are themselves affected by persons outside of these micro-systems (e.g. parents and their working colleagues): this is called the exo-system. These interactions also have indirect effects on the developing individual.. (To take an example from your personal life again: have you noticed any differences in your best friend's behaviour towards you depending on the state of his or her love life?)

Finally, the wider culture, laws and norms of the particular society in which the individual lives all have a powerful influence at all levels (i.e. the macro-system) (see figure 2.1).

The 'ecological' key to Bronfenbrenner's theory is not the division of influential environments into systems, but his claim that the interactive influences are multidirectional. Individuals affect the surrounding systems as, in turn, they are affected by the systems, so that 'the characteristics of the person function both as an indirect producer and as a product of development' (Bronfenbrenner and Morris, 1998: p.996). At the same time the various systems are also interdependent on each other – affecting and being affected. Development is not something that just 'happens' to the individual person, but an interactive, dynamic process that involves all the system levels of a society.

As an example, a new-born child affects its parents at least to the same extend as they influence their baby. Consequently, it is not only the child that develops, but also the whole micro-system, and while this particular micro-system changes, other interacting systems (like the parents' workplace, their social network, and even the childcare policies of the country) can be affected as well.

Hence, this ecological view is a more sophisticated extension of several of the theories discussed above, in which the individual is simply regarded as concentrating on a few substantial developmental

Figure 2.1   Examples of interactions according to Bronfenbrenner's theory

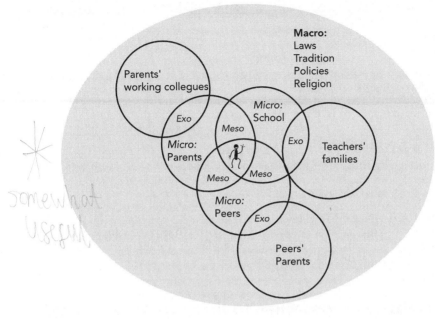

tasks in a one-to-one interaction. In contradistinction, Bronfenbrenner emphasizes the multi-layered interaction of various systems. This idea can also be found in the 'person-context-theory' presented by Magnusson and Stattin (1998). They emphasize the interactive processes evolving within the individual as well:

> According to a modern interactionist perspective, here designated holistic interactionism, psychological events reflect aspects of two types of inter-active processes: (a) the continuously ongoing, bidirectional processes of interaction between the person and his or her environment, and (b) the continuously ongoing processes of reciprocal interaction between mental, biological, and behavioural factors within the individual [p.694].

Similarly, from the stance of dynamic system theory, Valsiner (1997) discusses development as an interactive dynamic process:

> Biological, psychological, and social systems are open, and open (not closed) systems are capable of development. This important feature of develop-mental phenomena – their open system nature – leads to the necessity for all developmental research to be systemic and ecological; it has to study the target object interdependently with its environment [p.24].

Within Valsiner's framework (as in Bronfenbrenner's), there are four major kinds of environmental change that interact with the process of development:

- those that the individual's own actions produce
- those that people around the individual create
- those that are instigated by social groups on a higher societal level
- those that are caused by uncontrollable events (e.g. natural disasters).

Thus, the environment is dynamic, as it undergoes constant changes, and so is the process of the individual's development within it. Further, Valsiner emphasizes the role that conflict plays in development, promoting the idea of a 'goodness of misfit' by proposing different kinds of conflicts, one leading to the emergence of novel states and the other to breakdown:

> If we try to explain the process of development by way of oppositions (and conflict), the oppositional parts of the same whole need to be related in ways that lead to construction of novel organizational form, rather than to the breakdown of the whole. So we would argue that there are two kinds of conflict (from the perspective of development): good conflict (an oppositional relationship between parts of a developing system that leads to the emergence of novel states of that system) and bad conflicts (the clash or war of exclusively competing opposites that devastate each other, thus leading to the extinction of the whole in which they are parts) [Valsiner and Cairns, 1992: p.32].

Unfortunately, and in spite of his criticism of developmental psychology often being treated synonymously with child psychology, Valsiner himself (1997) concentrates all the examples of his theory within child development (as does Bronfenbrenner).

Theoretical approaches to lifespan development

One of the modern pioneers of life course theory is, without doubt, Glen Elder Jr. Inspired by the findings of his study *Children of the Great Depression* (1974), he developed a new way of looking at social change, life pathways and individual development as modes of behavioural continuity and change. In detail, he proposes the following four principles of life course theory (Elder, 1997, 1998):

- The principle of historical time and place. The life course of individuals is embedded in, and shaped by, the historical times and places they experience through their lifetime.
- The principle of timing in lives. The developmental impact of a succession of life transitions or events is contingent upon when they occur in a person's life.
- The principle of linked lives. Lives are lived interdependently, and social and historical influences are expressed through this network of shared relationships.
- The principle of human agency. Individuals construct their own life course through the choices and actions they take within the opportunities and constraints of history and social circumstances.

To summarize, Elder (1997), as all the others, sees the importance of 'life transitions' (i.e. challenges) in shaping development: 'People bring a life history of personal experiences and dispositions to each transition, interpret the new circumstances in terms of this history, and work out lines of adaptation that can fundamentally alter their life course' (p.957).

In contradistinction to earlier scholars, however, Elder does not want to focus certain events on certain age stages, but regards them, as well as the individuals' differential reactions to them, as a function of historical period, place and time during the life course. Furthermore, in line with Bronfenbrenner's (1979) ecological model, he emphasizes the inter-dependence of life courses within the same micro-systems. Extensive research during the last 20 years lends a strong body of empirical support to his principles of development.

At around the same time as Elder was working out his theories in the US, Baltes and his colleagues (e.g. Baltes and Goulet, 1970; Baltes, Reese and Lipsitt, 1980) in Germany began to elaborate their particular approach to lifespan developmental psychology. The four central tenets of this approach, as outlined by Smith and Baltes (1999) are:

- to provide a framework for understanding the overall structures and sequence of development across the lifespan
- to encourage research on the interconnections between earlier and later developmental events and processes
- to identify mechanisms that underlie life course (age) trajectories
- to specify the biological and cultural factors that facilitate and con-strain lifespan development and the ageing process of individuals.

As the term suggests, lifespan theory postulates that development extends across the entire life course, and that lifelong adaptive processes are involved. Apart from a certain temporal priority of earlier events in life, changes can have the same powerful impact on development through-out the lifespan (Smith and Baltes, 1999). Each age period is expected to have its own developmental agenda, and both continuous (cumulative) and discontinuous (innovative) developmental processes occur.

Similarly to Elder, Baltes and his colleagues claim that development is embedded in larger historical and cultural contexts. They distinguish three sources of contextual influences: normative age-graded influences, normative history-graded influences, and non-normative influences (Baltes, Reese and Lipsitt, 1980) (and we will return to this categorization in chapter 4).

Furthermore, Baltes (1987) postulates the concept of multidirectionality, emphasizing, on the one hand, that development always involves losses as well as gains and, on the other, that developmental changes do not have to proceed synchronously across, or within, domains of functioning. Losses, deficits and limitations are seen as serving as catalysts for positive change, because they cause the individual and/or the environment to respond. Thus, they can bring about an adaptive capacity. Successful development is, accordingly, defined as the 'maximization of gains and the minimization of losses' (Baltes, Lindenberger and Staudinger, 1997). Finally, there is the basic concept of plasticity, referring to 'within-person variability' as an indication of the individual's latent potential for different levels of functioning. A distinction is made between 'base-line reserve capacity', which identifies the current level of plasticity available to individuals, and 'developmental reserve capacity', which is aimed at specifying what is possible (in principle) if optimizing interventions are employed (Baltes, Lindenberger and Staudinger, 1997). These ideas presented for ongoing development in old age appear to be very similar to Vygotsky's 'zone of proximal development' in child development.

The resources an individual possesses are, according to Baltes (1997), allocated differently across the lifespan. In early life, they are allocated to functions associated with growth (reaching higher levels of functioning). During adulthood, they are directed towards maintenance (sustaining normal levels of functioning in the face of contextual challenge or a loss in potential). In later old age they are allocated to the regulation of loss when maintenance or recovery are no longer possible. In this context, individuals seem to prefer avoidance of loss rather than enhancement of gains. Tentatively, Baltes, Lindenberger and Staudinger (1997) suggest a model of development involving a selection (of developmental goals), optimization (generating and activating goal-related resources) and compensation (functional responses to the environmental or age-related loss of goal-related resources). This is an important set of ideas in relation to the developmental challenge model (see the next chapter, and there is a discussion of these issues at greater length in chapters 10 and 11).

In summary: for Baltes, development is the result of the successful confrontation with contextual life challenges and/or losses and deficits. What exactly these challenges are, and how they will impinge on the individual, will vary with context, age and culture. Whether or not they are met successfully is dependent on a wide range of factors, amongst others on the adaptive capacity of individuals. As with other scholars, Baltes and his team see a challenge as a necessary trigger to development. This challenge, however, does not have to originate in the individual's social environment. It can also be a loss of function or a deficit in the individual that calls for action and, thus, possible growth and development. In agreement with Elder, development is described as a lifelong, dynamic process of interaction.

Conclusions

Having seen how these theories have built towards an understanding of lifespan development in an ecological, historical, multidirectional and multifaceted way, we now move on to summarize their common key elements. Throughout the book these will emerge as the cornerstones of a holistic model of human lifespan development, applicable within and across historical times and cultural settings. We are, of course, not oblivious to the fact that the theories we refer to briefly above have many more differences than similarities. Nevertheless, the aim is to distil – admittedly simplifying – and emphasize similarities in order to find what might be the core features of the process of human development that emerge from the separate theories presented above.

We suggest the following elements as the key principles:

1. There needs to be a challenge (task, crisis, stimulus, loss) to stimulate development.
2. Development occurs through the successful solving of this challenge.
3. 'Unsuccessful' solving of a challenge leads to some kinds of problem in meeting future challenges.
4. Solving challenges is an interactional, dialectical process that leads to changes either in the environment, in the individual, or both, and thereby stimulates development.
5. Individuals have differing amounts of resources to meet challenges.

There are other similarities among the theories we have mentioned, such as the importance of security and the preponderance of early learning, which will appear within subsequent chapters of the book.

At this stage we need to admit that many of the theoretical contradictions among the various theorists cannot be integrated into one all-embracing eclectic framework. Plato and Aristotle could not agree; neither were the ideas of Skinner and Maslow compatible, and we do not attempt to square this circle. There were, and are, substantial philosophical and scientific differences between different theoretical schools of thought that cannot be ignored. For instance, how can the ideas of stage-wise, discontinuous development and notions of continuous progress be combined? Or how can the concept that development is completed by early adulthood be set against claims that development is lifelong? How can we resolve the dilemma that many developmental theories claim to be universal, but do, in general, only fit white Western middle-class males of the twentieth century?

The answer is that here we end our diplomatic eclecticism and choose a side to join in the theoretical debate. The position we select originates from the ideas of life-course theory that have evolved since the 1960s. With this, we join a growing trend within the social sciences that possibly emerges in response to the rapid changes that are taking place in modern society. As Buchmann (1989) suggests: 'The emergence of the ideology of life as a continuous development process, which only ends with one's death, can partially be interpreted as modern culture's response to contradictory developments in the social structure' (Buchmann, 1989: p.63).

Hence, in the following chapter we introduce the lifespan model of developmental challenge, which has as its foundation some of the major elements of the theories we have described above: the idea that lifelong individual development results from the dynamic interactions between potential challenges and individual resources within the ecological context of different psycho-social systems.

3 Introducing the lifespan model of developmental challenge

Introduction

Picture for a moment a young woman poring over a textbook in her bedroom, preparing for the exams that will take her to an English university; a child trying to write its first words with a pencil; an Argentine mother preparing an evening meal for her family; a middle-aged woman deciding to leave her husband of 20 years; an old man considering moving from Norway to Spain in order to enjoy the benefits of a warmer climate.

In all these scenarios we can perceive the idea of someone meeting a life challenge in order to survive and progress. This can be a big episode in one's life – like the clash between individuals' needs and the psycho-social demands of adjusting to the norms of a particular society, which at least temporarily leads to a crisis (as Erikson's theory proposes). Alternatively, it can be a very small challenge, like an unknown stimulus that does not yet exist in the individual's schemata (Piaget), such as a child experiencing snow for the first time in its life; or a stimulus to which the individual has not yet learned to respond in an appropriate way (Skinner), as when someone has been given a new computer but does not know how to operate it. Thus, it is clear that the individual will, in one way or the other, respond to a presented challenge, and by doing so will change as an individual. To some extent, how tasks are resolved as we grow up and mature through the lifespan will influence how we cope with the rest of our lives, and, with increasing age, will create greater differences between individuals. What this implies has to do with whether the task is met successfully or unsuccessfully, and this in turn depends on the resources an individual possesses. Hence, development means dealing with the large and small challenges that we meet in our life from day to day, and learning from them. If the number of challenges we meet is restricted – or if we seek to avoid them – we run the risk of limiting our developmental potential and draining the resources that enable us to survive.

In this chapter we present the various elements of a model of human development – the developmental challenge model – that revolves around the concepts of 'challenges', 'resources', 'development', 'stagnation' and 'decay':

- We begin by describing some of the potential resources individuals possess, and how these relate to potential developmental tasks they might meet throughout their life course.
- We go on to examine the significance of situational characteristics such as timing, biological state and motivation on the interplay of potential resources and potential tasks.
- Next, we discuss one of the preconditions of development, namely the perceived feelings of security that come from an awareness of possessing a sufficient array of resources to meet challenges successfully.
- We define what it means to 'meet a challenge successfully', and how challenges are sought proactively by the individual.
- Finally, we give consideration not only to successful development, but also to the limitations on individual development.

Individual differences in potential resources: components of the resource 'pool'

The start of life is not the same for all individuals. Already, a new-born child utilizes a 'pool' of potential resources to cope with the challenges of life. Many of these resources are innate, such as certain reflexes, and others are learned, since learning starts in the first seconds of life and will go on until death. Still others are structurally determined, such as nationality or social class. Just as a certain number of potential resources exist from the very first moments of life in the womb for every individual, so too does the inequality in the distribution of these resources. Already, new-born babies differ from each other in the number and quality of resources they have for coping with the challenges in their lives. These differences can later widen or narrow, depending on the individual's lifetime experiences.

In the following section we present some examples of what these different potential resources can be, and how they importantly interact with each other. In particular, we look at the following kinds of potential resources and their implications for the individual (see figure 3.1):

1. Biological dispositions (e.g. genetics, health ,'personality').
2. Social resources.
3. Skills in various domains.
4. Self-efficacy.
5. Structural resources.

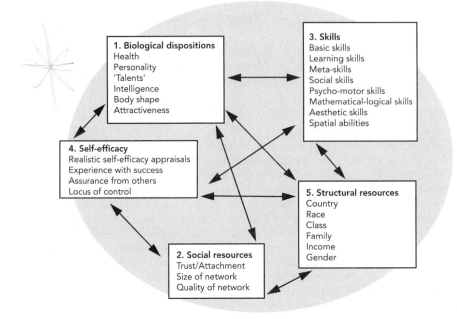

Figure 3.1   **Examples of interacting elements in the resource 'pool'**

Biological dispositions

Firstly, there are the resources nature has provided children with: genetic endowment, potentials for developing different talents, dispositions to certain diseases, personality characteristics, body shape, attractiveness and so on. These predispose children towards the kinds of skills they will be able to learn and how well they will learn them (e.g. taller boys may have a better chance of becoming good basketball players, musically talented children are more likely to take up playing an instrument). These will also determine how others will act towards them. For example, 'irritable' babies cause their mothers to become less involved, to have less visual and physical contact, and to be less soothing (van den Boom and Hoeksma, 1994), and for some families, problems with 'colicky babies' may evolve into a more generalized 'persistent mother–infant distress' syndrome, especially if additional risk factors are present (Barr, 1998). Further, personal characteristics will influence how children meet daily experiences (e.g. fearful children will exploit the physical environment less). As life goes on, these biological predispositions will increasingly interact with learned behaviours and the social environment, and thus be transformed. In particular, good health, which seems to be one of the most important and influential resources throughout the lifespan, is heavily influenced by lifestyle and environment.

Social resources

Already the act of being born involves social interaction. During our whole lives we will be dependent on other people, we will have to interact with them at least at a minimal level, and they have an enormous potential for helping us to cope with challenges. Thus, our social networks and the quality of our social relationships have to be seen as important resources. The quality of these social relationships depends mainly on two factors: the availability of social networks and the individual's social skills.

The greater the number and variety of people to interact with, the higher the probability that they will enrich the individual's resources with emotional, informational and practical support, whenever this might be needed in order to meet a challenge. To initiate and sustain social relationships, individuals need social skills, beginning with elementary skills, such as how they react to others, or how to seek and keep eye-contact, all the way through to highly complex and elaborated series of skills like how to solve a conflict or how to be a good lover. It has been known for a long time that even new-born babies who fail to respond adequately to social cues (e.g. do not respond to their care-givers' contact-seeking behaviours) are less liked by others than are 'normally' reacting babies (e.g. Bell, 1968). Erikson (1959) stresses the important role of learning to trust other people during the first year of life. Similarly, Bowlby (1969) pointed out how important the learning of early attachment is for the formation of later relationships. 'Insecure attachment' during childhood, as Ainsworth (1979) calls it, seems to influence an individual's way of relating to others throughout the life-span. However, secure attachment histories are no guarantee of positive adjustment later in life, nor are insecure early attachments a condemnation to poor adjustment later on (Fagot and Kavanagh, 1990).

Skills in various domains

In order to solve problems and meet challenges, a vast array of skills is needed. These skills should exist in many different areas, and the rule of thumb is that many different skills in many different areas seem to be a better resource than a high specialization of skills in a few limited areas. Generalists have a higher risk threshold because they can more easily compensate for loss of resources by utilizing other resources from their wide range of developed skills. These have been learned in the accomplishment of meeting previous tasks successfully. One can cope fairly successfully using specialized skills, but if significant changes occur, adaptability is the key for successfully meeting life's challenges. However, in certain cases a high specialization in one area could compensate to some degree for deficiencies in others ('specialization' will be discussed later in this chapter, under the heading of 'Development, stagnation and decay').

Particularly important are basic survival skills for the society in which the individual lives. These are skills such as psycho-motor skills, reading and writing (in most societies), economic budgeting, hygiene and self-maintenance skills. To these basic abilities we would like to add 'meta-skills', meaning all the generalizable skills that enhance the learning of new behaviour and the accomplishment of new tasks, like appraisal, self-evaluating or planning skills (Kloep and Hendry, 1999a). These are basic to the acquisition of any other skills, which, refined and adapted to new contexts, become a potential resource for meeting future challenges. As Fürntratt and Möller (1982) claim, the ideal person should not be *homo sapiens* – a mainly passively knowing individual – but *homo excercens*, an actively exploring, constantly learning individual with a broad repertoire of skills, comprising, among others, motor, social, artistic and cognitive skills, learning skills for further development, and the ability to specialize in at least one or two areas of expertise.

Self-efficacy

The assured confrontation with challenges needs a certain amount of self-efficacy or self-esteem, the feeling that one will be able to cope, or that one can actively solve challenges with one's own resources (this is similar to the idea of 'internal locus of control' described by Rotter, 1966). We learn the degree of self-efficacy partly through social feedback – others praising or criticizing us – and partly through experience – the successful or unsuccessful completion of tasks. We observe our own behaviour and evaluate our ongoing performance in terms of our standards and goals, or in comparison with the achievements of others. In this way, we arrive at generalized conclusions like 'I am hopeless in mathematics' or 'For my age, I am still pretty good at running up the stairs.' Bandura (1986) calls such judgements self-efficacy appraisals. He believes that our self-efficacy appraisals exert powerful effects on our level of motivation. We search out challenges and work persistently with tasks we think we can cope with, while we are more likely to avoid challenges or to give up on tasks when we doubt our abilities. According to Bandura (1986), self-efficacy appraisals are based on four sources of information:

1. The most important sets of information are the results of our actual performance. If we repeatedly succeed at tasks, our sense of efficacy increases, and temporary failures do not worry us too much. As Weiner (1972) has suggested, repeated experience with success will lead us to attribute temporary blunders to a lack of effort and to try again. But repeated failure and resultant low efficacy expectations are likely to evoke the attribution of failure to a lack of ability and cause the individual to give up.
2. Self-efficacy appraisals are also influenced by vicarious experiences, which means observing other people's success and failure at certain tasks.
3. Verbal persuasion, such as pep-talks and repeated affirmation of one's abilities by others is another source of high efficacy expectations.
4. We also adjust our efficacy evaluation to physiological cues. For example, we are able to interpret fatigue as a sign that a task is becoming too difficult for us.

Realistic self-efficacy appraisals are valuable preconditions for deciding whether or not a task should be approached, and how much energy should be invested in it. Particularly under conditions in which there are limited resources at the individual's disposal, it is an effective coping strategy (and a meta-skill) to select only manageable tasks and to concentrate on these.

Structural resources

Finally, another set of potential resources the individual has are those stemming from the cultural environment. These are often called 'structural variables', and encompass factors such as material resources, nationality, gender, race, personal or public status and social class. For example, money can make up for the lack of other resources (one can simply buy them from others), or the fact that one belongs to a minority group might mean that one needs far more skills than others in order to achieve a certain status in society.

Dynamic interaction within potential resources, and between potential resources and tasks to be faced

None of the variables within these different categories can be seen in isolation from the others; rather they have to be regarded as highly inter-active (see figure 3.1). Biological and socio-structural variables, for example, interact with acquired skills, and together form the base of self-efficacy, which in turn enhances the learning of new skills.

For instance, Elder, Van Nguyen and Caspi (1985) have shown that physically attractive children get more attention and positive responses from their parents, which enhances their feelings of attachment, and as a consequence their social skills. The number and quality of skills a person possesses will, in turn, have an effect on their self-efficacy beliefs. Further, people with high self-esteem are usually more likeable than others, and will thus have a broader social network and more opportunities to learn and practise their social skills.

Apart from being ecologically intertwined with each other, these potential resources are highly dynamic: they can be lost and gained and varied, and any change in any of these will affect the other variables of the individual's resource 'pool'. Biological characteristics can change, health can be damaged or regained, talents can be trained or neglected, social relationships can be built up, destroyed and rebuilt, so that the ingredients of the resource 'pool' are never static, but in flux throughout the whole lifespan. Importantly, at any point of the lifespan, the number and nature of these resources is predictive of life outcomes and functioning in the following years. Klohnen, Vandewater and Young (1996) report that in their middle-aged US sample, the generalized capacity for flexible adaptation to stressors, a sense of mastery within a wide range of life domains, and having effective interpersonal skills were the predictors of successful living over the next nine years of the life course.

Note, however, that no potential resource is a resource solely on its own (see figure 3.2). For instance, no-one can tell whether the Ace of Spades is a good or a bad card to play without knowing what card-game is being played. Similarly, any characteristics of the person can be a resource (being tall as a basketball player), irrelevant (being tall and trying to solve a mathematical problem) or a disadvantage (being tall and trying to sit comfortably in an economy class transatlantic flight). In other words, any of these potential resources only become actual resources through interaction with the kind of task that has to be met. The tasks the individual encounters define whether or not a potential resource turns out to be a real one. On the other hand, the number and kind of potential resources within an individual's resource 'pool'

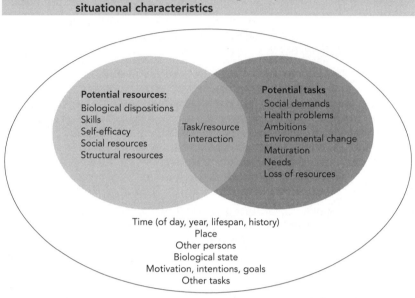

Figure 3.2   **Potential resources interacting with potential tasks and with situational characteristics**

determines whether or not a task an individual meets turns out to be a routine chore, a challenge (or, as Bandura [1986] calls it, a 'realistically challenging task'), or a risk.

The 'goodness of fit' between tasks and potential resources and the influence of situational factors

A range of variables determines the goodness of fit between potential resources and task difficulty. The kind and amount of potential resources in the individual's resource 'pool', as described above, are crucial. In addition, situational characteristics influence both the task demands, the strength of potential resources, and the interaction between tasks and resources (see box below for examples). Among others, fatigue, low motivation and competing goals can alter some of the individual's potential resources, and the presence of other persons or additional tasks can affect task difficulty. Another situational characteristic is time when – during a day, during a year, during a lifespan or in history – a certain task appears makes a difference. Obviously, getting pregnant without being married is different for a middle-aged woman and for a teenager, and is different for a modern woman than for one in the middle ages.

Elder (1986, 1987), for example, has shown that during the great depression in the US, having to do military service had a differential impact on young men depending upon when in their life course it happened. It had positive effects on younger men, who had just left high school, because it saved them from unemployment and gave them the opportunity to learn entrepreneurial skills, which were important for their future careers. Nevertheless, the same military service had negative effects on older ones, because it disrupted their careers and their families.

To illustrate the interaction between potential resources and potential challenges in different situations, consider the following examples:

- The Albanian schoolteacher who used her leisure time in the 1980s to learn Swedish, a skill that her husband regarded as superfluous and potentially dangerous in a society that was hostile towards any Western influences. But that turned out to be a most valuable resource when the country opened up for foreign investment and desperately needed interpreters (one of the few job openings in times of high unemployment).
- The Norwegian clerk for whom finding his way home from his community office has become a well practised routine task, but for whom the same task turns out to be more difficult to solve after a few Aquavits with his office companions.
- The gorgeous American actress who all her life got anything she wanted from others by exhibiting her pretty smile, and who after her third facelift has to admit to herself that this strategy does not work as a resource anymore, and that she desperately needs to acquire different social skills to make herself attractive to others (which, of course, is possible).
- The immigrant from Ghana who has been highly esteemed for his collective values and his caring attitude towards his extended family in his homeland, and who now has difficulties convincing his German girlfriend that all his nephews and cousins are resources and not a financial and social burden.
- Or imagine that you are sleepy and do not have the resources to get up and answer the phone when it rings. Suddenly a burglar appears in your window, and you have more than enough resources to get up, scream and fight (due to the sudden rush of adrenaline caused by his appearance). In other words, the 'pool' might appear sufficiently full to cope with the burglar, but too empty to cope with the ringing telephone. Furthermore, you might not have very sophisticated fighting skills, but your social relations with your neighbour are so good that he rushes in on hearing your first scream and helps you to overpower the robber.

Another important variable can be the number of different challenges the individual has to cope with at the same time:

> The multiple role trajectories of life patterns call for strategies of co-ordination or synchronization. Various demands compete for the individual's or family's scarce resources, time, energy, money....To cope with simultaneous, linked trajectories, the scheduling of events and obligations becomes a basic task in managing resource and pressures [Elder, 1997: p.956].

Young people, for example, who can space the different relational tasks they have to solve during puberty (relations to peers, romantic partners and parents) have a much smoother transition to adulthood than those who have to struggle with several relational issues at the same time (Coleman and Hendry, 1999).

The goodness of fit between potential personal resources and certain challenges is different between individuals, but also within individuals, because of situational factors: something that is easy for one person is not necessarily easy for another; something that was too difficult yesterday might be easy tomorrow.

What we have said up to now is that potential resources are inter-related and relative, and in the end determined by the kind of task the individual meets, that they are dynamic in their interaction with these tasks and can vary over time.

We can also see that there are individual differences in the number and kind of available potential resources. Some individuals can cope easily with a wide array of different challenges, even go and search them out, while others are upset and frightened by tasks which for most appear mere routine.

In summary, the properties of a task determine – in combination with situational characteristics – which of the qualities of the person can be used as a resource, and whether or not the demands of the task exceed these resources.

Consequently, we choose to call tasks that just match or slightly exceed the individual's resources 'challenges'. The less demanding ones we call 'routine tasks', the more demanding ones 'risks'. Hence we allow the kind and amount of the individual's potential resources to define whether a task is relatively easy or difficult (see figure 3.3).

Figure 3.3   Relationship between task demands and resources

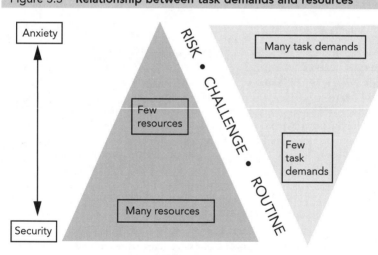

Potential resources and feelings of security

The subjective feeling of having a relatively full resource 'pool' and a sufficient range of resources to cope with nearly all the tasks and challenges of daily life elicit feelings of security. Or, as we would argue, feelings of security are a signal of a sufficient amount of resources to cope with actual challenges. New situations, unfamiliar tasks and problems to solve are all frightening to a certain degree, disturbing an individual's secure state (see below for a discussion of different aspects of security). Only from the position of a particular level of security will an individual choose to approach new challenges. If that feeling of security does not exist, the individual is most likely to try to avoid any challenges. This is in some way a clever choice, because anxiety lowers the level of competence for most (particularly more complex) tasks, and makes success more difficult.

Perceived security and development

The feeling of security – or the lack of it – can come from different sources. Paralleling the different categories of potential resources outlined above, security can be affected by biological, social, cognitive and structural variables. Here are some examples.

Personality psychologists tell us that people differ from birth in the degree of anxiety with which they react to the surrounding world: introverts appear to condition more easily to fear-provoking stimuli (Eysenck and Eysenck, 1985), individuals with a high degree of trait anxiety feel less secure in all situations (Spielberger, 1966), and sensation seekers and extroverts feel more at ease in new and challenging situations than other personality types (Zuckerman, 1979). While some people loathe change, others are open to new experiences (e.g. those scoring low and high, respectively, on the personality dimension 'openness to experience' of the Costa and McCrae Big Five measure of personality, 1988).

Apart from biological/genetic predispositions to insecurity, fear and security, reactions can also be easily learned. Behaviourists have shown in numerous experiments with animals and humans, that stimuli associated with, for example, pain or discomfort will gain the property of eliciting discomfort by themselves in future similar situations: they become conditioned fear stimuli. Similarly, stimuli that are associated with anxiety-free, comfortable situations will become conditioned security stimuli (Fürntratt, 1974): a student appearing for an oral examination might have the first signs of panic already by detecting the sign 'QUIET! EXAM!' outside the door of the examination room (i.e. a conditioned fear stimulus). On the other hand, his level of anxiety might drop a little when he sees his favourite professor approaching, the one known for being 'soft' with students (i.e. a conditioned security stimulus).

Crucial in skills learning is whether or not the learner's trials are successful. If the tasks are too difficult, the learner is confronted with failure, which is always more-or-less fear-provoking: repeated failure leads to reduced motivation, fear of failure (McClelland et al. 1953), low self-efficacy appraisal, and avoidance behaviour towards this specific, or similar, tasks (Kloep, 1982). While behaviourists claim the detrimental, anxiety-provoking effects of unsuccessful task-solving on further learning, psycho-dynamic-oriented psychologists go a step further. They state that the unsuccessful solution of stage-determined conflicts leads to anxiety-ridden neuroses for the rest of one's life (Hall, 1954), or at least have a negative impact on the tackling of future life crises (Erikson, 1959). Further, Maslow (1970) regards feelings of security as one of the basic needs that has to be satisfied before self-realization can occur. Once again, though the terminology differs, here is one common element that keeps appearing in most developmental theories. The significance of security – or the detrimental, cumulative effects of anxiety and repeated failure – is crucial to the way we deal with developmental tasks.

Just as the potential resources in the resource 'pool' change and interact with each other and with potential challenges, the state of experienced security and anxiety is highly variable both between situations and throughout the lifespan. Feelings of insecurity transpire whenever the level of resources in the 'pool' is low in comparison with the demands of the task (see figure 3.3). For example, if someone falls ill, feelings of security are immediately reduced (i.e. there is a perception of fewer resources), and the individual starts to behave 'childishly', seeking the security of familiar things, such as 'wanting to go home', wishing to be cared for and to be 'treated like a baby'. Put simply, regression to lower developmental levels – of guaranteed security – occurs. With globalization, multinational hotel chains and restaurants are well aware of the important role that familiarity plays in security and thus for popularity. There is no risk involved, for instance, if you choose to dine at Burger King or sleep in a Best Western hotel: service might not be special, but at least you know what you get!

On the other hand, when a person's skill level is perfectly balanced with the challenge level of a task that has clear goals and provides immediate feedback, this can lead to the experience of 'flow' (Csikszentmihalyi, 1975, 1997). People enter a flow state when they are fully absorbed in an activity in which they lose their sense of time and have feelings of great satisfaction – a state beyond boredom and anxiety. This experience in itself is so rewarding that people invest huge amounts of energy and time in achieving it and staying in the flow channel.

Whether or not a new task is perceived as being boring, challenging or panic-provoking is the result of the individual's level of self-efficacy appraisal: do they feel secure and competent enough to meet the task, or does the task by far exceed their resources?

As these examples show, security can be seen as both the base-line and the outcome of a range of resources an individual possesses to cope with challenges. The more perceived resources, the higher the degree of perceived security, and the more likely it is that the individual will approach a challenge and successfully cope with it (thus adding further resources to the 'pool'). This level of security, stemming from a relatively full resource 'pool', is regarded by some scholars as a personality characteristic, severally called hardiness, stamina, persistence and resilience, all meaning the presence of generally stress-resisting qualities. People with such resources will be able to appraise a threatening situation, and in doing so feel challenged and self-confident, seeking out and using support actively (Henrard, 1996).

When is a challenge met successfully?

Before we answer this question, we need to clarify our definition of a challenge: any new task an individual meets that just matches or slightly exceeds his or her current resources.

This task can be the problem of how to find the bathroom in an unknown building, how to attract the attention of that gorgeous man in the outdoor café, how to put on your clothes with your arm in plaster, how to rebuild a home in a war-stricken country, or how we can find a better example to clarify our next point! A task can be a simple problem that takes a few seconds to solve (like asking someone if there is a bus to Panzano in Chianti), or a complex one, consisting of numerous sub-tasks, that can be seen as a series of processes, taking several years to complete (like leaving that man from the outdoor café you foolishly married). It can be a completely new task, or a routine task performed under new conditions. The task can have positive connotations for you, like learning a new hobby or making new friends, or it can contain negative elements that nevertheless can lead to growth. In particular, stressors that disrupt the continuity of your life can act as 'catalysts for change' (Fiske and Chiriboga, 1991). Therefore, a certain amount of stress can even be regarded positively from a developmental point of view, because it can lead to the gaining of new skills (Aldwin, 1992).

However, it is not the event in itself that is positive or negative: it is the process and the outcomes of interactions between the individual's resources and the task that determine, in the main, if the result leans more towards development than decay.

Something as undesirable as going blind has, for some people, been the antecedent for enormous personal growth, and something as apparently desirable as winning a large amount of money in the lottery can turn out to be disastrous for people who cannot cope with new-found wealth. The same is true for minor daily events.

All tasks carry the potential for both challenge and risk. Being aware that the resolution of any task contains both losses and gains for the individual, it is difficult to decide when or how task resolution is generally 'successful' in lifespan terms. For instance, some strategies can be effective in the short run for the individual, but can lead to disaster after a period of time (like dampening your anxiety with a dram – or four – of whisky, then driving your car). Some resolutions might be seen as highly successful by the individual, but not by members of the wider society (like a highly lucrative bank robbery); and some, finally, might lead to gains in one area of one's life and to losses in another (like when your lover leaves you because you use all your time studying computer technology).

So now is the time for us to state clearly what we mean by 'successful solution' of a task. Borrowing from Gore and Eckenrode's (1996) inter-pretation of successful coping, we consider a challenge as being met successfully when the process of solving it does not drain the individual's resources but adds to them (or, as Baltes would put it, maximizes gains and minimizes losses). On the other hand, risk occurs when the task drains the resource 'pool'. Hence, development ceases, and turns into decay when the continual meeting of challenges drains resources so that in the end the individual cannot deal with them anymore.

To consider this idea of gains and losses further, take, for example, a person coping with a hip operation by retiring into a wheelchair and exploiting their entire social network for help. They might solve the task of overcoming some of the problems of their handicap (gains), but might alienate and deplete their social network drastically (losses), so that their resource 'pool' is seriously drained. This would not be seen as a totally successful strategy. On the other hand, if a person resolutely trains their muscles until they are able to walk again, this would be a successful

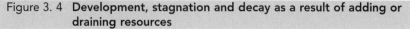

Figure 3. 4 **Development, stagnation and decay as a result of adding or draining resources**

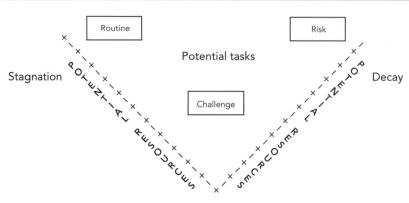

solution to the challenge, because it adds to the resource 'pool' (in the form of new skills and heightened self-efficacy) instead of draining it.

Thus, not all our attempts to meet challenges are entirely successful. However, only when the resource 'pool' is constantly emptied does this become a serious risk to further development. When the meeting of challenges continually drains resources (in the short, but particularly in the long run), development ceases and turns into decay. In the end, the individual does not have enough resources anymore to cope even with minor daily challenges. Furthermore, as noted above, an individual's resources consist of many categories that interact with each other. It is fully possible, that meeting a challenge drains one category of resources while topping up another. For example, if an individual has chosen to tackle a task that turns out to be too difficult, so that failure ensues, this can have negative effects on feelings of self-efficacy. At the same time, it can also have positive effects by adding to appraisal skills: in such processes, individuals will in the future be able more accurately to choose tasks that fit their skills level. As long as meeting challenges leads to 'net gains', by adding further potential resources to the resource 'pool', we can talk about development rather than decay.

Our comparison of potential individual resources to a 'pool' might evoke the picture of a static reservoir of resources that at any time is full or empty. Nothing could be further from the truth. Whether or not the 'pool' can be regarded as full or more-or-less empty depends on the interaction with potential challenges. Though some parts of the resource 'pool' might be comparatively empty, others can be quite full, and thus can act to compensate.

So again, we want to stress that a task becomes a challenge or a risk only in relation to the individual's characteristics (i.e. potential resources). In the interaction with this task, the individual is somehow transformed, and moves on from this task with a gain in, a loss of, or unaltered resources.

Figure 3.5   **Individual transformations in meeting tasks**

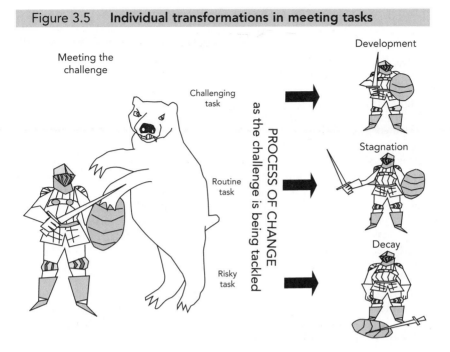

Depending on the result of this transformational process, we can say the individual has developed, decayed or stayed relatively unchanged by the experience (see figure 3.5). Furthermore, if resources are added, the likelihood of future successful task solution has increased, thus starting a process of accumulation of advantages. Similarly, any draining of resources decreases the probability of successful coping in the future, and thus may start a process of accumulation of disadvantages. For instance, a lack of social skills can firstly lead the individual to isolation from peers in school, then to leaving school as soon as possible with few qualifications, and in the end to unemployment and further problems associated with lack of education and money.

Seeking out challenges

Up to now, we have mentioned mainly challenges that appear incidentally in normal daily living, whether the individual wishes them to appear or not. But individuals can also seek out challenges voluntarily. Why and when does that happen?

We have compared the sum of an individual's potential resources to a 'pool' that can be filled and drained. If the 'pool' is relatively full, a state of contentment, a feeling of security, is reached. This in itself is a pleasant state of well-being which, however, after some time can lead to feelings of boredom: the individual does not feel sufficiently 'challenged'. One possibility is that this might have a biological explanation – all higher animals seem to get bored if the environment does not change, indicating something like an innate drive for stimulation (Fürntratt,

1974). In humans we observe that new-born infants (and even 36-week-old foetuses!) get bored and react with habituation (i.e. stop moving as a reaction to stimulation) when they are presented with the same stimuli all the time, and prefer to be entertained with different ones (Madison, Madison and Adubato, 1986). Another possibility is that it might be a socially conditioned phenomenon in our Western societies, where the longing for ever-changing experiences is a prerequisite for the success-fully functioning fashion and entertainment industries.

These are some possible explanations for a state of high security being experienced as boring after a time, leading the individual to set out to find new excitement and stimulation, a new challenge. The bored individual might go and search for something to be challenged by, to attempt to overcome the challenge, and thereby add new resources to the resource 'pool'. Thus, a dynamic and accumulative process occurs. The more and better potential resources an individual can count on, the higher the experience of security in relation to new challenges. As a consequence, the individual is more willing to seek out new tasks and if meeting them successfully, will add more resources to the 'pool'. Similarly, a downward spiral can occur. The fewer and weaker the resources individuals have, the higher will be their anxiety when confronted with new tasks, and the lower the probability that they will voluntarily seek out new challenges. As a consequence, their capacity to solve them successfully will decrease further as fewer new resources are added to their 'pool'.

These challenges that people might seek out if they feel 'boringly' secure can be anything from little daily tasks, such as trying to repair the bathroom light or experimenting with a new recipe, to more sensation-seeking ones like watching the neighbours through binoculars or speeding on the motorway, or going on an adventure holiday alone, to real 'life shifts' like selling one's home and going to live on a houseboat or in another country.

Development, stagnation and decay

According to our definition, development happens any time when the 'pool' of potential resources is added to and resources are strengthened. By contrast, a state in which no new resources are added to the 'pool' we call stagnation. And finally, if the challenges an individual meets in life continually exceed the potential resources, and thus drain the 'pool' ceaselessly, we can speak of developmental decay (see figure 3.4). This last state can be reached at any age during the lifespan – or may never be reached.

According to our definition then, development is a series of continuous changes that occur across the lifespan – not a series of transitions through stages. Within this definition of development it is clear that we do not view maturation as development in itself. Maturation is just another (biological) challenge that the individual has to cope with: a changing body-shape in adolescence, for example, does not constitute development in itself, but the challenges it creates for the individual in a variety of social, emotional, physical and cognitive contexts are triggers for development. The way the individual copes with maturational changes determines whether maturation is a step towards development (i.e. if it leads to strengthened resources), or towards stagnation and decay. In this context (and fully in line with Smith and Baltes' [1999] concept of multidirectionalism; see chapter 2), it does not matter if maturation involves changes that are commonly regarded as growth (as the gain in body weight in small children) or loss (as losing body functions in old age): any change is a challenge!

Neither should we confuse the notion of development with enhanced life quality. Constant development does not guarantee subjective happiness: one can be perfectly happy in a state of stagnation. The only negative connotation of stagnation is that it can put one at risk in possible future challenges that demand more than the resources available to meet them. Thus progressive development is just like a life insurance policy against possible challenges that might – or might not – occur. One way of shielding oneself against challenges or changes that are too high and demanding is to avoid them. This is fully possible, and might well create an effective way of living – for the time being. However, it will not contribute to 'the filling of the resource "pool"', so this strategy does not contribute to development. Within our model it leads to what we call stagnation.

Whether or not this strategy adds to one's life satisfactions has to do with the reasons why the individual chooses it in the first place. If it is selected as a strategy simply because a lack of resources leads to a limiting of alternatives, it usually has two major drawbacks. The first is that the individual is 'condemned' to more-or-less accepting life as it is, because there are not enough resources to change it. The second is that it is often combined with a high degree of anxiety, because individuals know they would not be able to cope with sudden changes. Any small challenge that might appear could be a threat to the individual's already drained resources, and hence to their well-being. We all know of the middle-aged family which has lived in the same small town for 30 years (and individually hate it). They spend their yearly holiday in the same uninteresting resort in a neighbouring country, and would see it as a minor catastrophe if somebody planted different sorts of flowers in the park across the road. We see this lifestyle (which is not completely self-chosen, because there are no perceived alternatives) as a form of 'unhappy stagnation' which does not lead to a particular good quality of life.

Our concept of stagnation is similar to Whitbourne, Sneed and Skultety's (2001) description of two adult identity styles:

> 'Identity assimilators' are theorized to possess externally strong but internally weak identities. To the outside world, they seem sure and self-confident, but their self-definition is based on a defensive rigidity that prohibits them from acknowledging their shortcomings. When confronted with experiences that threaten to challenge their identities, they rely on identity assimilation to distort the information so that it no longer causes them to question their abilities or importance to others. 'Identity accommodators' have weak and unstable identities that are heavily based on the evaluations of other people. They change readily in response to experiences because they lack internal consistency.

In their model, only those with a 'balanced identity' are able to alternate flexibly between identity processes, and thus maintain a stable sense of self, while changing in response to events that challenge their sense of self.

The notion of stagnation is also similar to Maslow's (1970) ideas about 'deficiency orientation', a state in which individuals are solely occupied with the satisfaction of their basic needs and can not engage in further development. This is opposite to 'growth orientation', in which individuals have their basic needs fulfilled and have enough resources to engage in self-actualization.

Not all stagnators, however, are in a state of involuntary, unhappy stagnation. Individuals might choose not to meet further challenges, simply because they are perfectly contented with the current resources in their 'pool' and their current lifestyle. One example of this might be a farmer, whose daily work has followed the same general routine for years. He or she carries out the job efficiently, loves the countryside, and has a reasonable social network. This farmer is too content ever to want to have anything else to do in life, because he or she 'knows' nothing can be better than this. He or she chooses not to change this life, though being not completely without challenges: every day, beyond routine tasks, there are small challenges, but ones that can easily be mastered, refining and improving skills from one specialized area of the resource 'pool'. This self-chosen state of stagnation can very possibly mean a high quality of life, at least as long as it is not disturbed by sudden external changes that 'force' the farmer to adjust and readjust (such as economic difficulties, growing urbanization, or natural catastrophes).

To take another example: it has been possible for whole cultures to build on a 'no-change' philosophy for a long time, and to venerate tradition. China, until its recent transition into a market economy with concomitant social changes, had many elements of such a society, both in its social and cultural life. For instance, Chinese opera, unlike Western theatre, has not changed for centuries – and is not meant to. For an equally long time, strong family traditions maintained social security for old people, who were venerated and supported by their adult children. A sudden change in legislation – the 'one-child-per-family' policy – has made this impossible, and led to a social breakdown in care of the elderly. Several massive political shifts have created considerable changes for the Chinese population's way of life, and adjustments and adaptations at the individual level will take some time to be made. Those individuals (and nations) who, for whatever reason, try to avoid any change are at risk simply because a life of 'no change and no challenges' cannot (and need not) lead to development. Thus, it makes them vulnerable to externally induced changes: contented stagnation can easily be turned into unhappy stagnation.

Sometimes it is not easy to decide whether an individual, or a culture, is in a state of unhappy or contented stagnation. There are, however, some indicators of unhappy stagnation: if, for example, tradition has to be enforced by rules, and possible change is banned, it shows that change is considered as threatening and dangerous by those in power. This can be regarded as evidence of unhappy stagnation, born out of anxiety, rather than of choice. New Year parties on 31 December are part of an enjoyable tradition which is voluntarily celebrated even by cultures with a different calendar. The wearing of a *shador* (black, unrevealing clothing, including a veil, worn by some Muslim women), on the other hand, has to be enforced by law and repression, and can hardly be seen as a happily adopted tradition. In the case of individuals, similar rules apply: habits and lifestyles that are kept mainly because a change would be punished in one form or another (e.g. by social disapproval or threats) point towards unhappy stagnation. Tolerance towards change in others, even while a lifestyle of no change in oneself is adopted, seems to suggest a lifestyle of contented stagnation. Unhappy stagnators have to avoid tasks they cannot cope with, while contented stagnators are not interested in other tasks than the narrow range of those they love. Thus, they often become specialists who develop in only a few life domains.

Specialization is a similar concept to stagnation, because it comprises a similar risk, as individuals narrow their range of skills. They continue to experience challenges, but the accumulated resources are often too one-sided or concentrated, so that a sudden loss of these resources could be catastrophic for the individual's overall development. For instance, consider the model who loses her good looks as she grows older, the violinist who breaks his hand, the microbe researcher who loses her eyesight. These all have little with which to compensate their loss, if they have not previously developed resources in other life areas. This puts specialists in the same risk position as contented stagnators. It is like the game of roulette: spreading one's chips can lead to small but more certain gains, while putting all one's money on one number is a high risk (with the possibility of a highly improbable big gain as the outcome). Of course, in both cases something is potentially 'lost'. In one instance, the individual will never have a big win. In the other, the risks are so astronomical that a loss is almost inevitable.

The constant chasing after change, on the other hand, is not necessarily a sign of development either. It depends on why a particular challenge is sought – is it a search for something or a retreat from something? Development is more likely to happen if challenges are sought from a state of security and with adequate resources to cope. By contrast, if the constant seeking for change is simply a strategy to evade other concurrently challenging situations which are difficult for the individual to handle, it will drain the resource 'pool' in the long run instead of adding to it. Quitting one's job and finding a new position each time one meets difficulties at work, leaving each new partner after the first quarrel, or giving up any new hobby for another after realizing it requires time and regular practice are examples of avoidance behaviour that seldom leads to development.

Furthermore, in reality there are not simply 'pure' types of responses to challenges, but rather all kinds of 'hybrids' and mixed types of responses in various life domains. Additionally, the four possibilities we propose theoretically, namely development, contented or unhappy stagnation and decay, are not stable over time (i.e. they are not personality traits), and they are, perhaps, better seen as being points on a continuum from development at one pole to decay at the other.

It is, for instance, possible to stagnate in one area of one's life (e.g. one's family role) and to continue developing in others. But if stagnation occurs in many domains, the risk is cumulative and the 'pool' will drain exponentially. However, for most individuals it is usually somewhat domain-specific. The individual's resources can be almost completely drained within one life area (e.g. being unskilled in physical activities), be just sufficient to be happily stagnated in another (e.g. in one's social life) and be continuing to develop in a third (e.g. doing one's job efficiently). So at least it is possible for one domain to compensate partially for other less endowed life-skill areas. For instance, Quinton and Rutter (1988) could show that positive experiences at school – though not necessarily academic ones – made it more likely for children from disadvantaged backgrounds to develop planning skills, which in turn were an important step towards leading a successful life:

> The mechanisms remain ill understood but probably what is happening is that success in one area gives people positive feelings of self-esteem and self-efficacy that make it more likely that they will have the confidence to take active steps to deal with life challenges in other domains of their lives.... The implication is that the experience of pleasurable success is probably helpful in enhancing those aspects of the self-concept that promote resilience [Rutter, 1996: p.26].

Whether or not individuals search for change, or challenges come to them, is not important in itself. The crucial element in meeting the future challenges of life is possessing the potential for change. The world is changing, more and more rapidly. Hence, being adaptable in as many life domains as possible – in other words possessing many resources in a variety of areas – provides this potential.

If resources are constantly drained, either because individuals meet too many concurrent challenges, or because single challenges cannot be met due to an initial lack of potential resources, stagnation can, over time, turn into decay. That means the beginning of a downward, cumulative spiral in which resources drain, with individuals increasingly over-whelmed by tasks that cannot be coped with. Even the state of decay, however, is not irreversible. 'Turning-points' that bring about an influx of new resources can transform the process into a positive one again. Take, for example, a widower in his early fifties, caring for three daughters, who suddenly loses his job. Disillusioned and bitter he spends his days on the sofa, watching TV and drinking beer and arguing with his children. He is clearly in a process of decay. But a sudden event, such as an unexpected job offer, can turn this process around: he might renew his self-esteem, gain enthusiasm by starting work, lose weight, re-engage with his family and find a girlfriend in the process. In the ebb and flow of living it is never too early and seldom too late in life to replenish the resource 'pool', and to turn a downward spiral into an upward one.

Conclusions

In this chapter, we have focussed on developing a holistic theoretical model, which is relevant for understanding the whole of the lifespan in various cultural settings. This 'lifespan model of developmental challenge' emerges in an innovative way from some of the ideas of other theories, and provides new insights into the way various factors and processes influence the life course.

To summarize the key points of the model:

- There are individual differences in potential resources. These resources interact in meeting both day-to-day problems and larger life events. Development occurs each time life challenges are met successfully, and further resources are added to what we call the individual's resource 'pool'.

- Considering the individual's resources as a 'pool' that can be filled or drained, we can say that a state of dynamic security is reached if the 'pool' is relatively full. After some time, this state can lead the individual towards feelings of contentment and, as a further step, towards boredom. One way of avoiding such feelings is to approach new challenges that just match (or, better still, slightly exceed) the individual's competence and resources. Hence, the goodness of fit between the extent of the individual's resources and the perceived challenge is determined by certain factors, such as the difficulty and timing of the task and the kind of corresponding resources the individual possesses. This goodness of fit between resources and particular challenges can vary between individuals, between different life domains, and also within the same individual in different contexts. The individual's resource 'pool' and its level is always in a dynamic state.

- A challenge is successfully met when the process of solving that challenge does not drain the individual's resources, but rather adds to them. On the other hand, when the task drains the resource 'pool' the individual's resources are somehow depleted and development ceases. Additionally, this can turn into decay when the continual meeting of challenges drains resources more and more, so that in the end the individual cannot deal with them anymore and competence decreases.

- Avoiding challenges can lead to stagnation, or at least to some limitation of the developmental potential. Stagnation can be of two kinds. There is contented stagnation, in which individuals are happy with their lifestyle and do not wish to seek out any further major challenges, and unhappy stagnation, in which individuals simply do not possess the resources to meet further challenges and thus try to avoid them. Specialization is where development occurs only in one or a few narrow areas, to the neglect of development in other domains.

- We can stagnate, and our development can even turn to decay, if our skills are not continually tested and our resources strengthened. But even that is not always irreversible: we can add resources at any time in our lives, given support and/or learning opportunities. As every challenge changes the individual's resources with which they meet further challenges, development is a dynamic lifelong process.

- The model of developmental challenge is valid for understanding the process of human development throughout the lifespan. However, it is also relevant for studying development cross-culturally. Which challenges stimulate development varies across cultures and over time. Yet the mechanisms of development are the same, irrespective of time and place.

4 Challenges associated with normative and non-normative shifts

Introduction

Having discussed the contents of the resource 'pool' in the previous chapter, we now move on to consider the elements of challenge that face individuals across the lifespan. Apart from the minor problems that have to be dealt with on a day-to-day basis, and that cumulatively can create relatively massive psycho-social development, there are a number of major changes occurring during the life course of any individual. What are these more extensive challenges, or 'developmental turning-points', as Elder (1998) calls them, which an individual will meet in a lifetime? All of us will have to tackle some of these tasks; others, only members of certain groups, cultures or societies will meet; and a few will be experienced by a relatively small number of people. Equally, we will search out some of these tasks ourselves, while others will come and meet us, whether we choose them or not.

The chapter starts out by describing different kinds of developmental shifts, namely maturational, normative social, quasi-normative and non-normative shifts. Then the various developmental consequences of normative and non-normative shifts are outlined. The chapter then offers empirical examples and discusses the theoretical considerations of coping with such challenges in the light of the developmental challenge model.

Developmental shifts

Baltes, Reese and Lipsitt (1980) distinguish three forms of developmental shifts: normative age-graded (maturational and environmental) ones, historical ones, and non-normative influences on development. We believe these categories are insufficient to explain fully lifespan changes, for three reasons:

- In order to stress cultural differences more forcefully, we want to divide the age-graded shifts into both maturational and normative social changes.
- We see the need to add a category, which we call 'quasi-normative shifts'. These quasi-normative shifts are more-or-less predictable events, taking into account the changing values and norms of different societies.
- We consider historical influences as simply one of several forms of non-normative shifts, due to the fact that they are – like other non-normative events – less predictable in normal life trajectories than normative shifts (see table 4.1).

Table 4.1   **Developmental shifts**

Shift		*Description*	*Examples*
1.	Maturational shifts	Shifts caused by normal biological changes, and experienced in more-or-less the same age range by all human beings. Thus, they are predictable, expected and shared with peers.	Growing teeth Puberty Losing hair Menopause
2.	Normative social shifts	Shifts prescribed by law for a well-defined group. They apply generally for all members in this group (society, culture). Thus, they are predictable, expected and shared with peers.	Starting school Age of majority Military service Pensionable age
3.	Quasi-normative shifts	Shifts common in a certain well-defined group, which are normally expected to happen within a certain age range. There are seldom laws to enforce these shifts, but certain social pressures may occur. Thus, these shifts occur for a majority of members in that group within that age range, and are thus fairly predictable, expected and shared with many peers.	Leaving home Marriage First job Parenthood
4.	Non-normative shifts	Shifts that in this particular form do not occur for everyone.	

continued over

Shift	Description	Examples
4.1. Off-time shifts	Shifts that are non-normative, not because of their quality, but because of their timing. They occur to many people, but at an earlier or later time in their lives. Thus, they are not very predictable or expected, and are shared to a certain degree with people of another age-group.	Teenage pregnancy Early death of parents Late marriage Early retirement
4.2 Historical shifts	Shifts due to historical events that occur to everyone in a particular group. They are not often predictable or expected, are shared with all other people in the group. There are seldom readily available role models.	War Economic crisis Natural catastrophe Inventions, such as the contraceptive pill
4.3 Self-instigated shifts	Shifts that do not happen automatically to people, but that have to be actively initiated. Thus, they are often expected and planned for by the individual. The more 'non-normative' (unusual) they are in a certain social group, the more stigma may be associated with them.	Divorce Emigration
4.4 Idiosyncratic shifts	Shifts that happen to only a few people. They are not often predictable or expected, and shared by few others. There are seldom readily available role models for coping with these shifts.	Handicap or serious illness Winning the lottery Being divorced
4.5 Non-events	These are maturational, normative or quasi-normative events that form a challenge in an individual's life by *not* happening, although expected to. There are seldom readily available role models.	Unwanted childlessness Unemployment

Thus, linked to the lifespan model of developmental challenge, we propose the following categorization of lifetime shifts, as shown in Table 4.1:

1. Maturational shifts. These consist of biological changes, such as the onset of puberty, or the menopause, and are common to all healthy individuals. Even if there are certain variations in the onset, duration and side-effects of these maturational changes between individuals within the same culture, and between cultures, the processes involved, and the biological outcomes, are pretty much the same for all human beings. Because these shifts are inescapable, they are also fairly predictable, and individuals can expect them, and be prepared to meet them. Furthermore, as the experiences are shared by other age-mates, and have been encountered by older friends and members of family, social support and role models for coping are readily available. All these maturational changes have, of course,

social implications, which vary between cultures. (These we will consider under normative and quasi-normative social shifts.)

2. Normative, social shifts. These are common for most individuals in certain social or cultural settings, and are often closely related to age and maturational shifts. These are most often legally prescribed social events, like compulsory school attendance, legal ages for adult status and the state pension. Age-graded procedures like these, which influence individuals differentially, are to be found in every society, though their content varies considerably by culture. For example, with school attendance, some European countries have almost 100 per cent of children in the appropriate age ranges enrolled in school, and regularly attending it. In other countries, children might be enrolled in school (or not), but not attending, school attendance may depend on the child's gender, and on the parents' economic resources. To take another, more extreme, example: while female circumcision is illegal in some countries, it is obligatory – normative – in others. Further, even within the same country, there can be differences between social groups as to which events are considered normative and which are not. Conscription into military service in many countries, for instance, is only obligatory for males. Certain religious rites are only required from members of that religious sect, not the whole population. What is common, however, for all these normative social shifts is that, in spite of their variations, members of the particular social groups know when and how these events will occur. In other words, these social changes are fairly predictable; individuals can expect them to happen and do not have to meet them unprepared. Additionally, as they happen to other group members at the same time, the individual can count on social support as well as on the relating of previous, shared experiences from older group members. Though different between cultures, the developmental experiences of those within socio-cultural groups in one culture are fairly similar, shaping development in a normative way for all group members.

3. Quasi-normative shifts. These are similar to normative shifts, and are age-graded events, common for most individuals in certain social or cultural groups. By contrast, they are not prescribed by law, although they often operate through unwritten rules and norms. As a consequence, there is always a (smaller or larger) minority within the same socio-cultural group that does not experience these shifts. Normative and quasi-normative shifts closely resemble Havighurst's (1972) developmental tasks, Erikson's (1959) psycho-social crises and Levinson *et al.*'s (1978) developmental transitions. The one proviso is, however, that we do not want to restrict the nature of these changes to a number of specified events, only typical for a certain culture, in a certain historical time. We want to allow for cultural variations in what is normative and what is not normative for certain individuals. These shifts vary across cultures and cohorts, while the mechanisms for meeting normative and quasi-normative events will not. Not too long ago, for instance, becoming a member of the Communist Party in the eastern part of Germany was quasi-normative. Nowadays, it is highly non-normative. At various

times historically, divorce, or the birth of children out of wedlock, was a non-normative event in most societies. But recent figures from Scandinavia show that both events are on the brink of becoming normative. These changes contribute to so-called cohort effects: for one generation, events that may have been normative cease to be so for the next, and so have totally different developmental effects on the two cohorts.

4.   Non-normative shifts are changes experienced in a particular way or at a specific time by relatively few people, and can take different forms. Whether or not an event is non-normative can depend on the time, place or nature of the event.

4.1. Off-time shifts. According to Neugarten (1968), normative life events are transitions that somehow follow an approximate age-appropriate social timetable. Part of the cultural socialization process is to teach members of a society 'age expectations', including notions about the timing and order of certain life transitions. Individuals create an internalized social 'clock' that tells them whether they are 'on time' (or not) in following the psycho-social schedule of that particular society. Experiencing a normal shift at a distinctively different time in the lifespan than most other people gives a non-normative 'off-time' character to this event. On the one hand, this is stigmatizing; on the other, it carries with it other difficulties, such as the absence of role models or clashes with other life transitions. For instance, a man in his forties, who is a father of three small children whilst in the midst of his career, will encounter many more difficulties if he becomes a widower, than a retired man in his seventies. The same widower, falling headlong in love with a young woman 20 years later, will find much less understanding and support among his family and friends, than he would have in early adulthood (see box below for further examples).

Two examples of off-time events

When puberty starts off-time for one girl (e.g. much earlier than for the rest of her peers) she is confronted with a number of extra challenges. She might not yet have learned the social skills involved in heterosexual relationships and might, therefore, be embarrassed by any sudden interest taken in her growing breasts by much older boys. She has not learned how to react to an adult world which is starting to treat her (however inappropriately) as a young woman, while in most of her interests and views she still perceives herself as a child. She also lacks role models among those in her school class, and will often start to associate with girls much older than herself. She is also likely to share their sometimes risky leisure activities – activities in which she, according to her age and her level of resources (but not her physique) is too young to participate. Stattin and Magnusson (1990) have shown that many – but far from all – girls in this situation do not cope well with these non-normative challenges, and might manoeuvre themselves into an accumulation of risky challenges, such as heavy drinking, leaving school or teenage pregnancy.

Another example of an off-time event is a late, first pregnancy. Apart from the heightened biological risks for the woman, the 'non-normality' of this event can add other challenges. A woman in her mid-forties might receive less understanding and support from friends, family and employer than a twenty-something would in the same situation. She might not have many (or any) same-age girlfriends to chat to about pregnancy and giving birth. She might feel isolated by her age among all the young women attending a breast-feeding course at the local health clinic. Additionally, it might not be easy, after all those years, for her to adjust her career, lifestyle and leisure time to a new, demanding family member.

4.2. Historical shifts. These are developmental influences arising from changing events in the macro-system. These can be incidents of a time-limited nature that have to be dealt with, or occurrences that will change the life of individuals in that society forever. Examples of the first are economic crises, socio-political breakdowns, wars and natural disasters. Examples of the latter are the invention of the contraceptive pill, the rapid development of computerization or the end of apartheid in South Africa. Usually, these shifts affect all members of a cultural group, are often quite unexpected and, at least initially, prepared for by only a few. Thus, seemingly, all are in the 'same boat'. Hence, there is often a great deal of social support available. However, people will deal with these changes and challenges differently, so that the same historical shift can have a different impact on individuals' life courses (see, for example, the discussion about the impact of economic crisis in the following chapter). On some occasions, what has started as a non-normative historical shift turns into a long-lasting situation. In this way, for instance, the war in Northern Ireland must seem more normative than non-normative for those born during its long duration.

4.3. Self-instigated shifts. The individual is not always a passive victim of change. Often life trajectories are planned and chosen within existing social and historical constraints. Elder (1998) sees planned alterations to one's life course as an expression of human agency, closely linked to perceptions of self-efficacy. As we will discuss in the next chapter, it makes a clear difference whether or not a divorce, for instance, is the result of a careful planning process or if it comes as a surprise. Though these self-instigated shifts might be easier to deal with than those that take us by surprise, they are nonetheless a challenge, and require coping resources. No matter how long and thoroughly planned, the decision to move to another town, to learn to play the piano, or to quit smoking will involve the individual in many different tasks, with obstacles to overcome, which will drain or add to resources.

4.4 Idiosyncratic shifts. These comprise all the life events that happen to only a few people. As such, they are not only in many cases stigmatizing, they also leave the individual relatively alone in coping, and without the support of others who have gone through similar challenges. Furthermore, they often happen unexpectedly. Thus, they might be among the most difficult life challenges individuals encounter. For instance, societies' structures and buildings have in the main been constructed for the comfort and convenience of healthy bipeds. Being different from this physical norm can be an extra challenge for the individual with a handicap, whether this is due to birth damage or impairment, or to an injury later in life. As with all other non-normative events, handicaps pose a set of challenges that can lead to development, stagnation or decay, dependent upon the way the individual copes with these various life situations. As with normative shifts, non-normative, idiosyncratic changes need not be ones that have a negative impact on resources. Events that are generally perceived as positive, such as getting a promotion or inheriting a large sum of money, are also changes in our normal lives that need adaptation. They challenge our coping responses in a way similar to negatively perceived events, like an illness or the death of a near friend or close relative.

4.5. Non-events. There are also non-events that happen to 'almost everybody else', but not to us. Since everything that causes us to deviate from social norms induces a stigma, non-events do this for us because we are not undergoing the same life events as everybody else. In particular, 'desirable' events that happen to many other people but not to certain individuals can constitute a severe coping challenge. For instance, we hear regularly about the incredible efforts undertaken, and the enormous sums of money spent, by couples who cannot, but dearly want to, conceive a child.

These shifts can all be developmental 'turning-points' (or maybe better, 'turning-processes') and, particularly if they are early transitions, can have enduring consequences. By affecting subsequent transitions through a process of cumulative advantage or disadvantage, they are significant life shifts (Elder, 1998). However, we should keep in mind that many of these transitions do, in reality, consist of multi-phasic processes of relatively long duration, frequently comprising a succession of several points of choice, and not single, short-lived events (Elder, 1998). Thus, these shifts present the individual with a whole host of challenges, and each of these can be dealt with more-or-less successfully. This might be why the occurrence of life events alone is a weak predictor of psychological well-being, while the number and perceived adversity of 'daily hassles' is a more effective one (Bolognini, Plancherel and Halfton, 1996).

Normative and non-normative shifts: a comparison

When we consider how 'maturational', 'normative' and 'quasi-normative shifts' all present the individual with challenges, and thus act as 'triggers' for development, we see that what these shifts have in common is that they happen to all, or nearly all, people of a certain age range in a particular society. That means that they are fairly predictable, and individuals can prepare themselves more effectively to meet these changes. Certain countries, for example, devise ways of helping groups of people to adjust to these changes. There are special programmes to prepare nursery school children for the start of formal schooling; seminars for young couples contemplating marriage or parenthood; many companies have their own courses for senior employees, to facilitate their transition to retirement. In other cultural contexts, such preparation happens in the family or community, when, for example, young girls are prepared by their mothers or older women for their future role as wives, or young boys accompany their fathers or older mentors to the work-place to learn their future trades.

Such organized events provide the individual experiencing them for the first time with a number of role models and possible sources of emotional and social support. Learning or experiencing the same as everybody else in the group does not involve any stigma. To take an example of a maturational shift, it is not too terrible to lose one's front teeth early in one's elementary school career, when the same thing is happening to all one's age-mates. It would be more difficult to cope with if, for some reason, it happened at age twenty (however, such an event might be seen as quite normal again about 50 years later).

The point we want to make here is that, no matter how dramatic or exciting normative shifts might appear to the individual, in reality they do not constitute a particularly powerful challenge. Coping with them is largely facilitated by their predictability and by the support the individual receives from social networks and the various sub-systems of a society.

By contrast, the challenges that are more difficult to cope with are the non-normative shifts that often hit unexpectedly the unprepared or unsupported individual, and making them 'deviant' from the societal norm. These non-normative shifts not only present a greater challenge to the individual than the rather more predictable normative ones, but – as a consequence – also offer a greater potential for growth. Fiske and Chiriboga (1991) arrived at a similar conclusion following a 20-year longitudinal study of US adults:

> Curiously, we found that the normative transitions defining the study did not themselves provide much in the way of a catalyst for change. Normative transitions, by their very nature, can be anticipated long before they occur and thus give people ample time to prepare. Moreover, most normative transitions are either ambiguous or positive. Thus it was the unanticipated events that most often brought upheaval and change [p. 285].

Coping with challenges

Dealing with all challenges, but particularly non-normative ones, has much in common with general coping in stressful situations. For instance, coping has been defined by Lazarus (1993) as 'ongoing cognitive and behavioural efforts to manage specific external and/or internal demands that appear as taxing or exceeding the resources of the person', a definition that parallels our concept of meeting challenges. Another example is Aldwin's (1992) description of stress and coping in relation to age:

- Stressful events constitute a context in which adult development can take place.
- The experience of stress is universal, even though the content of the experience may differ according to culture.
- Coping with stress can provide people with skills and capacities, in other words develop their practical knowledge.
- There cannot be a universal sequence of development, as development is an issue of volition; the choices we make when facing a problem (i.e. to cope with it or not) affect our adaptive processes.

Stress, as Aldwin (1992) points out, can be seen as a positive factor from a developmental point of view, since it can lead to learning and the promotion of new skills:

> the process of coping with stress may provide a means through which development can occur in adulthood. That is, as people cope with stress, they can – although they do not necessarily – develop capacities and skills that are prized by a given culture [p.101].

According to her, three developmental trajectories may occur as a result of coping with stress: the individual can become more 'frail', can return to homeostasis, or develop increasing resources – or, in our terminology, can decay, stagnate or develop.

Coping with all kinds of challenges means dealing with different degrees of stress and is, therefore, a vital part of the developmental process. Whether or not the coping strategies turn out to be successful depends – according to the developmental challenge model – on the individual's resources. In a review article, Ruth and Coleman (1997) emphasize that for facing up to challenges a range of similar personal and structural capacities are needed, which they call maturity, optimism, coherence, locus of control, coping strategies, social support, higher education and social economic status.

No matter how one deals with the challenge, the resultant changes essentially make the individual a 'new' person. However, as Rutter (2000) put it, most single experiences, like most single genes, have scarce and limited effects. The main impact comes from a combination of risks, where chronic rather than acute stresses cause long-term effects. Of course, both early and later experiences are influential, but, to an important extent, early experiences shape the later ones. The same seems to be true for the successful negotiation of minor and major life events. Fiske and Chiriboga (1991) observed this in their longitudinal sample, and describe it in this way:

> It appears that a lifetime of experience in dealing with social stressors often results in some expertise in coping with problems – or at least a habitual approach to deal with them, whether it to be to indulge in an alcoholic binge or take direct action [p.284].

Rutter (1996) compares these non-normative experiences, which are difficult enough to challenge the individual's resources but not impossible to cope with, to the effects of vaccinations on the body's defences. By vaccination, small amounts of noxious substances are injected to create antibodies and strengthen the immune system against future infections. By analogy, he calls these challenges 'steeling experiences', small 'injections' that prepare the individual to cope with different, more demanding challenges in future life.

One significantly illustrative example of this is the repeated finding that single women in their old age find themselves more effectively adapted and content with their life situation than divorced and widowed women of the same age. Perhaps the process of single living itself explains the apparent gift many of these people have for nurturing friendships. Singles may simply have practised their social skills more, and in more varied circumstances, than married couples. Further, single individuals stress self-reliance – making do with one's inner resources – and self-assertiveness as assets in coping with retirement. Like a facility for making friends, this may be the product of a life without marriage (Miletti, 1984).

Similarly, Csikszentmihalyi (1990) describes how negative life events can lead to personal transformation by forcing the individual to focus their efforts and skills on the demands of coping. This he calls the process of 'cheating chaos'. As we have pointed out before, many challenges are not single events, but processes that comprise a range of different challenges. Often one set of challenges leads on to others in a sequence of processes. At each step, there is a possibility for failure or success, so that the relationship of 'losses' to 'gains' is sometimes positive and sometimes negative. If we consider different and various life domains, we see that some lead to stagnation or even decay, while others create massive and significant development. Thus, challenges are not only a set of different tasks, but they also result in a set of different outcomes.

Conclusions

There are a number of normative shifts expected of individuals in different age phases. Some of these shifts are biologically determined and happen sooner or later to all healthy human beings. Others are socially determined (and often age-related) and depend on the laws, rules and traditions of particular cultures, at certain historical times. We saw that no matter how dramatic normative shifts might be for the individual, in reality they are not necessarily exceptional challenges. Given their predictability and the support the individual can receive from members of his or her social network and the various sub-systems of a society, they are frequently not particularly difficult to resolve. By contrast, the challenges that might be more troublesome, and even risky, to meet are the ones that are not prescribed within normal life trajectories.

We then discussed how dealing with challenges has much in common with general coping strategies. Thus, when the challenges faced exceed the individual's resources, risks occur for the individual. It is then that the situation becomes difficult and anxiety-provoking. The individual is forced to react in ways that do not add new resources to the 'pool', but rather drain it. This can result in the risk of stagnation, or even decay in the longer term.

Finally, we stressed that it is important to realize that most challenges are not necessarily events, but processes that may actually comprise many different challenges. In a similar manner, most challenges do not lead to a single outcome, but rather to a series of positive and negative, short- and long-term consequences in the various life domains.

In the following chapter we further illustrate the phenomenon of non-normative shifts, by offering two extensive examples of these processes, namely divorce and economic crisis.

5 For richer, for poorer? Two examples of non-normative events

Introduction

You probably have some more-or-less detailed plans on how your immediate future life should be: what to study or whom to work with, where to live, whom to love, your appearance, how much money you have, what you will do next weekend and so on. Now imagine something happens that overturns most of these plans: an illness, a natural disaster, a death, a new love, a large sum of money or something like that. Suddenly, you will have to adjust all your plans, maybe your whole life, because of this event – and not only you but many people around you will also be affected. What you are experiencing (together with those in your micro-systems) is a non-normative shift. Whether or not this is a change that you initially regard as positive or negative, it will challenge your resources, and the outcome for you personally can be anything from extremely good to totally disastrous.

The number of possible non-normative shifts that happen to people across the life course is nearly infinite. Therefore, before moving on to consider mainly normative shifts of the various life phases in subsequent chapters of the book, in this chapter we want to look more closely at two non-normative occurrences as detailed examples of the impact of such shifts on the resource 'pool' and on the micro-systems individuals inhabit. These examples allow clear illustrations of the interactions and ecological components of challenges, tasks, risks and resources in the face of non-normative events.

We focus firstly on divorce, an idiosyncratic (and often self-instigated) event, because divorce is still non-normative in most societies. This event can have wide implications and repercussions for all members of the families involved and beyond, into the micro-systems of the participants. Then, to illustrate the variable impact of macro-system shifts on individuals within the different micro-systems of a society, we have chosen to look at the events surrounding a critical historical event, namely a major economic crisis, and at possible factors that lead to resilience and the building of resources even in the face of massive disadvantage.

The challenges of separation and divorce

Divorce is affected by – and clearly affects – more than one psycho-social system within a culture and, like many other challenges, it is a process, not a single event. As such, it is an excellent illustration of how the developmental challenge model can be used to describe and understand people's different adjustments to a particular set of challenges at a particular time in the life course. Further, an extensive research literature exists around the topic of divorce, making it easy to build our presentation of the developmental challenge model's various components on a strong empirical base. We start by describing divorce as a non-normative event, then outline some of the resources that can be brought to bear in the process of readjusting life after separation, and describe how divorce affects other members of the micro-system, namely grandparents and children.

Divorce and the macro-system

We regard divorce at the present time as a non-normative event, because it does not happen to everybody. Even in the industrialized countries of the Western world, people do not expect that it will happen to them, and have divergent opinions about it. A study by Hays (1994) shows that in the US and six European countries men are more disapproving of divorce than women. In Scandinavia, Knudsen and Wærness (1996) found that older women are more sceptical about divorce than younger ones, and those with strong religious beliefs are more negative about it than those with few or no religious affiliations. In other cultures, such as China (Liao and Heaton, 1992), divorce is often regarded as 'abnormal', with consequently low divorce rates, in spite of a liberalization of marriage laws. What these studies illustrate is that the experience of divorce means different things to different people, to each gender and in different cultures. Thus, for some the process still remains a non-normative shift, whereas for others it is *almost* regarded as normative. How can we possibly say anything generally valid about divorce with such a diversity of cultural patterns, except that it poses a variable and divergent challenge to the individuals involved?

Many decisions that are made on the individual level and within various micro-systems are nevertheless powerfully influenced by the macro-system. Divorce is no exception. Several researchers reveal that socio-economic development, women's social status and the sex ratio in a society (e.g. Trent and South, 1989), the participation of women in the labourforce, geographic mobility, the number of available alternative marriage partners (e.g. South and Lloyd, 1995) all influence divorce rates. But the association among these factors is not always simple. Even some patriarchal societies, in which female status is lower than that of males, have high divorce rates, for instance the Hausa, a traditional Muslim community in Nigeria (Solivetti, 1994).

Industrial countries demonstrate a steep increase in divorce rates over the last three decades. This may suggest that macro-social developments could make divorce a quasi-normative shift in the near future, at least in some Western societies. Already now, the fact that divorce is not an especially rare event in the West means that divorced partners are not particularly stigmatized or without role models (McKenry and Price, 1991). Divorcees find that friendships with others in the same position are especially important. These relationships provide a source of emotional support, an opportunity to share experiences, and a feeling of mutual acceptance. Divorced friends can be a ready source of help because such assistance is viewed as more spontaneous and less obligatory than help from family members.

Potential resources and added challenges in experiencing divorce

At this point, we are already discussing the resources that can make individuals cope effectively with the various challenges of divorce. In appraising this, we should keep in mind that divorce, as other life issues, is not a discrete life event, but rather a process that starts long before the actual divorce begins (Pledge, 1992), and that it is by no means ended with the signing of legal documents. Chiriboga (1991) concludes from his longitudinal data:

> Marital separation and divorce, in the long run, is not the solution to problems, but only a beginning of solutions. For many it was relief from the chronic duress of an unhappy marriage, for some it was also a crisis, but for all it posed a challenge to forge for themselves a new life. The process initiated by the decision to divorce in essence is the beginning of a transition that is successfully concluded only with the construction of a new and more satisfying life [p.292].

If a process consists of many different challenges that have to be met by using many different resources, as we have claimed, then it is not easy to formulate a general recipe for the 'successful' divorce. Many factors interact, though we can show from research that certain of these repeatedly appear as outstanding resources, as proposed in the developmental challenge model: higher self-esteem, family cohesion, social support (Farnsworth, Pett and Lund, 1989; Garvin, Kalter and Hansell, 1993), together with a sound economic situation. Additionally, the developmental challenge model would predict that those with a more flexible approach to living should cope better with separation than more-or-less 'stagnated' persons. Empirical findings support this claim: partners who have less traditional sex-role orientations during their marriage (Pledge, 1992), those with an androgynous lifestyle (Chiriboga, 1991) and non-conventional women (Hetherington, Law and O'Connor, 1997) are found to have fewer problems in adjusting to divorce than more traditional, conventional (possibly stagnated?) people.

There are a number of stresses that are specific to divorce, and these can further tax the individual's coping abilities because of their cumulative impact, or because of changes occurring in different areas of the individual's life within a short period of time (Pledge, 1992). For example, when health is already poor, divorce is more threatening to well-being and difficult to manage (Farnsworth, Pett and Lund, 1989). Furthermore, divorce leads to multiple and simultaneous changes in living conditions, finances, household routines, residence and custody of children. Each of these are quite difficult challenges in themselves (Hetherington, Law and O'Connor, 1997). For example, findings from the US suggest that the economic position of mid-life women whose marriages end can be seriously eroded. Most of these women experience a decline in their economic position, regardless of whether they are widowed or divorced, though the risk of falling into poverty is even greater for widows than for divorcees (Morgan, 1989).

Those coming from long-term marriages usually suffer from more post-divorce stress and poor adjustment. We would describe these couples as having previously stagnated within a certain kind of lifestyle, not having had the chance to learn alternative ways of living. Additionally, those for whom the pre-decision period is short and who are thus not necessarily well enough prepared for change, also experience stress (Barnet, 1990). Often, women endure more pre-decision stress, and take more time to reach a decision than men, but in turn seem to adjust better after divorce (Barnet, 1990). Furthermore, the partner who does not initiate the divorce, and has not perceived warning signs (and thus is undergoing an idiosyncratic non-normative shift, see table 4.1), may experience more conflict and deterioration in well-being (Gander, 1991).

A summary of the existing empirical findings in relation to the developmental challenge model can be seen in figure 5.1. As the figure shows, the interaction of resources and challenges plays a significant role over the period of the divorce process, and also indicates the importance of other situational factors.

Figure 5.1   **Potential resources interacting with potential tasks and with situational characteristics in the process of divorce**

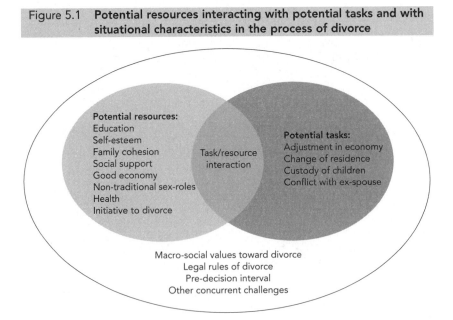

Potential resources:
Education
Self-esteem
Family cohesion
Social support
Good economy
Non-traditional sex-roles
Health
Initiative to divorce

Task/resource
interaction

Potential tasks:
Adjustment in economy
Change of residence
Custody of children
Conflict with ex-spouse

Macro-social values toward divorce
Legal rules of divorce
Pre-decision interval
Other concurrent challenges

A similar model to ours has been constructed by Tschann, Johnston and Wallerstein (1989) on the basis of their findings (see box below).

Tschann, Johnston and Wallerstein's 'divorce process' model

The 'divorce process' model of the various factors that can predict the extent of family adaptation to a crisis shows the cumulative effects of stresses and strains both before and after divorce. The model indicates factors that contribute to adaptation, such as personal, family and social resources, available or developed, to meet the demands of the crisis, and the family's general orientation to the total situation. The resources with which the separating partners meet the demands of divorce include structural assets, such as education and occupation; personal assets, like pre-separation psychological characteristics; and social assets, such as social activities, social support, and a possible new intimate relationship. Lack of these resources not only makes men and women more vulnerable to the stresses typically accompanying divorce, but, for men in particular, makes it less likely that they will develop the social resources further to enhance adaptation to life as a divorcee. Greater stresses (e.g. decreased income) and strains (e.g. conflict with their ex-spouse) accompanying the marital separation impair men's and women's adjustment, both directly and by increasing mutual animosity.

Hence, whether the final outcome is positive or negative depends on the form and quantity of resources the individuals possess. Research has given us examples of both. Hetherington, Law and O'Connor (1997) state that the strong negative emotions evoked by divorce usually disappear within two years. However, Lorenz *et al.* (1997) found that divorced mothers show more stressful and depressive symptoms than married women do, even three years after divorce. They conclude that divorce either accelerates additional stressful events, or that stressed mothers get involved in a series of events that accelerate divorce.

Divorce affecting other people in the micro-system

Seen from an ecological perspective, it is obvious that divorce affects – and is affected by – more than one psycho-social system. Beyond the divorcing couple, it is mainly children and grandparents who are caught up with the maelstrom of the event. The way they are affected by divorce is again dependent on what resources they have to cope with this situation, and how many different challenges the process of divorce creates for them. For example, in the first year after a divorce, mothers tend to be less nurturing to their children, less sensitive to their needs, less supportive of their efforts to deal with the day-to-day challenges of school, peer relations, homework and family life (Chase-Lansdale and Hetherington, 1990). Nevertheless, it has consistently been found that children adapt better in a well-functioning single-parent family or in a family with a step-parent than in a conflict-ridden family of origin. Totally in line with the developmental challenge model, and after more than two decades of research on marital transitions, Hetherington (1989) describes the possible variety of children's adjustments:

> Depending on the characteristics of the child, particularly the age and gender of the child, available resources, subsequent life experiences, and especially interpersonal relationships, children in the long run may be survivors, losers, or winners of their parents' divorce or remarriage [p.12].

In the same way, during divorce children can be a resource for their parents, an additional problem, or even both at different phases of the divorce process. In a review of the literature concerning individual responses to divorce, Pledge (1992) points out clearly that in many cases children do help their parents to displace their anxiety in making the adjustments to a single lifestyle. But this buffering effect might be offset later by increased stresses resulting from continuing contact with the ex-spouse over the children.

In the transition out of marriage, grandparents also play a decisive role. Those divorcing benefit hugely from a relationship with their own parents characterized by a strong degree of approval, as well as emotional and financial support. In turn, this has a positive effect on the children. Children with supportive grandparents are better adjusted mainly because their mothers are also better adjusted to the situation (Isaacs and Leon, 1987). However, sometimes the grandparents' role in their child's divorce can be perceived as an unwelcome interference (Myers and Perrin, 1993). Divorce can painfully disrupt the image grandparents have built up about their life and the unity of their extended family:

> A principal theme developed is that divorce exacerbates the role losses, challenges and ambiguities that naturally arise as a person ages. The grandparents' reaction to the divorce of their children involves not only grieving for the loss of their constructed image of the marriage...but can precipitate shame, anger and guilt [p.144].

Furthermore, as Gray and Geron (1995) identify, grandparents might be 'propelled back into an active parent role, physically, financially and psychologically'. For an increasing number of grandparents this means even taking on the role of surrogate parents for their grandchildren. In the US, for instance, there has been an increase of more than 40 per cent in children living with their grandparents in the decade before 1995 (Robertson, 1995). In a review of the existing research, Emick and Hayslip (1996) conclude that many grandparents are left ill-prepared to take on the role of 'custodial' grandparent. The role is a tenuous one, lacking formal norms, and permits individuals the freedom to define the role as they wish, yet with little guidance on how to do so:

> On balance, one might consider custodial grandparenting a potentially stressful role, whose demands with which some individuals are more able to cope than others, in light of concurrent influences as health, social and economic resources, the specific demands of the grandchild, marital status, and access to full-time/part-time work or respite care [p.145].

A number of studies suggest that care-giving grandparents have an increased risk of emotional and physical health problems, social isolation, family conflict, and legal and financial obstacles. At the same time, they report that grandparents can derive substantial emotional rewards from their child-rearing activities, and a renewed sense of purpose in bringing up another generation of young children (e.g. Burnette, 1998; Giarrusso, Silverstein and Bengtson, 1996).

As in other non-normative shifts, several challenges can accumulate and make the task more difficult to cope with, while added resources can facilitate the process. For care-giving grandparents in the US, for example, the task is aggravated by financial difficulties, as more than half of those still working had to give up their job (Pruchno, 1999). They have lower mean and median incomes than 'normal' grandparents, being 60 per cent more likely to report incomes below the poverty line (Fuller-Thompson, Minkler and Driver, 1997). Additionally, most of the grandparents' friends no longer have any children at home, and might not regard the inclusion of grandchildren into their joint activities with enthusiasm (Morrow-Kondos *et al.*, 1997). This can eventually lead to social isolation.

Thus, it is evident that the process of divorce can put grandparents at risk of draining their resources. This illustrates how risks and stresses can encompass various (or all) members of connected micro-systems, and how resources can be drained from different individuals in the face of a multifaceted challenge. How the non-normative challenges involved in being a custodial grandparent are tackled also depends to a great extent on reactions from the macro-system, particularly from public opinion and community acceptance. As Morrow-Kondos *et al.* (1997) conclude from the findings of their study:

> If a person moves into the role of raising grandchildren and society labels this as normal, the transition is likely to be smooth and easy. However, if the new role is considered unusual or unexpected by family and friends, the transition will be obscure and the person may experience difficulty [p.43].

This conclusion is strengthened by findings that black custodial grandmothers in the US are more likely than white ones to have friends who also live with their grandchildren, or to have lived themselves in their grandparents' home when young. Thus, feeling supported by their community, they less often feel trapped in their roles than their white counterparts, are less tired and isolated, and are less likely to feel that their social life and their relationships have suffered (Pruchno, 1999).

The role of a care-giving grandparent can be self-chosen, but it is often demanded, or even assumed, by other family members. In many cases, grandparents are quite unprepared, and take some time to adjust to their new role. A quotation from an interview in a study by Jendrek (1994) illustrates the initial disappointment and subsequent struggle of the grandparents:

> This is what we had planned and so forth, and it's just not fair for this to happen to us. I think it's mostly because we are so tired, we do have so much to do, and we did want so much. We know now if we're going to have any of it, we're going to have to try harder, and there are some things, which are just not going to happen. It's a self pity thing that I'm trying very hard to overcome [p.215].

While some grandparents get more involved in the divorce of their children than they might wish, others find themselves being excluded and separated from their grandchildren, since the parent can prevent the grandparents from having contact (Giarrusso, Silverstein and Bengtson, 1996). This has led a considerable number of grandparents in the US to seek legal help in order to achieve visitation rights (McGreal, 1994). We are fairly certain, however, that this does not occur to the same degree in regions such as Scandinavia, where even 'warring' parents often share custody of their children after a divorce.

Potential psycho-social outcomes of divorce

It is common to experience anxiety and negative emotions whenever one is confronted with the challenges a massive change elicits. But success-fully dealing with the challenges leads, more often than not, to feelings of personal development. This is particularly true for women, who frequently perceive divorce as a move from dependence to independence (Colburn, Lin and Moore, 1992). They view divorce as a sign of personal growth, and as a new start (Campbell, 1995) that leads to more autonomy and freedom (McKenry and Price, 1991). From the findings of a longi-tudinal study, encompassing several age cohorts, Chiriboga (1991) describes the process as follows:

> What we encountered, as we looked at the lives of these men and women, is that the stress context of divorce often prompts a growth experience...for many people, especially those in the middle years, the course of life had essentially been set when they married. Life scripts had been written, and the expected life course was more or less a certainty. Divorce upsets the expectable lives of our participants, adding uncertainty about the future to the troubles they already faced in their marriages. During the impact phase the majority of our participants were distressed...three and a half years later, it was a vastly different story. Many, if not most, of these people responded to the challenge, discovering in the process abilities and strengths they often had been unaware of [p.282f].

Thus, on many occasions, and dependent upon a number of factors, the experience of divorce can be considered more of an achievement than a failure, as a source of joy or other positive emotions rather than despair – a challenge well met. The quality of the experience is dependent on personal attitudes towards divorce, personality, age, gender, the level of independence during marriage, the length of the decision period, whether or not there is a continuing relationship with the ex-spouse, income level and social networks (Veevers, 1991). Hence, if the number and type of resources a person can mobilize matches the number and kind of challenges of the divorce, it can be a successful developmental process. On the other hand, if the goodness of fit is poor, it can be a mixed or even a distressing experience: 39 per cent of a Norwegian sample considered their own divorce as a 'very positive' event (though the process might have had negative aspects), while 25 per cent considered it as 'very negative' (Kloep, 2000). In Kloep's study, more women than men were positive about divorce – maybe for men, who always had other opportunities for personal growth outside a marriage, a partner-ship is more of a resource than a challenging process. As early as 1966, Musgrove commented that women got little from marriage except financial security, whereas men were provided with an 'in-house' therapist to assuage their cares and worries. Therefore, men lose more, and suffer more in separation and divorce. Little seems to have changed since then, as Hetherington, Law and O'Connor (1997) describe:

> Re-partnering is the single factor that contributes most to the life satisfaction of divorced men and women; however, it seems more critical to men. Divorced fathers are less likely than divorced mothers to show marked personal growth and individualization while they are single. Men show more positive development in the security of a marriage [p.184].

By utilizing the developmental challenge model, we have been able to show that a non-normative process such as divorce, which from the outside might seem like a painful and negative experience, can be a 'turning-point' leading to individual growth for the separating couple – or the direct opposite. Additionally, the events of divorce link the lives of other members of the micro-system into the process, so that even they can be enriched or have their resources drained by the challenges involved.

Influences from the macro-systems, in the form of public opinion and legal regulations, also affect the circumstances surrounding the divorce. All these different factors in concert, and dynamically interacting with each other, determine in the end whether the event of divorce turns out to be a step towards development, stagnation or decay.

An example of a historical shift: economic crisis

It might not be too surprising that divorce can turn out to be a positive event in the life of many people, leading to a new start, development and growth. On the other hand, it might seem quite incredible that a difficult, non-normative event such as a major economic crisis in a society could have beneficial outcomes. Nevertheless, this can be the case, as Elder (1974) has shown in his analysis of the different developmental pathways of children growing up during the years of the Great Depression in the US. In the following years, he and his colleagues could point out several important factors in the interplay between external economic change on the macro-social level and micro-social family experiences:

- Families differ in the material resources they have at the beginning of a national economic crisis, and in the way they are affected by it. Some families suffer hardly any decrease in income, while others have enormous financial problems.
- For some children of the Great Depression, the economic crisis turned out to be a 'steeling experience'. These were the children, who were affected by income loss, but who had enough family resources not to experience the event as a total catastrophe. The psychological health of middle-class children, who had suffered a considerable income loss, was better in their later adult years than that of middle-class children unaffected by the crisis. This indicates that they learned to cope effectively with such difficulties, and in the process learned resilience. In general, however, the psychological health of these middle-class children developed better than that of members of the working classes, for whom the economic crisis might have been too much of a challenge for their already scarce resources.

- Not all families that suffer economic hardship react alike, but rather use different coping strategies that lead to different long-term outcomes (Moen, Kain and Elder, 1983). For instance, postponing the birth of a second child may reduce for the time being the impact of economic loss, but may also prove to be a decisive act in creating forever a one-child family. Economic adjustment strategies that involve an element of loss – such as selling possessions, reducing purchases or using up savings – tend to have a more negative psychological impact on families than other arrangements, such as growing one's own vegetables, mothers working part-time or doing overtime whenever possible (Elder *et al.*, 1992).
- The situation, as defined by the participants, plays a decisive role. Whether or not individuals feel in control of their lives helps to shape how they believe that even a difficult situation can be dealt with competently (Moen, Kain and Elder, 1983).
- The timing of the crisis has an impact on how relatively easy it is to cope. Families with small children might have more problems than families with adolescents, who can help to stimulate the family economy by various means (Moen, Kain and Elder, 1983).
- If the country's economic crisis is exacerbated by a political crisis on the macro-level (as was the case in former European communist countries), families will also have to deal with 'internal' value clashes. These conflicts can occur where political differences, changing ideologies and a sense of 'anomie' can intensify family problems (Kloep and Hendry, 1997; Kloep and Nauni, 1994).

So far, we have been dealing with the response of the family microsystem to macro-social challenges. As Bronfenbrenner's (1979) ecological model would anticipate, interactions on the meso- and exo-level can also play a part. This is the case, as has been shown in various studies from the US (Elder *et al.*, 1992, Elder, van Nguyen and Caspi, 1985; Flanagan, 1990; Lempers, Clark-Lempers and Simons, 1989; Skinner, Elder and Conger, 1992); Germany (Silbereisen, Walper and Albrecht, 1990) and Albania (Kloep, 1994; Kloep and Tarifa, 1993a). All these indicate that economic difficulties generally affect children indirectly through the reactions of their parents (see figure 5.2). Typically, it is the father who responds to economic difficulties with increased hostility and acts more negatively towards his spouse. Additionally, negativity within the marital relationship, in association with financial difficulties, leads to more punitive, arbitrary and rejecting parenting. These changes in parental behaviour can, in turn, result in more temper tantrums and difficult, irritable behaviour among young children, and can increase the risk of aggressive behaviour and depressive feelings among adolescent boys and girls. However, if parents' marital relationships are unaffected or even strengthened by economic difficulties (particularly the case for couples with strong bonds before the crisis), this downward spiral need not be initiated, and children do not suffer in the same way. Furthermore, whether or not children develop behaviour problems can in turn have an effect on the parents' marital relationship, and might affect the family's economy even more negatively (see figure 5.2).

Figure 5.2   **Mechanisms that link economic crisis and child behaviour problems**

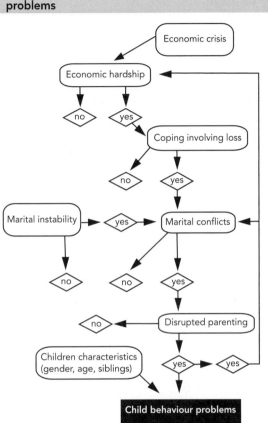

The risk of chronic poverty and resiliency resources

Almost all these examples are taken from relatively affluent countries that have only suffered a limited period of economic crisis. Chronic poverty has even more detrimental effects on people (e.g. Takeuchi, Williams and Adair, 1991), because it cumulatively drains an increasing number of resources, or prevents young children being given the opportunity to develop them. Even in the comparatively rich parts of the world, such as the European Union, 20 per cent of all children are assessed as being poor (UNICEF, 2000b). If children's poverty is defined, in relative terms, on the basis of households with incomes below 50 per cent of the national median, then we find that poverty in children ranges from 2.6 per cent in Sweden to 22.4 per cent in the US. Countries such as Italy, the UK, Canada, Australia and Ireland are in the lower (i.e. poorer) end of the scale; Sweden, Norway, Finland, Belgium, Luxembourg and Denmark are towards the upper (UNICEF, 2000b).

Poverty in its most extreme forms – which is certainly not rare across the world – can mean malnutrition, brain damage, child labour under health-damaging conditions, disease and a lack of formal education. These are conditions that drain available resources profoundly, so that even small tasks can become irresoluble obstacles. Poverty to that degree can seldom be seen as a challenge, but is rather a menacing risk that can deter most development.

However, even under such extreme conditions some individuals manage not only to survive, but can actually utilize resources to develop. Werner and Smith (1982) followed a cohort of Hawaiian children from birth into their late teenage years. They found that a number of these multiply underprivileged children, against all odds, underwent relatively normal development. In investigating the factors that made these particular youths resilient, they discovered that they proactively sought and received help from a great number of sources (see for comparison Philip and Hendry's 1996 study of disadvantaged adolescents in a Western culture). It seems as if, regardless of all deprivation and disadvantages, the chances for positive developmental outcomes were greater for those who possessed a wider range of personal and structural resources. These protective factors included the following:

- being reared by somewhat better educated mothers
- having received attention from primary care-givers during the first year of life
- growing up in multi-age households that included members of the grandparent generation
- having had age-appropriate perceptual-motor, communication and reasoning skills when tested at the ages of two and ten years.

Resilient children also reported a significantly smaller number of cumulative life stresses, such as problems in family relationships, maternal mental health problems, absence of father from the family home, financial problems, serious illnesses or accidents, teenage pregnancy and early marriage. Among other characteristics, social orientation, nurturing and a 'healthy androgyny' figured significantly. As Werner and Smith (1982) point out, their study replicates the findings of many others, and reflects the biographies of poets and writers who, throughout history, surmounted deprivation, poverty and persecution in their early lives:

> All give us a glimpse of the universality of the enduring forces that allow the human species to overcome adversity.... These families were poor by material standards, but a characteristically strong bond was forged between the infant and the primary care taker during the first year of life. The physical robustness of the resilient children, their high activity level, and their social responsiveness were recognized by the care-givers and elicited a great deal of attention.... The strong attachment that resulted appears to have been a secure base for the development of the advanced self help skills and autonomy noted among these children in their second year of life [p.155f].

The number of protective factors that discriminated between positive and negative developmental outcomes in this cohort increased as relative stress and deprivation increased. In other words, as disadvantages increased, more protective factors were needed by the children to counterbalance risks.

Following members of the cohort into their early thirties, Werner and Smith (1992) described how one third of the high-risk sample – the 'resilients' – developed into competent, confident, determined adults with a positive vision of their life course. It appears that even those who had been 'delinquescent' teenagers and those with mental health problems had, by and large, adapted and adjusted in adulthood. This is not to say that all had met life's challenges and developed. One quarter of males and ten per cent of females had criminal records at the age of thirty-two years. As other studies have shown (e.g. Farrington, 1989), there seems to be a trend that engaging earlier and in more criminal activity in adolescence is associated with more adult crime.

One of the most important findings to emerge from this study that bridged a substantial number of years is that there is a cumulative effect of resolving challenges through the life course. The authors interpret development as occurring through the use of various protective factors, which come into operation in developmental sequence and which enable successful adult adaptation:

- Early childhood characteristics that evoke positive responses from adult care-givers lead to the development of autonomy and social competence in the toddler.
- Added to this are the essential roles of parental competence and care-giving (especially from the mother) and the possession of a sound support network, both for the individual and the family.
- Later, scholastic attainment and 'good' behaviour at school (i.e. 'staying out of trouble') seem to be keys to progress in middle childhood.
- In late adolescence, setting realistic educational and vocational goals leads on to low levels of distress and emotionality in adulthood.

Overall, the findings suggest that resilient individuals are capable of actively selecting social environments that reinforce culturally appropriate competencies. Hence, while individuals range from resiliency to vulnerability across the lifespan, there are important 'turning-points' in the life course, at which the strategies used in performing tasks or meeting challenges can begin to initiate a cumulative process towards either development or decay.

One of the most important resources, which contributed to effective coping amongst the 'resilients' in adulthood, appeared to be a personal confidence that challenges could be surmounted. Some children developed this positive quality early in life through caring adults, but many of their troubled teenage peers had a 'second chance' at developing a sense of self-worth in adulthood, for example through encounters with persons who opened up opportunities, acted as mentors, and gave them meaning in their lives.

Thus, early events in life are not the only ones that affect later adjustment to the world of work, relationships or parenthood. The optimistic message from these findings is that it is possible to compensate for some resources that are lacking by replacing them with others. In fact, if the existing, remaining resources can interact in a highly positive manner, they can, under certain circumstances, turn even extremely stressful, disadvantaged situations into settings for challenge and growth.

Conclusions

In this chapter we have examined the impact of non-normative shifts on the resource 'pool', and on the micro-systems the individual inhabits, by examining closely the experiences resulting from the process of divorce and of economic crisis and poverty in society. These examples of divorce and economic hardship, in which the outcome for the individual depends on a complicated interplay of challenges and resources, are illustrative in relation to the developmental challenge model. These experiences can lead to a draining, maintaining or strengthening of future potential resources, and can enable us to see the dynamics of challenge and coping responses in interaction with various psycho-social systems.

Firstly, we outlined the various factors enabling divorce to become a relatively positive experience, providing added resources for the individual's future life. Some of these characteristics included maturity, optimism, coherence, locus of control, coping strategies, social support, extended education and social-economic status. Such elements were relevant for all those affected by the divorce process, including children, grandparents and friends.

Secondly, we considered the effects of economic crisis on individuals and families. For those suffering from economic loss, different factors were influential on the psycho-social outcomes they experienced. These were factors like timing in the life course, feelings of control, choice of coping strategies, and the impact of economic hardship on marital satisfaction and parenting styles. We also looked at the characteristics of resilience in disadvantage and poverty, and saw many reflective aspects of the developmental challenge model in these empirical findings from early childhood through adolescence to adulthood.

Both examples also illustrate Bronfenbrenner's (1979) ecological model by showing the strong impact of the macro-system on decisions that are actually made within micro-systems, and the influence on and by 'linked lives' within these. They support the developmental challenge model by demonstrating that if the number and type of resources a person can mobilize matches the number and kinds of challenges, then even difficult non-normative shifts, such as divorce or economic hardship can become adaptive and positive processes that enable future successes and create added resources.

6 First encounters with the world: the challenges of childhood

Introduction

When the new-born child first views the world it will immediately meet a whole range of developmental challenges (though of course development actually begins long before birth). Never again in life will the human being be confronted with so many maturational shifts as during childhood. From soon after birth, body dimensions and proportions change rapidly, forcing the child to interact with the environment by continuous bodily adjustments and fine-tuning of skills.

We begin by considering the development of psycho-motor skills, so evidently the significant integrative vehicle for early childhood learning, in order to illustrate the coherent nature of these early learning processes.

Then we look at social skills as another example of the co-ordination of perceptual, cognitive and motor modalities in the child. For this we consider the various levels of Bronfenbrenner's (1979) social systems, to show how early learning progresses from the level of social groups to institutions: in early childhood the micro-system of the family is essential, later to be followed by peer groups, and finally the school system and other institutions. Thus, in discussing this period of the lifespan we focus on three important types of maturational shift and social challenge:

- maturational changes and the learning of psycho-motor skills
- social skills involved in 'vertical' and 'horizontal' relationships
- the normative shift of beginning formal schooling.

From the framework of the developmental challenge model, these examples depict how early development evolves from the ecological interactions of the child's initial resource system with the various psycho-motor, social and cognitive challenges it meets during the first years of life.

Maturational changes as challenges to learn psycho-motor skills

The skills to be learnt in relation to the changing body are normally referred to as motor skills, but are, in fact, much more sophisticated than that. Movements are an integral part of a highly complicated behavioural puzzle of interacting perceptual, cognitive, emotional and/or social skills: they are, as Welford (1968) and Argyle (1967) called them some years ago, psycho-motor skills.

This becomes quite obvious if one observes for a while how a child reaches out, grasps a rattle and shakes it: a highly complex pattern of co-ordinated perceptual, motor and cognitive skills in such a small movement. In order to perform this movement, children need to have learned head control, upper torso control, to extend the arm toward distant objects – not to mention skills of attention, motivation and memory – a repertoire that takes several months to acquire (Spencer *et al.*, 2000).

Using the terminology of the developmental challenge model, the wish to grasp the rattle implies a challenge, and to cope with it involves the interactive utilization of parts of the resource 'pool', mainly integrated behavioural patterns of different categories of skills. Any new skill (whether it is perceptual, motor, social or cognitive) will constitute a new resource that might become useful in learning other, even more complex, skills – and will thus be an addition to the 'pool'. In other words, in observing the child playing with its rattle, you have just become witness to a developmental process.

The challenge of moving around

Whoever has observed a baby for a lengthy period must have noticed that what the little child wants to do most of all is to move around and explore the environment – leading literally to the first steps in further development. The ability to change position in space allows perceptual information to come to the child from a multiplicity of environmental sources and aids integrative learning. Not surprisingly, infants who move around in the environment (by crawling or using a wheeled-walker) have better spatial abilities, show increased attention to their environment and socialize more with other people than children who do not move around or crawl on their bellies (Thelen and Smith, 1998).

In order to accommodate the large human brain, babies are born with a head a quarter of their total body size. They are also relatively fat, to make up for the fact that, unlike the young of many animals, they do not have fur to keep them warm. Further, they have not built up muscles strong enough to cope with gravity while floating around in the womb: in all, babies do not have many initial resources with which to meet the challenge of moving in the physical environment. This does not, however, mean that the baby's movements are best characterized as involuntary, purposeless, or even as simple as an excited thrashing of the limbs. In a series of experimental studies, van der Meer and her colleagues 1996, 1997a) have shown that new-born babies, given the oppor are in fact capable of producing quite sophisticated and pre controlled arm movements. They move their arms more when thc, ___ see them, and they can keep their arms in full view even when small weights are placed to pull them down in the direction of their toes. Additionally, placed in a darkened room and only allowed to see their arms in a narrow beam of light, within minutes they are able to reach towards that spot of light. This is strongly indicative of the fact that new-born babies learn extremely quickly, and are capable of combining visual and kinaesthetic feedback as aids to learning and to remembering movement patterns.

A different challenge presents itself when it comes to the child adjusting its locomotion to changing environments, and new ways of meeting these challenges have to be learnt. For instance, children who have learned to judge whether or not a slope is too steep for them to crawl down have to evaluate this perceptual-motor task all over again when it comes to walking instead of crawling down the slope (Adolph, 1997). Thus, babies 'learn to learn', they do not learn facts. They learn to adjust their balance according to their postural situation, and they have to learn this over and over again for each new postural task (i.e. crawling, sitting, walking), because a different co-ordination of body parts is involved in each activity, eventually building up a general kinaesthetic schema.

Earlier researchers thought that a kind of 'stepping' reflex existed in neonates, because a new-born child, held upright with feet touching the ground, will make 'walking' movements. This reflex disappears for some months within the first year of life. Researchers believed this happened because of the reorganization of the nervous system during the time until the child learns to walk 'for real'. However, Thelen (1983, 1984) gives a quite different interpretation of this phenomenon. Her findings show that babies put on so much body weight for a period of time that they cannot perform the stepping reflex due to lack of strength, but 'regain the skill' when they have grown again to the appropriate body proportions. In an ingenious series of experiments (Thelen *et al.*, 1982, Thelen and Fisher, 1982), she and her colleagues made babies artificially lighter (i.e. submerging their legs in water) or heavier (by attaching weights to their legs). As Thelen had predicted, she could remove and reintroduce the 'stepping reflex' simply by manipulating the babies' weight and body proportions. These results show that it is not simply maturation at work, but the kind of challenge that is being presented interacting with (however temporary) available resources, such as having the right body proportions or environmental features, that facilitate or hinder the attempted resolution of a particular challenge. This is, of course, not only true for growing infants. Anyone who has closely observed a teenager just after the growth spurt, or a heavily pregnant woman, will be aware that it is necessary to adjust movement skills in order to meet the challenges of changing body features and proportions. A great deal of interactive learning is necessary in order for these developments to take place. For example, we now know that a baby takes between 500 and 1500 steps an hour on average, on a variety of different surfaces, in order to learn to walk steadily (Adolph, personal communication, 2001).

Bladder control, which involves highly specific muscle control, is another example of a task that in Western cultures has long been regarded as a completely maturational process. The general view in the West is that toilet training should not be started too early, in order to avoid frustrations in the child. Hence, the average age of the fully toilet-trained child in Europe, America and Japan has increased quite dramatically in recent years (van der Meer, 1997b). To meet this demand, nappy producers have flooded the market with ultra-absorbent brands that look like real underwear. In the face of such attractive commercial resources, it is neither an attractive or urgent challenge for the child or its care-giver to put effort into learning the necessary skills – an example of how even a highly personal skill like bowel control is under the influence of macro-social mechanisms.

By contrast, in many African and Asian societies infants are expected to be toilet-trained (day and night, bladder and bowel) well before their first birthday. In these cultures it is believed that babies have to pass all the major psycho-motor milestones, including bladder control and spoon use, really early in life. Mothers in Mali, Korea and among the Bambara in Africa, for example, have expectations that their children's development should occur at much earlier stages than European mothers (Bril, Zack and Nkounou-Hombessa, 1989). They use massage techniques and baby gymnastics, keep their babies more often in an upright position (even during sleep) and have them interact much more with the environ-ment than babies in the West. As a result, babies born into these cultures are advanced in their motor development by comparison with their peers in industrialized societies (Bril, 1997). Healthy physical development can serve as the most extreme example of maturational shifts. However, as we have seen, not even this development is purely maturational, but heavily influenced by other 'acquired' resources, such as body shape, skills training and learning.

Psycho-motor skills as a resource for understanding the world
Hand-in-hand with these bodily changes and the accompanying acquisition of psycho-motor skills comes an increasing exploration of and learning about the environment. Things are seen, touched, smelled and tasted, and cognitively ordered into schemata according to the practical meaning and function they have for the child. Children learn to ignore an object's irrelevant features and to respond to those that have 'action potentials', such as a chair for sitting in, a pen for drawing (Gibson, 1991). Perceptual categorizations go across division lines such as 'edible' or 'non-edible', 'pleasant' or 'unpleasant', 'useful' or 'useless'. Children learn within days to distinguish the sight, sounds and smells of their mother from other human beings. It will take them considerably longer to discriminate between 'bow-wows' and other animals, and most of them will never learn the difference between a swallow and a swift, because the distinction is not important in their daily life. Learning these differences is not a cognitive task alone, but is, as are all tasks, interwoven with perceptual-motor skills. So, Thelen and Smith (1998) argue that movement *per se* should be considered as a perceptual system, and that there is little or no learning or development that is strictly within one modality. Even in a simple task, like perceiving a visual stimulus,

the edges, colours and motion of the scene are joined by precise and synchronous activation of eye movement detectors:

> Movement...must be considered the common primitive of cognitive development, and may well be the dynamic control parameter in the emergence of many early skills. If self-produced movement is critical, then dynamic category formation – the infant's basic organization of the world – must be paced and constrained by the ability to produce and control that movement.... At the same time that these motor skills are critical for understanding, the increased perceptual specificity learned through movement also contributes to more accurate and efficient actions....As infants learn about the properties of cups – that they hold liquid, afford drinking from and putting small objects into, are graspable by the handle or with two hands – they also learn dynamically the appropriate motor responses by which to accomplish these actions...infants must learn...the match between their own abilities and the qualities of the world that support action within it [p.194f].

As is well known, the Innuit have many more words for snow than people living in less icy areas. However, simply being able to name the different weather conditions does not help them. It is necessary for them to differentiate between these conditions because of the behavioural implications such a distinction has: what to wear, how to dress, whether or not to go hunting. The learning of different concepts, the ability to categorize them and to react accordingly, is the basis of all skills learning, and happens daily for as long as we live.

The meaning different concepts have for daily life in our culture has a strong impact on what we learn, how we think and how we act. For a long time researchers assumed, for example, that people from some indigenous tribes are less intelligent than modern Western people, simply because they achieved lower scores on Western intelligence tests. Further analysis by cross-cultural psychologists (e.g. Glick, 1975) revealed that this is not a question of greater or lesser intelligence, but of different thinking categories dependent on different cultural needs. Asked, for example, to pick out three matching pictures from a set of four (a saw, an axe, a shovel and a piece of wood), Liberian peasants chose on the basis of the concrete situation in which they would use the objects: to cut a piece of wood, one needs an axe and a saw. Westerners, on the other hand, categorized the objects saw, shovel and axe together, using the abstract category 'tools' (and were rewarded IQ scores for this kind of reasoning). This example shows how the demands and procedures of daily living in different cultures shape different concepts and different ways of thinking.

Even in the same culture, there are different concepts and ways of thinking between, for example, age-groups, dependent on the significance certain concepts have for the life of individuals. These different social contexts, rather than maturation, affect perceptions and reasoning. Piaget (1970), however, assumed that small children think in a qualitatively different way from older ones, and are unable to form certain types of concepts or learn certain principles (such as conservation and class-inclusion) before a given age. The work of more recent scholars, however, has shown that the inability of young children to solve some of Piaget's tasks is more dependent on a lack of motivation. If the tasks are transformed into more play-like activities (e.g. having a 'naughty teddy' play a role in the experiment) or if their solution is made more meaningful to the child ('Do you want all the sweets or all the red sweets?') than the original task ('Are there more marbles or more red marbles in the glass?'), children can problem-solve at a much younger age than Piaget had postulated (Donaldson, 1978). This shows that motivation determines what is regarded as meaningful, and thus what concepts are needed. Given the differences in daily life between children and adults, and between younger and older adults, it is not surprising that these differences obtain.

In order to learn different concepts, categorize them, and understand their interaction and interconnectedness, children have to solve myriad small tasks actively. From early on, they have been observed using and training meta-skills, such as repeating new words, rehearsing, talking to themselves and structuring tasks, imitating and experimenting. In a recent study, Matre (2000) shows that children act like small researchers in trying to understand the world in conversations with their peers. They evaluate new information critically, they mentally try out different consequences of different assumptions, they clarify notions and use creative thinking and logical reasoning in trying to solve problems (see box below for an example).

An example of a dialogue between two five-year-olds, showing their use of reasoning

(Matre, 2000: p.88, translated from Norwegian by the authors):

Per:	…and my daddy he is thirteen.
Hilde:	No, no, that's not possible.
Per:	Thirteen, yes.
Hilde:	No, because there is a girl, her name is Veronika, and she is thirteen…

Learning to build up social resources

Another developmental challenge that is vital for the neonate and for the growing child is that of forming different kinds of social relationships. As new-born babies are dependent on nurture from a care-giver, a social relationship with an older person is necessary for survival. Thus, initially the child has to learn how to interact with another human being in a hierarchical, vertical relationship from a position of powerlessness. This implies that in order to facilitate the relationship the child needs to develop a range of social skills such as:

- trust and attachment
- intimacy
- communication
- negotiation (e.g. being charming, testing boundaries, telling lies, blackmailing)
- obedience.

An example of extending social resources

Picture the little toddler, who on a visit to an unfamiliar flat clings to its mother's legs without looking up at anyone or anything for the first ten minutes. After that, the child has topped up its 'pool' with sufficient security and the environment has, accordingly, become less challenging. Cautiously exploring the nearest surroundings, the child investigates first with its eyes, then by crawling round its mother's feet, then by distancing itself some metres further, but still in eye-contact with mother. Finally the little imp is found in the bathroom exploring what happens if someone mixes Chanel No 5 with toothpaste in the toilet bowl…

Several researchers (e.g. Ainsworth, 1979; Bowlby, 1969) have highlighted the importance of trust and feelings of secure attachment to the care-giver (see box above for an example). The quality of attachment has a significant impact on the development of the child's social relationships later in life. Additionally, it impinges on whether or not the care-giver will be chosen as a role model in learning different skills (Bandura, 1977), or later, as a confidant to the teenager. 'Child disclosure', child-initiated communication and parental warmth are seen as the best predictors of positive adjustment in the adolescent years in Western societies (Stattin and Kerr, 2000; Trost, Stattin and Kerr, 2000). Mentoring relationships with one or several older people is also a basis for other resources (Philip and Hendry, 2000). Apparently 'powerful' adults, attending to the child's demands, let the child conclude that it has some kind of self-efficacy and control over social situations. This reinforces and strengthens self-appraisal skills. Since positive feedback comes from others, interactions with them will be seen as rewarding, thus adding new relationships (and more social skills) to the resource 'pool'.

Trust, together with the absence of social anxiety, is the most important resource to be gained in the early childhood years. This seems to be true not only for human infants, but for primates as well. Harlow's seminal studies (Harlow and Harlow, 1966; Harlow and Zimmerman, 1959) have demonstrated this convincingly: monkeys, raised on a steel imitation of a mother monkey, providing the little ones with only food and drink, but not with warmth and affection, suffered serious adjustment problems in their social development. So it would seem that if the care-giver can provide an aura of trust and security, children have enough resources to dare to meet the challenges of a relatively 'unknown' environment. Thus, they all learn some social skills within a hierarchical interpersonal relationship. However, cultural differences put so much variation into this relationship that a broad variety of skills are learnt:

- Children grow up in different forms of family units within the same society. Some children are raised in an extended family with many care-givers, others live in a nuclear family with parents (of whom one or both may not be their biological parents). Some live with only one parent, others in an institution with well educated, professional carers, or in one that only provides basic care, or are fostered out. Or they might try to survive in the street, without much contact with adults.

- Different parental styles will operate between different macro-social systems; thus, care-givers will react differently to children and have different child-raising methods in different cultures. For instance, in Sweden, for several decades now the law has forbidden corporal punishment, while some child researchers in the US (e.g. Baumrind, 1996) still promote its use under certain circumstances, claiming its educational effectiveness. In traditionally patriarchal societies, like Albania (where the prevailing social attitude says that *not* beating a child means that the parent does not care for it), the use of corporal punishment correlates slightly positively with child adjustment, while in Northern European it tends to correlate negatively (Kloep and Tarifa, 1992). Thus parents use different socializing styles, and children react differently to them, depending on the prevailing attitudes and traditions in their culture. Accordingly, the form and pattern of relational skills and the degree of trust children learn will differ hugely, dependent on the existing social and cultural conditions.

Interaction with peers

Having learnt how to deal with relationships from a less powerful position, the child is now ready to learn how to interact with peers. These 'equal' relationships demand a different range of social skills than vertical relationships with adults. Obviously, pestering, whimpering and temper tantrums do not have the same effect on peers as on parents. So the skills to be learned are competencies such as:

- negotiating
- taking turns in conversations
- sharing
- empathizing
- keeping promises
- mutual trust.

Egocentricity or just inexperience?

So-called egocentric behaviour, often ascribed to young children (such as bringing one's own mother to comfort a crying friend, even though the other's mother is actually present), might also be interpreted as a beginner's way of trying out new collaborative social skills. Children, like adults, generalize from situations they know, and apply that experience to new ones, trying out behaviours that have worked for them previously. To illustrate this, just answer the following question: what kind of present would you choose for a person relatively unknown to you? Probably something that you would like to have yourself. An egocentric act?

It takes some time observing others and rehearsing and trying out these 'horizontal' skills before young children easily take up the challenge of starting friendships. In many textbooks, a study by Parten (1932) is still quoted, suggesting that there is a time at which young children engage in 'parallel play', meaning playing side-by-side without interacting with one another. We suggest that children engage in these seemingly parallel activities because they still lack interaction skills, not because they lack interest or because they are too caught up by their own interests (see box above for a discussion of child egocentricity). Furthermore, even though they may lack the capacity for verbal communication, already one-year-olds can be observed having a multitude of ways of communicating, usually by 'doing' their relationships, using actions based on shared meanings in order to communicate non-verbally (Løkken, 2000).

Once they are willing to interact with peers, children start the long process of learning social skills within more-or-less equal relationships. Often they have to learn the hard way to negotiate reciprocal arrangements. In any playground, young children run to their mothers, bitterly complaining about having been hit by another child whose toy they had earlier confiscated, or crying that nobody wants to play with them, after dominating the other children too much! This is the time when vital social resources are laid down in the resource 'pool'. It seems as if children who do not learn the essential social skills that are necessary for 'equal' relationships in the early years have considerable difficulties later in life making up this deficit. A number of children who are already described as 'anti-social' by their nursery schoolteachers retain this behaviour for the rest of their lives (Loeber, 1985).

Patterson (1996) explains this process as follows: because of restricted resources on the part of the parents (social disadvantage, single-parenthood, lack of parenting skills and so on), children become both irritable and irritating, and effective parenting practices are disrupted. As a consequence, the child will not be reinforced for pro-social behaviour (i.e. friendly attention-seeking), but only for aggressive, anti-social acts. For example, the child either gets a great deal of parental attention, or can cause the parent to stop verbal or physical chastisement by contra-aggression. Consequently, the child learns social skills that most often lead to rejection by others (including the parents, who become increasingly irritated by their 'difficult' child). As a result, the child seeks out other anti-social friends among peers, and they continue to reinforce each others' anti-social behaviour, a trajectory that can lead to the early onset of delinquency.

Having failed to build up essential resources to cope with social challenges, these children can miss out on building up other resources that emerge from social relationships, such as attempting to acquire sporting, dancing or activity skills. Children who lack social skills are unpopular, are excluded from activities, and are 'attacked' rather than helped by others. In addition, they get little feedback to enhance their self-efficacy appraisals. Starting off with a serious deficit in certain resources can cause a cumulative draining of the individual's other resources, thus leading to a downward spiral of development from which it is difficult, though not impossible, to recover.

Under ideal conditions, children learn a range of effective social skills together with siblings or friends of their choice in a secure environment, sometimes with the help of an adult to advise them in difficult situations, and to guard them against the rougher treatment of older peers. If this is the case, they are ready after some years to face the next social challenge of integrating with and forming relationships with a wider, less self-selected peer group in the local community. Children are then prepared enough to meet and interact with new companions in school and leisure organizations. With practice in these new forms of socializing, children begin to feel more and more competent and self-assured with their new range of skills, and less and less need to feel the added security of adult assistance and organization. Eventually, in Western societies, as adolescence proceeds, they are ready and eager to meet their peers without the supervision of adults (Hendry *et al.*, 1993).

In this context, it is interesting to note that there are considerable gender differences in the way peer relationships are formed, and consequently in the developmental social tasks young girls and boys learn (Golombok and Fivush, 1994). In Western societies, girls and boys prefer to play and interact with peers of the same gender from a very early age, maybe because the two genders already prefer different activities. Later, it is more common for girls to have a few intimate 'best friends', with whom they share secrets, problems and intimacies. Boys are more likely to play in bigger groups and have many casual friends with whom they share activities but not close relationships. Thus, boys learn to compete, to organize, to co-operate in bigger groups, to be a 'follower' and a 'leader', whereas girls learn how to avoid and solve conflicts, to maintain a relationship and to communicate in dyads or small groups. These differential relationship patterns often persist for the rest of the lifespan.

There are, however, cultural variances in this pattern. In more collectivistic societies, for example, males regard it as much more important to achieve harmony again after a conflict than to use legal rules to solve it (a pattern that resembles the Western female's conflict-solving style). In individualistic cultures, males value compliance with legal rules considerably more highly than a consideration of moral rules or the recreation of harmony and friendship (Bierbrauer, 1994).

Learning in school and leisure

The next significant developmental challenge that awaits today's children is going to school. Nowadays, this is a normative challenge in many cultures, though formal schooling did not exist for most children less than two centuries ago. Before that time, children could learn all they required – and all that society needed them to learn for survival – at home. This is still true for some rural societies, where particularly women are prepared for their future roles by helping their mothers in the home and in the fields from a very early age. Only with industrialization did the level of skills demanded from workers become greater than could be learned by apprenticeship to adult craftsmen. Thus, formal schooling became necessary for the masses. With higher demands from industry for skilled employees, obligatory schooling became more and more extended, to its present length, which includes university education for many. Nowadays, almost all countries have a formal school system, even though rules concerning pupil attendance – and enforcement of these rules – vary widely across cultures, depending on their economic structure. In the extremely poor sub-cultures of many countries, parents cannot afford to send their children to school, because they need the children's help in earning money for the family budget (see box below). In traditional cultures, in which children are security for their parents' old age, and in which a higher education means a higher income, parents are more willing to invest in their offsprings' education. In modern welfare societies, in which economic support in old age is guaranteed, and children have more emotional than economic value for their parents, it is the state that enforces education in order to produce enough highly-skilled members of the workforce to compete in the global marketplace. An increasing institutionalization of education facilitates the burden of child-rearing, so that both parents are free to work (Jensen, 1994). Thus, the impact of different macro-systems on the lives of children is obvious.

Some macro-social conditions affecting children's development

- Every year, throughout the world, 12 million children under five die.[1]
- About half of these deaths are caused by five or six specific illnesses that can be easily cured at low cost. For instance, to vaccinate all US children against polio in a ten-year programme would cost $100 000 000. At the same time, it would save $114 000 000 dollars per year in healthcare and treatment of the condition.[2]
- Only 10 per cent of all development aid given by world governments is used to satisfy the most basic needs of poorer countries, such as health-care, education, clean drinking water and family planning.[2]
- One-hundred-and-thirty-million children, almost two thirds of them girls, are denied the right to primary education.[3]
- Poorer countries today owe about ten times as much to the rich industrial countries as they receive in resources from them (foreign aid, private investments and private loans taken together). This means, for instance, that countries in Africa pay more money in interest for their foreign debt than they can invest in their own healthcare and education.[1]
- The market protection methods introduced by rich countries (amongst them taxes and customs duty on goods) cost developing countries about the same amount again because of the reduction in their exports to Western countries.

All figures from UNICEF, The State of the World's Children
1 2001.
2 1992.
3 1999.

The school curriculum as challenge and risk

Most Western schools offer a curriculum that is rather detached from the child's own world of experience, and is tailored more towards the needs of future employers than to the child's own interests. This is also reflected in the social organization of learning – the 'hidden curriculum'. As Furlong (1991) says:

> Through our power we attempt to try to get children to accept certain values, to aspire to certain futures for themselves. Education structures are used not just to impose certain sorts of behaviour but to construct young people in particular ways. We do not use our power simply to force children to act in these ways. Rather we insist that they come to see themselves and organize their lives in these ways [p.304].

Furthermore, the teaching emphasis is on cognitive skills, whereas children enter school with differing needs, skills and existing resources. Classroom groupings are most often arranged by chronological age and not according to the child's skill level, despite claims for individually devised learning programmes in some schools. Attempts in pedagogics to design special programmes to motivate children's learning by, for example, more problem-based teaching, do not have the same effects on all children. In one study, Sander and Draschoff (2000) evaluated a computer-based interactive trigonometry programme designed to create cognitive conflicts in learners in order to motivate different solution strategies. The programme had very positive effects – but only on learners who already had satisfactory mathematical skills (and thus a high level of perceived security in that area). Those with less resources within this area were not at all motivated by the challenge presented (more likely, they were made anxious). This is a good example of the provocative statement of the German philosopher Lichtenberg about books, namely that they make clever people cleverer and stupid people more stupid! In our terms, Lichtenberg means that a challenge can cause a resourceful person to develop, while it can drain the resource 'pool' of a less resourceful person even more.

The school system as it works today builds on cumulative knowledge. Unfortunately, for those who miss out on the basics, this also means cumulative disadvantages: they might initially learn a little bit of addition, subtraction and multiplication, for instance, but before understanding the concepts are moved on to another set of problems, which they have no chance of comprehending. In this way, their initial weaknesses will be exacerbated instead of improved in course after course. Apart from destroying motivation and not providing the necessary skills for individual advancement, this downward spiral of accumulated school failure effectively drains self-esteem and other resources from the 'pool'. Given this, the normative shift to formal schooling is a highly risky event for many children.

By using the developmental challenge model, it is easy to see that some children will face challenges that far exceed their existing resources (and this will drain them further). On the other hand, others will be under-challenged and bored to such an extent that they will start to search for challenges elsewhere. As Andersson (1995) says about the Swedish school system: 'School is good for many students, but school is also bad for too many students' (p.113). This is echoed by writers such as Willis (1977) and Oldman (1994), who suggest that many children dislike school so much that they 'vote with their feet' and play truant.

However, most societies have decided that children must begin to meet the challenge of schooling somewhere between the age of four and seven, and by doing so have marked the transition from 'early' to 'middle' childhood. In this process, they confront children with many important, decisive, formal challenges, such as learning:

- a new form of communication, the written language
- concepts of numbers and mathematical procedures
- scientific thinking, in the form of hypothesis-testing and logical reasoning.

In addition, children are asked to:

- develop an interest in potential leisure activities for the future, such as arts, music or sports
- respond appropriately to the 'hidden curriculum' of discipline, time management and conformity.

To be fair to the schooling systems in most Western societies, authoritarian educational and teaching styles are diminishing, and the early independence of pupils' learning is an emphasized goal. Teachers try to create learning situations that demand independent and individual decisions from pupils, such as weekly planning of their own learning programme, project work and the selection of optional courses. However, these small adaptations do not resolve the need to provide more pupils with learning experiences that realistically match their capabilities and enable them to meet educational and social challenges in a manner that gives them even greater resources. Further appreciation of skills development, instead of a focus on pure reproduction of knowledge, testing and certification, is prevented by various macro-social forces, which differ in their image of an optimally socialized and educated citizen.

Furthermore, social behaviours learned in the family and in leisure-time may not match those required by the school. Children are less quiescent these days, and do not obey authority figures such as teachers just because of their formal social position. Nowadays, respect has to be earned, and motivation for learning has to be created, not enforced. This leads to clashes between schools, young people's values and 'resistance' behaviours, parents' expectations and employers' demands.

All this has consequences for individual young people. Much of the basic content of their resource 'pool' is determined during the school years, though not all skills they learn are part of the official curriculum, and might be more-or-less desirable for their society. Many valuable skills that should be learned in schools encompass meta-skills, namely skills of 'learning how to learn'. Here schools might actually play a detrimental role, if they constrain children's enthusiasm for learning or force upon them a 'stagnated', uni-dimensional way of thinking. This might well prepare children to fit into a society that values conventionality, conformity and only a modicum of individuality, but it hardly provides them with resources for change. Curricula and teaching techniques further the division of individuals into 'conventionalists' or 'adventurers', into 'developers' or 'stagnators'.

Some of the skills pupils learn, they develop in spite of, not because of, formal teaching. These skills might involve obviously risky behaviours like cheating and playing truant, but they can represent creative ways of thinking and acting as well, emerging as a 'quiet' rebellion against authority. While the school system claims to provide the same opportunities for all, the 'products' of formal education range from nicely adapted conformists to rebellious geniuses and losers who drop out. Once more, we have an example of how macro-social regulations (such as national curricula) interact with different micro-social conditions (such as teachers', parents' and peers' attitudes), and with individual young people's resources. All these combine to create a series of challenges that can lead to development, stagnation or decay.

Leisure and developmental challenge

However, learning about the world does not occur in school alone. Leisure time provides many opportunities for games and play, activities that fulfil several objectives for the growing child. Apart from being a time of recreation, leisure offers many possibilities for the enactment and trying out of future adult roles in a non-threatening context, for socializing with peers and rehearsing different social skills, and for using problem-solving and coping skills in a playful manner (Hendry, 1983). However, in modern Western societies, with their expanding artificial and technological environments, children move less freely and have fewer opportunities to learn to experience and manipulate their 'natural' environment. They are more and more confined to play-areas, clubs and commercial settings, designed by adults to protect children from the environment (or the environment from children?). Zinnecker (1990) calls this the 'manufacturing of the environment', augmenting the 'Verhäuslichung' of children in modern societies (limiting their lives mainly to the indoors). As a consequence, the number of children killed in road accidents in Britain, for example, has declined dramatically over the past 30 years – at the same time as the number of children allowed to move around freely in the environment (visiting leisure parks or crossing roads alone) has decreased at the same rate (Qvortrup, 2000). Qvortrup concludes that the price for reducing the number of children killed on the roads was partly paid by the children themselves, and he adds that '...the car is seen by (male) adults as the ultimate epitome of freedom, while for children it almost literally means curfew' (p.92). Earlier, Sutton-Smith and Heron (1971) wrote that adult society created the child's leisure environment in play areas and playgrounds by 'caging them in', and then believed that children could engage in 'free, expressive play' – the ultimate irony?

Growing artificiality in booming urban areas creates a totally different environment for city-dwelling children than for their age-mates in the countryside, thus providing rural and urban youths with different leisure practices and skills. Increasingly, artificial games substitute for real-life experiences: Western children feed their plastic dolls and play 'mother–father–child', or experience family life by manipulating virtual personalities on a computer screen, while their age-mates in other societies actually take care of their younger siblings (see figures 6.1–6.3) or help their parents in the fields. Adventure holiday centres and theme parks are attempting to substitute for real rivers to swim in, natural forests to explore, and fresh sea breezes to breathe. Adults might observe this development with nostalgic eyes, overlooking the fact that playing in an artificial environment provides children with exactly the skills they will need as adults for living in a more technologically artificial world!

Figure 6.1   **Mayan street-girl taking care of her younger brother**

Figure 6.2   **Mexican children swimming in a jungle river**

Figure 6.3   **German children diving in a middle-class bathroom**

Büchner (1990) considers that children today make the transition from childhood to youth sooner than previously this century. This may be because many areas of adult life and lifestyle are open to them at an earlier age, and they are 'encouraged' to participate in these by the fashion and music industries, the mass media and various types of global trading companies. Or perhaps they are forced to be more independent, since adults see their continuing dependence as a restriction to their own life development. The demand of parents for some time for 'their own lives' has an impact on children. Children have more and more areas of independent living, which demand individuality and the skills to decide and act proactively, and to demonstrate individual taste, for example in spending money, in time planning, selecting leisure-time activities, and in fashion and media consumption.

Nevertheless, an increasing number of children is sent to specially reserved places for leisure-time activities and hobby and cultural programmes, separated from the adult world but arranged and run by adults. This is true not only of kindergarten, but also of children's clubs and organizations and of their playroom at home. All these are specialized for specific child activities. Hence, children have to follow time schedules and be transported from one place to another. Leisure pursuits at relatively remote venues demand rigorous discipline. Often children, particularly middle-class city-dwellers, have 'no time' for genuine free time from a very young age. Traffic makes free play in the streets and meetings with mixed age and social-class groups virtually impossible, and this is substituted for by adult-led peer groups. The gain of independence in autonomous extra-family activities is lost through the prevalence of professionally planned leisure-time programmes. By moving from one type of activity to another, the number of social contacts grows enormously, but most of them are superficial and short-lived. They are similar to the transient 'throw-away relationships' of adults described by Maffesoli (1996), and in certain ways preparing the children for the possible pattern of their future adult lives.

This does not mean that children grow up without discipline or social control. Parents have delegated large parts of their educational competence to social institutions in and out of school. Qvortrup (2001) argues that all these factors contribute to the shortening of the period of childhood for modern children:

> Children are in other words typically enrolled in adult-like formal groups characterized by organizational structures in terms of bureaucratic admini- stration, clock-regulated time schedules, functionally defined and spatially organized boundaries and buildings. There is no doubt that institutional- ization as a tendency represents a mechanism for adapting children to norms and rules of modern society; by doing so it certainly also is an effective way of colonizing children's time. Besides their protective and care-taking qualities, institutions also deprive children of alternative options for using their own time. This is not necessarily deplorable, but it is a fact. Even outside schools – a time in principle at children's free disposal – children's involvement in so-called voluntary leisure-time activities is quite time consuming. Many children like these activities – but we do not really know if these were children's first choice, given the lack of alter- natives. We know that they are activities much desired by parents – because children are even here taken care of, controlled, and disciplined.

Examples of normative and quasi-normative shifts in childhood that are a challenge in developing important resources

- Developing basic psycho-motor skills.
- Understanding basic concepts, categorizing them and relating them to each other.
- Learning to communicate – first in oral, then in written, form.
- Learning to relate to adults, siblings, friends and peers.
- Coping with the challenges of school and leisure.
- Developing an increasing responsibility for one's own life.

What we have described here is of course a Western scenario of children's leisure time, as such only observable in affluent, industrialized cultures. More frequently, a limited domestic economy forces children to contribute to family earnings or household chores, thus engaging early in 'real life' rather than in artificial play. Children participate in daily life as competent and capable members of the family, sharing tasks and responsibilities with adults, and are treated to a certain degree as such, though not necessarily with full adult rights. While condemned from a Western point of view because of the dangers of abuse, child labour has not always and only debilitating consequences. In many cases, apart from creating a range of useful skills, it strengthens self-esteem, allowing engagement in meaningful activities, intensifies social bonds with the family, with and for whom the child works, and sometimes provides the necessary economic conditions for the child to attend school as well (Schrumpf, 2000). The ethnocentric view of Westerners in their well-intentioned campaign against child labour in Zimbabwe, for example, has left children without the opportunity of school education, when companies, under international pressure, decided no longer to admit children under 16 years into their system and thus not into the company school (Bourdillon, 2001). Only if work proceeds under health-damaging circumstances, incorporates abuse, or prevents necessary education does it drain more resources than it creates. Unfortunately, this is the case for more than 120 million children in the world today (International Labour Organization, 1998).

Conclusions

In this chapter we have reviewed the development of the neonate and growing child, and argued that all development was both integrative and interactive. We chose three areas of the child's life, namely psycho-motor development, social relationships and learning in school and leisure, to illustrate a number of themes (see box above for a summary). Firstly, when the child interacts with its environment and starts to learn, all sensory and cognitive modes are involved. Hence, social, cognitive and sensorimotor resources are (potentially) available to enrich the resource 'pool'. Secondly, the child begins to learn the various gradations of social relations, from 'vertical' to 'horizontal', and these are achieved

– or not – by interactions with parents, peers and other adults. Thirdly, the challenge of attending school and leisure activities brought into focus the necessary tension between self-efficacy and independent learning with conforming, 'fitting in' and learning from older authority figures. This third issue may be important as a forerunner in the development of both conformity (i.e. stagnation) and boundary-testing (i.e. development) in the next phase of the life course, that is adolescence.

7 Adolescence and the status of early adulthood

Introduction

Do you remember that day when you prepared yourself for the big party where you hoped you would meet the person of your dreams, and then, looking in the mirror, detected that a huge red pimple had developed on the side of your nose? Or that geography lesson, where the teacher made you look a fool in front of the whole class? The shock you felt when you realised that your parents where just 'ordinary', and perhaps not even as clever as you? The nights when you could not sleep, wondering if you had any future at all, if you had chosen the right school subjects? What you should do next weekend, or whether your new sweater made you look fat? If you remember these, or similar occasions, you still have a pretty clear picture of what adolescence is all about.

In many respects young people have borne the brunt of the rapid pace of change affecting most areas of social and family life (Coles, 1995). The array of choices, contradictions and risks confronting young people growing up in the West today is arguably greater than that faced by any recent previous generation (Chisholm and Du-Bois Reymond, 1993). Experimentation, with its resultant successes and (sometimes embarrassing) failures is a significant part of the picture. Frequently, relations with adults in authority can be ambivalent and turbulent, whether they are parents, teachers or the police. In the past three decades, research on adolescence has expanded greatly, and writers and theorists have devoted a great deal of effort to analyzing and interpreting the transitions of youth in modern societies. Because of this plethora of recent research and writing on adolescence, the first part of this chapter looks at the adolescent years selectively, and does not try to cover all aspects of them. In the second part of the chapter, we look at various aspects of life in early adulthood. With the initial entry into adulthood, the individual comes into a life phase in which there are few traditional or institutional constraints as long as one remains within the law.

In detail, the chapter comprises the following sections:

- puberty: the adolescent body, romance and societal images
- leisure and risk-taking
- the symbols of adulthood: the finishing touches of socialization?
- transition to young adulthood.

Puberty: the adolescent body, romance and societal images

The process of puberty, as an important maturational shift, heralds to some extent entry into adolescence, when the individual begins the relatively long physical and psycho-social transition from childhood to adulthood. What is clear in the teenage years is that the micro-systems surrounding the growing individual expand and change their structure. For example, there is a shift from hierarchical to horizontal relationships on the part of most teenagers as they socialize with parents, friends and teachers, even though these social encounters may not always be convivial. Additionally, interactions among their different social systems become more and more complicated as they experiment with and internalize the norms and values of their particular culture in the contexts of family, peers, school, work and leisure.

Part of the process of growing up involves the development of a sexual identity, and associated with this process is the creation of a personal body image. With the maturational changes of adolescence, young people become especially concerned with their body shape. Elongated limbs, developing breasts, increasing weight and stronger muscles all draw adolescents' attention to their own body and everyone else's. There are other sources of information about body shapes that young people pay attention to. It is impossible to ignore the tremendous coverage given to fashion icons and cult figures in magazines, newspapers and television. Further, the media emphasize the struggle these young stars of the fashion catwalks undergo to remain svelte and lightweight, suggesting that they are the modern saints and martyrs of dieting. In this position, they represent role models of an aspect of adult society so effectively that more muscular 'star' athletes, no matter how glamorous, cannot compete against them. With these fashion images of glamour and slimness, adolescents face a challenge to 'shape' their own body and create a satisfactory body image, while at the same time wishing to approximate the ideals held up by modern society. This is equally true for young women from more traditional societies, all of which have their own norms of female attractiveness. Although the 'desirable' shape may be different from that in the West, nevertheless the need to try to fall within a reasonable tolerance range of 'normality' and/or to approach the 'ideal' is still relevant.

This also influences adults and young men, though, to date, not as much as young women. There are three possible reasons for the increase in male concerns about physique. Firstly, the 'club scene' has developed dance styles and fashions that are revealing, so bodies are seen and looked at. Young men are no longer excluded from the 'body' parade of the nightclub or all-night rave. Secondly, male models, the promotion of male 'sex objects' in women's magazines and TV commercials, and male striptease shows make an impression on adolescent males. Thirdly, film stars and characters like Rambo and Arnold Schwarzenegger and 'competition' with male peers over muscle size and definition in body-building clubs put pressure on young men. In future generations, it may be that young men will be as concerned about having a 'perfect' body as many young women are today. However, research findings from many countries show that worry about appearance is still more typically a female concern, scores for 'negative body image' being one to two standard deviations higher for girls than boys beyond thirteen years of age (e.g. Kloep, 1998; Wichstrøm, 1999). Further, physical appearance figures very significantly among young women's life concerns (Kloep, 1999).

The emphasis on the body and its social meanings in adolescence can cause severe risks to certain adolescents. With body shape being of such importance, it is not surprising that teenagers of both genders try to slim or build their muscles in gyms, sometimes using illegal drugs to back up their 'body sculpting'. The number of girls in Europe suffering from anorexia or bulimia is estimated at 1 and 3 per cent respectively (Barnombudsmannen, 1997 for Sweden; Woodroffe *et al.*, 1993 for the UK). Shucksmith and Hendry (1998) report that young Scottish people believe themselves to be 'too fat', when they actually have an average body shape.

Experiencing puberty: gender differences

Young women and young men seem to experience puberty quite differently. Martin (1996) interviewed male and female teenagers about their experiences, and found that puberty means that boys look forward to becoming men, and to gaining strength, freedom and status. By contrast, for young women puberty has an ambivalent, if not negative, value, as they perceive that society demands them to identify with their adult female role and to accept a lower social status than young men. Furthermore, it means a limitation on freedom, because parents wish to protect their teenager daughters against the social-sexual dangers of harassment, pregnancy and rape. At the same time, young women feel the paradoxical expectation of having to be beautiful and seductive. Wichstrøm (1999) has shown that depression scores, which are highly associated with negative body image, increase remarkably around the onset of puberty for girls. Additionally, body image at thirteen (around puberty) seems to be a predictor of depression at age eighteen for young women, whereas body image at fifteen predicts depression at age eighteen for young men (Kraft *et al.*, 2000). During puberty, many young women develop a range of depressive symptoms, and their depression rate, which before puberty did not differ from that of young men, then becomes significantly higher, and stays at that level for the rest of their lives.

The development of a sexual identity becomes salient in the process of beginning and experiencing romantic attachments in adolescence.

However, we know that the process starts much earlier in childhood, as an interaction of innate characteristics, social symbols and gender-role learning, occurring in the family, school and playground. It is an accepted cliché to say, 'Pink for a little girl, blue for a boy!' Already, separate sexual identities begin to emerge from the reactions of adults to small children, depending upon whether they think the baby is a girl or a boy (irrespective of the real sex of the child), as Seavey, Katz and Zalk (1975) have shown in their classical experiment.

The hormonal changes and alterations in body shape during adolescence bring with them the challenges of sexual experimentation and the further establishment of sexual identities. For adolescents beyond puberty, physical and sexual maturation and heightened sex-drive increase interest in romantic relationships. During mid-adolescence, dating begins to complement activities with friends, and romantic partners become a crucial source of social support at this time. For both genders, the acquisition of romantic strategies and sexual techniques is problematic. Unlike most other aspects of social learning, family, schools or even peers offer little help and support to young people (Hendry *et al.*, 1995; Shucksmith and Hendry, 1998). As Kloep and Hendry (1999) have written, questions like what is required to be a good lover, how to make a socially competent (sexual) approach, or how to end a relationship are seldom mentioned to teenagers, or only covered inappropriately in teenage magazines or pornography. For both genders, sex education in schools does not appear to meet the needs of adolescents (e.g. Shucksmith and Hendry, 1998).

Like all skills, the abilities needed to relate romantically to others have to be practised. Many adolescents take up leisure activities not for the intrinsic value of the pursuits themselves, but as contexts for making and meeting friends and beginning romantic attachments. These activities take place in a whole continuum of settings, from pubs and clubs and cinema back rows to sports clubs, swimming pools and ski slopes. Commercial leisure venues are especially designed to enhance the ambience that enables romance to blossom (Alapack, 1991; 1999).

Leisure and risk-taking

Hendry (1983) and colleagues (Hendry *et al.*, 1998) have demonstrated that there are a series of leisure transitions for youths in Western societies. The first, in the early adolescent years, involves young people associating with a range of adult-led organizations and activities, such as Brownies, Scouts, sports clubs and so on, some of which have been participated in since childhood. Within this process, they learn to accept adult values and norms, as well as enjoying the activities and mixing with adults in their free time. Then, the general feeling among many young people, as they progress through the teenage years, is that adult-organized activities and clubs become too tame or over-controlled to appeal to them. This is followed by a stage of informal leisure pursuits in the company of peers, 'hanging around' in the street, shopping malls or the park, casual 'kick-abouts' on waste ground, or 'sleep-over' parties. At this stage an important issue of trust and confidentiality emerges. 'Entrusting' personal information and sharing secrets is a necessary risk. It is the experience of taking such risks and sometimes having one's trust betrayed that establishes friendships and social relationships. The ethic of reciprocity underlies trust relationships. In all cases, adults are not present, except as peripheral, background figures, and the purpose is to begin discussing and 'rehearsing' some of the behaviours and social skills and strategies necessary for acceptance in various sectors of adult society. Peers reaffirm identities, enable the individual to 'try out' certain social roles, and encourage transition to the next stage, which is the attempted acceptance into adult commercial leisure settings. Growing into adulthood demands that the adolescent tries out activities perceived as, or known to be, exclusive to adults. Pubs, nightclubs, discos, squash and fitness clubs, foreign travel, and even window-shopping to keep up with fashion trends which may be unaffordable, all feature at this stage. Further, it is clear that club cultures accommodate young people of different ages, social backgrounds and race under their roofs, giving them the early veneer of sophistication and adulthood (e.g. Rietveld, 1994; Thornton, 1995).

These leisure transitions ideally incorporate three stages of development, in each of which a consecutive set of new skills is learned within a relatively secure environment, releasing young people step-by-step into the world of adult relationships. The first step is concerned with conformity with adults and the observation and practice of 'appropriate' behaviour in the presence of adults. The second involves an apparent rejection of adult organizations for young people, with social learning taking place in the peer group. Finally, these learned social skills are tried out in adult settings. In this way, teenagers observe, rehearse and perform the skills and behaviours they perceive to be necessary for their absorption into the adult world.

Sharp and Lowe (1989) have suggested that young people's drinking is a part of this socialization process from childhood to adulthood, and a symbolic practice related to seeking social acceptance in adult society. So even apparently risky activities, like underage drinking, may contain elements of challenge, offering the potential for growth. Pape and Hammer (1996), for instance, suggest that young male abstainers, and men who are latecomers to drinking, show indications of a delayed entry into adult roles, and a reluctance to adopt adult role behaviours. Thus, according to the authors, perhaps getting involved in drinking for the first time in mid-adolescence is an ingredient in the normal developmental process. In rural areas in Scotland, Sweden and Norway, Kloep *et al.* (2001) found that teenagers said that one of their main reasons for drinking was to be seen to be adult and to be accepted into adult venues. Hence, there is supporting evidence for the key finding that, amongst other reasons for drinking (and smoking), it is the wish to gain adult status as soon as possible, at least symbolically, that leads many youngsters towards drinking (e.g. Pavis, Cunningham-Burley and Amos, 1997). The desire for acceptance into adult society seems to lie at the back of much teenage behaviour disapproved of by adults who do not fully realize that it is actually imitative and, as adolescents perceive it, a wish to be socialized 'conventionally'. These are some of the symbols of adult society, well advertised through the mass media, that attract many young people in a process of emulating adult role models and meeting the challenge of the normative shift to adult status.

Is it possible to suggest that illegal drug use can come into the same category? Certainly, 'soft' drugs are being perceived in a radically different way by politicians and the general public in a number of Western countries. Already, the use of such drugs has, to some extent, been 'normalized' in certain cultures. In the near future it is probable that they may not be regarded as illegal substances, at present theoretically carrying prison sentences for possession. Some scholars have suggested that more problems are caused to the lives of young people by the criminalization of drugs than by the drugs themselves (Christie and Bruun, 1996).

Young people do engage in under-age drinking, smoking and use of other drugs, although contrary to media images a great majority of adolescents drink very little alcohol and never take drugs (Coleman and Hendry, 1999; Kloep *et al.*, 2001). Further, these substances, both legal and illegal, are often presented to adolescents by adults (though this is illegal in most countries), and many youngsters simply and easily accept the risks involved in these adult activities in their pursuit of the signs and symbols of adult status. Young people take risks and weigh up the enjoyment and advantages of their various social and leisure activities against the dangers and pitfalls. This 'cost–benefit risk assessment', as Parker, Aldridge and Measham (1998) call it, is an elaborate psychosocial process in which the young person decides how far to go to get a 'buzz' from alcohol or drugs. For example, Kloep *et al.* (2001) report that rural youngsters in Norway, Scotland and Sweden go through several stages of painful discovery in learning how to drink sensibly.

Such risk assessment is in itself an important generalizable meta-skill, because testing the goodness of fit between challenge and resources – learning what challenges one can accept in relation to the resources one has – leads to learning how to assess whether one can cope with a challenge or not. This enables one to adjust one's aspirations or intensify one's efforts in response to a particularly demanding task. This skill may become particularly salient for many people in old age, when selection of tasks, optimization of efforts, and compensation for missing skills is one of the secrets of successful ageing (Baltes and Baltes, 1980, see chapter 10).

Risk-taking in adolescence

Given what has already been said in this chapter, can we simply say that risk-taking is part of the psychological make-up of youth – a thrill-seeking stage in the developmental transition – or a necessary step to the acquisition of adult behaviours, skills and self-esteem? Or is it a consequence of a societal or cultural urge in adults to 'marginalize' youth because in their transition from controllable child to controlled adult they are sometimes seen as troublesome and a threat to the stability of the adult community's values? Arnett (1998) has pointed out that Western cultures must accept a trade-off in socialization between promoting individualism and self-expression on the one hand, and promoting social order on the other. Western societies pay the price for emphasizing individualism and achievement by having higher rates of adolescent risk-taking in response to adults' attempts to ensure value- and behavioural conformity in the young before adolescence is over.

Is Arnett correct in his assessment of risk-taking? What are the components and purposes of risk-taking in adolescence? Are there differences between Western and more traditional cultures in the degree of adolescent risk-taking? Hendry and Kloep (1996) offer three categories of risk-taking:

Firstly, there are thrill-seeking behaviours. These are exciting or sensation-seeking behaviours which arouse and test the limits of one's capacities. Sensation-seeking is often the vital component of this, since too much security is boring to certain adolescents, so that they go out to create and seek challenges. Teenagers often choose different kinds of risks from adults and, moreover, have limited experience of their own capacities and the actual risks they are taking. Their self-appraisal evaluations may not yet be well formed. And this is exactly one of the objectives of risk-taking, namely to test the limits and to learn to estimate how far one's resources can and will go. In other words, risk-taking is one way of learning the meta-skills of assessing goodness of fit between one's abilities and the demands of a situation – though admittedly it is sometimes the hard way to learn.

Secondly, there is audience-controlled risk-taking. In order to be accepted, to find place in a peer group (and thereby gain the resources of social support and security) and to establish a social position, people have to demonstrate certain qualities and abilities. As we have discussed above, many young people imitate high-status groups in order to show, at least symbolically, that they 'belong' to that group – if necessary by taking risks. This may be the reason why adults do not engage so often in demonstrative risk-taking: they have the means of displaying their status in titles, expensive clothes or sports cars. Lacking these symbols, adolescents may turn to challenging activities that take them to the edges of legality, and thus assure them of police and media attention, as well as that of their peers.

Thirdly, there are risk-taking behaviours that are simply irresponsible. These are not performed because of the risks they involve, but in spite of them, in order to achieve other desired goals. Such irresponsible behaviours demonstrate the inability of individuals to see long-term consequences or, if these are apparent, their unwillingness to abstain from such activities because of perceived short-term advantages. It is obvious that behaviours such as getting drunk or failing to use condoms are not attractive because they are risky, but they are pursued for other reasons that are temporarily more important. Clearly, these are risks that adolescents share with adults in most societies, though, through a possible lack of meta-skills such as appraisal and control skills, teenagers may enter this risk zone more frequently than adults do.

What do teenagers in more traditional societies do to assess the goodness of fit between challenges and their skills and resources, and as a way of acquiring the techniques of self-expression and conformity? How do they give rein to self-expression and challenge where there is less demand for individualism? Anyone who has ever visited Turkey, Greece or Latin America can attest to the fact that, for example, teenagers drive motorbikes with even more abandon than in the West, and mostly without the use of a protective helmet. Their risk-taking matches, perhaps even supersedes in some areas, that of their Western colleagues, and is carried out for the same basic reasons. There are cultural differences, but the mechanisms of challenge and development are the same.

The symbols of adulthood: the finishing touches of socialization?

We have argued that security is a necessary component in our ability to face up to future challenges. But security also results from knowing that one belongs to, and is accepted by, a protective group. The price one pays for acceptance is having to conform to the rules, and to internalize the values, of that group, to a greater or lesser extent.

The rapid economic and technological changes in modern industrial societies – and the family influences in traditional cultures – are crucial structural frameworks within which young people face the challenges and risks of striving to achieve adult status and to gain civil rights. Identities are made within increasingly globalized media and youth culture, with time and place transformed through acts of consumption and identification, and with a mixture of cross-cultural symbols. Picture an Indian Muslim boy in Yorkshire, consuming black American jazz culture and supporting Arsenal Football Club, a white Canadian girl whose passions are Eastern philosophy and mariachi music, or a Mayan-Indian teenager in her traditional costume calling her boyfriend at the end of trading on market day, using a mobile phone.

Traditional cultures give young people security because their future work and social roles are fairly predictable and the pattern of future life is, to some extent, predetermined. On the other hand, because of the social and technological changes of recent decades, Western societies are undergoing many shifts, many norms are transitional or changing, and social and occupational roles are in a state of flux. Increasingly, this is also beginning to be true for more traditional societies due to growing globalization. A range of social processes, such as the development of a 'risk society' (Beck, 1992), 'de-traditionalization' (Heelas, Lash and Morris, 1996) and 'individualization' (Beck, 1992; Furlong and Cartmel, 1997) have had an impact on the meaning and experience of youth. These changes have led to a destabilization of the authority of traditional institutions such as school, state and family, giving rise to new forms of authority centring on the individual. This leads to a greater sense of insecurity in youths because they perceive their futures to be uncertain and risky (e.g. Parker, Aldridge and Measham, 1998). So, some young people seek out social or political organizations that appear to offer certainty and security in the form of an ideology and behavioural norms. These organizations can range from various religious sects, through Voluntary Services Overseas, to violent sub-cultures, in which territorial ideas and national unity can be expressed symbolically, for example by supporting particular football teams or neo-fascist groups. In this way, adolescents accept the offered values of their chosen group and/or seek to create their own norms in the face of societal uncertainty. Within such a fluid societal context, as Beck proposes, the potential for adults to support young people in negotiating their way towards adulthood may be simultaneously highly significant and problematic (e.g. Hamilton and Darling, 1989).

These ideas can be linked to Bourdieu's (1973) theory of 'cultural capital'. Originally, the concept was understood by Bourdieu to be a set of resources which enable certain groups to profit from education to the exclusion of others. These are made up of sets of attitudes and values implicit within the school curriculum. J.S. Coleman (1988) describes such cultural capital as essential to complement financial capital in helping young people to succeed within the school system. Thornton (1997) extends this idea to include 'sub-cultural capital', which she views as a means by which young people negotiate and accumulate status within their different social worlds. Thus, 'sub-cultural capital' can be described as a degree of 'street wisdom', plus a set of social skills, which enable young people to negotiate and survive in modern sub-cultures. As such, it is a measure of knowledge and control over the various social contexts in which they conduct their lives, in which a range of opportunities, risks and dilemmas are encountered. In our terms, 'sub-cultural capital' is akin to 'resources', and it is fairly obvious that as adolescence proceeds, most opt for the 'safer' strategies, which lead to relative conformity and conventionality as adulthood approaches, despite media images of 'reckless' youth.

The commercial world has cleverly understood young peoples' need for identity and security within a group, and promptly converted this need into promotional campaigns, offering their young clients the feelings of 'belonging' through association with their products. Millions of teenagers adapt to the lifestyle of the Coca-Cola generation and the dress code of Nike or Adidas. More recently, attempts to sell types of commercial conformity have been directed towards increasingly younger children, communicating the risks of appearing 'deviant' if they don't collect absolutely all the Pokémon figures, or if they 'fail' to be welcomed into the McDonald's family for their birthday party.

Mainstream Western societies today seem completely open and individualistic, creating a sense that 'everything goes'. But many different groups exist under this surface, each with their own (and often competing) norms and standards. To some of these groups, many young people are loyal for a great number of years, while others they might only be associated with for a short period. All this creates the phenomenon of 'serial conformity'. Whether by long- or short-term commitment, young people learn to conform in order to be accepted. Of course, this is not exclusive to adolescents. It starts in nursery school with Teletubby T-shirts and ends with golf-club ties at the members' annual general meeting.

In trying to 'socialize' young people, the desire in adult society to protect the young from all kinds of risks and threats has never been so highly prioritized. On a societal sea swell of uncertainty and change, and with little stability in the norm structure of industrial societies, a contradictory tendency can be observed: adult social institutions (like schools, youth organizations, and safety laws) as well as parents tend to act over-protectively towards young people. From nursery school onwards, leisure time is safeguarded and organized for young people (instead of by them) (Kloep, 2001). All challenges of an unplanned, self-organized, exploratory kind on the part of children are actually carefully arranged and designed by adults to ensure that no-one is hurt, and so most get easily bored. This continues into adolescence, so that many of those adolescents, who already have a great deal of security, feel the need to alleviate boredom by creating their own challenges. This may conflict with society's values, and even at times with the law – thus confirming the nightmare vision some adults have of 'teenage monsters'. The popular image is focussed on the young person as the perpetrator of violence: young people mugging old ladies, joy-riding in stolen cars, bullying younger peers. These stories are currency for the mass media, following a long tradition of adult anxiety about the lifestyles of the young. While there is nothing new about this, the expansion and acceleration of media culture means that moral panics have become an everyday part of modern life, a 'non-stop media show' in which representation and reality merge (Davis, 1990; McRobbie, 1994). If a moral panic is perceived to happen, then adult societies lose the mask of patriarchal love and show an iron will in demanding conformity to their values. This can even take the extreme form of sending under-aged offenders to a kind of concentration camp (like the boot camps promoted by certain American TV shows), or having them killed (like the Brazilian street children).

The developmental challenge model and adolescent identity development

We suggest that early and total conformity to the norms of adult society, something that within the framework of the developmental challenge model could be a sign of early or premature stagnation, is somewhat similar to the phenomenon Marcia (1980) describes as 'foreclosure', the early and conflict-free adaptation of an identity by adjusting to the wishes of others. He points out that while foreclosure is not beneficial for identity development in Western societies, it might well be a sign of positive psycho-social adjustment in more traditional societies, where feelings of collective identity are more highly valued than the establishment of individual identity. Recently, advances in identity research have revealed other similarities with the developmental challenge model, now extending identity development beyond adolescence to cover the whole of the lifespan. Adolescent identity structure is no longer regarded as a more-or-less permanent structure, but as an initial and preliminary entity. This initial structure will be challenged later in adulthood by events that cause potential 'dis-equilibrium' throughout the adult lifespan, and to which an individual may react in a constricted or constructive manner (Marcia, 2000; Kroger, 2000).

Identity achievement is the only status which maintains both exploration and commitment at the same time, allowing for continued reorganization and refinement of identity, which might also be called continuous personal growth. If either exploration or commitment, which are the underlying processes of identity formation, is lost, an adult who had reached identity achievement might fall back into an earlier identity status (Stephen, Fraser and Marcia, 1992).

Even though we use a slightly different phraseology, we can, yet again, agree with other scholars about some vital features of lifespan development.

Thus, there are strong forces in society that pressurize young people towards conformity. This is somewhat in contradiction to Beck's (1992) individualization thesis, which has been influential in interpreting youth transitions. He argues that traditional structures of education, family and work have become fragmented, and that this has led to a blurring of social roles. Thus, young people simultaneously face a range of choices and risks in relations, education and work. Since traditional networks of support in the family and neighbourhood no longer offer clear-cut guidance, as in previous times, and extended formal schooling has led to a marked segregation of young people from adult life, there are restricted cross-age experiences for individuals (Elder, 1975). Young people there-fore have to invent individual developmental strategies. While this may open up opportunities for some, there are fewer safety nets for them. The attendant risk of stress and uncertainty may cut across traditional lines of class, race and gender.

Nevertheless, a number of problems arise in relation to the individual-ization thesis. It is clear, for instance, that structural inequalities of class, race and gender, far from disappearing, may even be widening (Coles, 1995; Hendry, Kloep and Olsson, 1998; MacDonald, 1997; Wyn and White, 1998). So while it may be true that new independence and choices are available for those who can access consumer markets, this is reliant on the young person having an income. It seems as if the argument that young people construct their own biographies beyond traditional constraints is somewhat flawed. Young people today are caught up in a network of schooling programmes, unemployment and semi-legal work on the black economy to secure an income, which is very often below subsistence level (e.g. MacDonald, 1997). The lack of job continuity, the changed relationships between work, non-work and leisure, together with a world of permanent under-occupation, have led to new forms of survival. Young people are to a large extent lost, powerless and margin-alized, often criminalized, in the series of national and international reactions to the structural problems of the labour market. Cashmore (1984) described this 'luxury gap' already in the 1980s:

> Tantalos was a mythological Greek king who was condemned to stand in the abyss of Tartarus, surrounded by fruit and water, which he craved but could not reach. Similarly, youths find themselves in a position in which they are shown goods, yet denied access to them; like the Greek king they are tantalized by things that are out of their reach [p.80].

Today, this picture has not changed much. On the contrary, it is particularly true for youth in the former communist states of Eastern Europe, who are daily reminded of the enormous poverty gap between their own countries and those of the West by countless TV channels (Kloep and Hendry, 1997).

The implications of adolescents' transitions
The psycho-social implications of puberty are necessary to our under-standing of young people's transitions to early adulthood. Adolescence has been described by Erikson (1968) as a 'psycho-social moratorium', whereby young people are given the 'licence' to experiment and explore various facets of life and living, and test the boundaries of 'acceptable' behaviour. Yet, as we have exemplified above, there is little doubt that

most societies provide a set of rewards and punishments, through the family, schools, churches and even penal institutions. So it is reasonable to 'expect' that most teenagers have learned to conform to social rules, written and unwritten, by the time adulthood approaches. In this way, even rapidly changing societies ensure a degree of both conformity and conventionality. Many emerging adults internalize these sets of 'rules' and values, and accept them, in general terms, for the rest of their lives, even in the face of macro-level changes. This was referred to many years ago by George Mead (1934), when he described the learning of social values. He used the idea of the 'generalized other' to refer to the individuals' conception of the general attitudes and values of those people within society with whom they interact. It operates as an important constraining influence on individual behaviour. It emerges through 'feedback from others' in their (micro) social networks, through social interaction and through the playful trying-out of different social roles in childhood. This 'generalized other' is akin to Durkheim's (1893, 1964) 'conscience collective', and reflects aspects of the macro-system in Bronfenbrenner's (1979) theory.

Some normative and quasi-normative challenges in adolescence

- Puberty and body changes.
- Developing romantic relationships.
- Extending micro-systems and creating new ones.
- Increasing independence from parents and leaving home.
- Augmenting legal rights.
- Choosing education and career.
- Exploring pathways towards an adult identity.

These ideas also have links to the developmental challenge model. It is possible that the security provided by being integrated into a society makes the 'breaking' of rules, written or unwritten, a perceived risk – an added challenge – which might prevent some adults choosing unconventional lifestyles in order not to lose the security of total, incontestable membership of that society. We have suggested that one of the challenges of the teenage years is to face up to this conflict between the fairly immediate and relatively unquestioning acceptance of adult values, and the process of forging one's own personal views. This 'identity-formation' process comprises meeting challenges, carrying out an exploration of life experiences, undergoing an experimentation of lifestyles, making mistakes (i.e. trial-and-error learning), and testing behavioural 'boundaries'. During this course of action, there are always elements of risk and failure within the many tasks and challenges adolescents seek and encounter (see box above for a summary).

The transition to early adulthood

We have seen, in examining adolescence from the perspective of the developmental challenge model, in Western societies the signposts and symbols of approaching adulthood are inconsistent and difficult for the young person to understand and interpret. This, as we have pointed out, is because post-modern, fast-changing societies are in a state of flux, with few stable norms or behavioural role models for young people to imitate. The consequence of these shifts is the de-standardization of the life course. Hence, traditional developmental tasks (e.g. Havighurst, 1972), such as gaining independence from parents, and perhaps independent living arrangements, orienting to a career, developing a different set of relationships to parents, peers and the opposite gender and so on, present today's youth with significant challenges in gaining adult status. This is mainly because these normative shifts become less age-related in modern times. Present-day lifestyles make it possible to be a mother or holding down a responsible job in one's teens, to be still a student at twenty-five, or a middle-aged bachelor of forty still living with his parents. Which one of these has, in fact, reached full adult status? It is clear that shifts rather than chronological age determine when we move from one life phase to another in modern societies. Sociologists such as Buchmann (1989) even state that:

> The distinction between youth status and adult status is gradually blurred ... over the last fifteen years, the behavioural differences between youth and adults have drastically diminished. In a growing number of life spheres (sexuality, political behaviour, etc.) young people behave like adults or claim the same rights as adults [p.85].

At the same time, adults behave like youths: going back to school, falling in love with a new partner, starting a new kind of job, having exciting leisure pursuits, following 'youth' fashions, a situation that Fiske and Chiriboga (1991) describe as follows:

> Next time you visit the supermarket, you may encounter ... newborn infants with their mothers who are aged fifteen and sixteen and newborn infants with mothers aged thirty-five to forty.... You may encounter, in fact, grandparents in their early forties as well as parents in their sixties and seventies [p.286].

Within this de-standardized life course, decisions taken towards the end of adolescence are no longer once-and-for-all lifetime choices. This instability is created by a number of macro-social factors, such as changing customs and practices, fluctuating and uncertain job markets, demands for higher qualifications at the same time as there is a deflation of academic titles and a greater need for qualified women in the workforce. Allied to this there are burgeoning leisure industries, many fragmented social groupings with different sets of values, which young people join inter-mittently in their leisure time, and fewer age-segregated pursuits (e.g. Maffesoli, 1996). Furthermore, the state has taken over several functions previously fulfilled by the family. Instead of former collective production, family members today share only collective consumption (e.g. Buchmann, 1989). However, in this state of volatility, there are few, if any, normative shifts required on the part of young adults. As Featherstone and Hepworth (1991) put it:

Adult life, then, is a process – a process, we must emphasize, which need not involve a predetermined series of stages of growth. The stages or hurdles which are placed in front of people and the barriers through which they have to pass (age-specific transitions) can be shifted around and even discarded [p.375].

For the young adult, there are many choices to be made and a relative freedom to choose what they will make of life and what they will pursue in employment, leisure or in relationships, within the obvious constraints of the macro-system's laws, traditions and economic state in different countries. The advantage of having the freedom to choose from a *smorgasbord* of life options, however, at the same time involves a pressure to choose. Every choice means 'choosing away' something else, and implies the risk of choosing 'wrongly', and missing out on other opportunities, which may have influences on later phases of the life course.

This is the time when young people can explore the whole array of adult activities as a 'real' adult (with rights) after the tentative, and sometimes illegal, experimentation with some 'adult' pursuits in adolescence. This stage of the lifespan creates a wide range of possibilities for facing 'challenges' and achieving 'tasks', but can also introduce risk behaviours into one's life. Lifestyles stabilize: for instance, alcohol or drug misuse, crime or vandalism on one hand, or regular exercise, meaningful leisure-time activities or active participation in voluntary care organizations on the other hand, which have often been started in adolescence, may continue and have psycho-social implications both currently and later in the lifespan. Here it is interesting to note that when soccer hooligans are apprehended, newspaper reports reveal that the perpetrators are often aged in their twenties, or even early thirties, but the headlines and editorials still discuss the problems of teenage violence!

In early adulthood, challenges abound not only in seeking career openings, but also in leisure and social settings and in the realm of romantic relationships. In this connection, commercial leisure venues, more than in adolescence, become important social contexts within a 'singles' life for the initiation of friendships and social relations. The various commercial leisure industries have been quick to exploit these needs of early adulthood, and a flood of nightclubs, bars, contact clubs and agencies advertizing exotic holiday tours exclusively for the 'under thirties' has appeared in cities and towns in most Western societies.

There are no clear-cut maturational shifts of note during this life period. However, there can be normative pressures, so that, for example, within a relatively stable romantic relationship, or within a first marriage, a young couple may be asked if they are 'ever going to set up house together' or 'Are we going to become grandparents soon?' There are also questions such as 'Are you ever going to finish your studies?' posed by parents, aunts and neighbours, who have not quite grasped the de-standardization of modern life trajectories.

From the young adults' perspective, at this time of life there is a considerable amount of 'changing partners' within more serious relationships than existed in the 'serial monogamy' of adolescence. These can be seen as a prelude to establishing a possibly stable association with a 'final' mate. This can be likened somewhat cynically to shopping in the supermarket where there is an array of assorted goods to be considered, before making one's selection of purchases! Or, expressed in a more serious way:

> Instead of commitment to one's life choice, the ability to develop in love relationships and to experience personal growth – a process that may involve continuing choices – becomes the yardstick for successful identity formation. Lifelong attachment to a cause is replaced by the capacity for flexible adjustments to new demands and for exploring new experiences. Self-realization, as a reflective process involving one's needs and interests, to which a love relationship contributes, is more highly valued than personal fulfilment through selfless giving to a love partner [Buchmann, 1989, p.61].

Early adulthood, social class and cultural differences

In former times (and in less 'modern' societies), the pathway to adulthood was relatively clearly marked out. Nowadays, modern society offers young people at least the illusion of flexibility and variety, and that in social life 'anything goes': to marry or not marry; to live in a partnership with a same-sex or opposite-sex partner; to have children as a teenager, as a middle-aged adult or, as seems to be more than possible in the near future, even as a retired woman; to have a job first and a higher education later, or the other way round, or to alternate between the two. Almost all choices are reversible – partners, jobs and dwelling-places can be left and replaced.

On the one hand, individualization leads to greater autonomy and an increasing number of life options. On the other hand, it is linked to a heightened risk of failure, insecurity and stress. As Jones and Wallace (1990) point out, the choices in young adulthood are not all individualized, but still depend to a high degree on social origin and gender. There are clearly better options for some wealthy middle-class youths (Furlong and Cartmel, 1997). For the rest, mainly from the working classes, career options are reduced and risks are heightened by an uncertain labour market and the consequent danger of low incomes. Additionally, the modern individualization thesis applies more to men than to women, whose autonomy is restricted by parental control, part-time employment, lower wages and gender biases in the job market.

What has been written so far applies only to Western cultures, and the picture can be totally different in other societies. The life events in Western societies that were previously regarded as markers for the transition to adulthood – leaving home, finishing one's education, finding a job, starting a family – happen earlier and are more often predictable and seen as a normative shift in traditional cultures (Zinnecker, 1991). Furthermore, the Western stage of individualistic 'adult independence' might never be reached, or even pursued, in these societies. Instead, social norms and parental authority and decisions determine much of the future life of these young adults, and the age at which adult responsibilities start. There is not much opportunity for individual selection of challenges or choices. Cultural differences in the transition to adulthood have been noted in several research studies. In the US, differences have been observed as to when and why young people from different cultural backgrounds leave home. Catholics leave home later than all other groups, while fundamentalist Protestants leave home at a fairly early age for marriage, whereas liberal Protestants do so to go to college (Goldscheider and Goldscheider, 1994). Similar cultural differences are found within Europe. A very high percentage of young Italian adults, for instance, leave home only to marry (Rossi, 1997), while in less traditional cultures the transitional pattern to full residential independence is relatively early, gradual and with several intermediate steps. These steps can include cohabitation, living alone, or in rented accommodation with peers, including repeated returns to the family home. Even when individuals are supposedly living independently, they may still rely on family resources for the washing of clothes, ironing, meals and so on (Goldscheider, Thornton and Young-DeMarco, 1993; Thornton, Young-DeMarco and Goldscheider, 1993). In traditional cultures, adult responsibilities are thrust upon adolescents at a much earlier age, and expectations are high that they will continue to contribute to the family's income in various ways into early adulthood and beyond, either by working within the family's occupational structure or acting as child carers. Young adults in traditional, more collectively oriented cultures are not expected to develop the same kind of independence that is associated with adult status in Western societies. They stay highly involved with their family of origin, and even after leaving home, Greek and Turkish daughters, for example, consider independence as 'taking on responsibility for their family', while German daughters would interpret independence as 'taking responsibility for themselves' (Papastefanou, 1999). Traditional societies thus create their own challenges through which young people fulfil their true developmental potential. There are more normative shifts for them to make and, at the same time, they have more role models and more (and different) family support and guidance when making these transitions than young Westerners do in gaining adult independence.

A particularly difficult transitional shift, with an added number of challenges, might await young adults who experience a clash of values between their own traditional ideals and Western ones. Nauni (1999) shows in her study of Kosova-Albanian refugees in Norway how they try to adopt a double conformity. This implies maintaining an Albanian cultural identity, and at the same time exhibiting day-to-day conformity to the rules, laws and customs of Norwegian society. Young people, for instance, solve the problem by respecting their parents and their cultural values in the family, but by being more 'Norwegian' outside the home. Parents make an effort to adjust to the values of their new society and bring up their sons in a spirit of autonomy and independence. However, girls are granted less 'space' for independence than boys. Restrictions are explained by parents as age-restrictions, but are in fact most often requirements appropriate to Albanian patriarchal culture, such as protecting their honour (i.e. their virginity) and acknowledging the primacy of the male gender.

Value confusion can be prominent among second-generation immigrants to the West, as this example shows, or for young adults in countries that are suddenly heavily influenced by Western values, such as the former communist countries of Eastern Europe (Gurko, 1997; Kloep and Hendry, 1997).

Conclusions

Adolescence and early adulthood differ in their developmental tasks and challenges, and yet share a number of common features. Adolescence, from the onset of the process of puberty, can be shown to have a number of psycho-social implications. Young people are influenced by media images of physical beauty, and respond to these in a range of appropriate and maladapted ways. On the basis of physical development, adult society treats them as adults (or not) in daily interactions, while young people themselves are still striving to attain adulthood in a variety of other life domains. Hence, young people receive conflicting messages about their current social status. While testing the boundaries of 'appropriate' adult behaviours, they imitate adult role models' behaviour on a continuum from highly approved activities, such as taking on political and community responsibilities, to highly disapproved and risky adult entertainments such as drinking and sex. All of these essentially involve a quest for adult status and a need for some resolution of the tensions between individuality and conventionality, perhaps the major challenge of adolescence, and one which may have important implications for the building up of resources and for the effectiveness of the resource 'pool' later in the life course.

Entry into adulthood provides the individual with a series of societal rights. Within the laws of a particular society, it is a time in the lifespan when there is a great deal of freedom of action and limited social responsibility. Unlike the teenage years, after the very obvious and significant maturational changes, early adulthood is a relatively quiet time biologically, though the individual continues to grow in strength and power until physical maturity is reached. There are no normative shifts for the individual to attempt in Western cultures; nevertheless, it is a time of individual choices and challenges, made keener because of current societal changes at the macro-level.

The pattern of choices and restrictions for young people in more traditional cultures is of a different order. It is designed to give the young adult a great sense of security, but at the same time grants the parental generation a great deal of power in decision-making processes and control over the future work and marital life of young adults, to ensure acceptance of adult responsibilities. These secure an unchanging style of inter-generational development, and provide support and care from a relatively large family in the parents' old age. However, globalization has introduced market forces into some traditional societies, and changed their economies from a mainly agricultural to an industrial base. These rapid social changes have introduced severe challenges to former ways of living and to the traditional choices of early adulthood.

Middle adulthood: conventional lifestyles or new challenges

Introduction

Imagine those middle-aged couples who begin their day by eating breakfast together, without talking or even looking at each other, each sitting behind their section of the newspaper, reading (he the sports pages, she the gossip columns), the silence interrupted only by the noises of chewing toast or sipping coffee – married bliss? Are they really happy and contented with this style of living? Have they accepted their less-than-perfect relationship? Are they silently suffering, without the courage or the skills to end what has become unhappy stagnation? Or is one of them already secretly preparing his or her way out of the relationship, hoping for a new beginning elsewhere? In sum – are they typical of couples in mid-life?

After the relative freedom accorded to young adults in Western cultures, we can see how various expectations and pressures within the occupational and relational spheres of their lives begin, over time, to direct them towards the next period of the lifespan. Middle adulthood brings with it the beginnings of restriction of choice. For example, it is already too late to develop certain physical abilities to a high degree: most sporting records are achieved by young adults, not the middle aged. In business, whilst not impossible, it may be difficult to gain further qualifications with which to seek promotion or pursue a different kind of career. Again, some life choices will no longer be reversible: for instance, it is not easy to get rid of the kids once you have them! Challenges in earlier years appear to come to the individual, but challenges in mid-adulthood may have to be actively sought. Sooner or later in young adulthood the day comes when student days are over, or when it is not possible to stay in the family home any longer, so that young people are inevitably forced to make some choices and to start new episodes in their lives. By contrast, in mid-life, adults are often settled, and have already made their most important life choices. Only occasionally do non-normative events, like job loss or one partner's death, confront them with 'turning-points'. In the main, those in mid-adulthood have to create choices and life changes themselves if they want them to happen. In other words, further development is now very much in the hands of the individual.

In this chapter we discuss the following aspects of middle adulthood within the framework of the developmental challenge model:

- evaluating one's life and the so-called 'mid-life crisis'
- parenthood and the 'empty nest'
- career and unemployment
- the mid-life moratorium and the importance of leisure.

Evaluating one's life and the 'mid-life crisis'

Middle adulthood is a time for looking, Janus-like, both backward and forward over the life cycle, and of evaluating what has been achieved so far, and (possibly) assessing what is yet to be (see figure 8.1). A number of essential life decisions have been made by now, and people can choose if they want to abide by them, or change. Generally, nothing perforce pressurizes people into making any additional life decisions now, if and when they have found a job or a source of income, a place to live, a partner with whom to share their life or a chosen solitary existence, and have made the choice whether or not to have children. On the contrary, there is a certain social pressure towards following a conventional lifestyle.

So, many respond to the approach of mid-adulthood by accepting a 'comfortable' and conventional life pattern, having little interest in seeking new challenges, and creating the possibility of 'stagnation' in their lives. Yet, there are others who continue to develop by actively changing the parts of their life they are dissatisfied with by constantly adding new experiences and competencies. Thus, there are decisions to be made concerning 'challenge' or 'consolidation' in middle age. Though evaluating one's life is not confined to mid-adulthood – it happens continually – it attains to a certain necessary importance in the middle years, because there is still time enough to reconsider one's life decisions and initiate possible new beginnings.

Those who, for whatever reason, are not happy with the lifestyle they have may not have the resources to change it. They may lack skills, money, health or courage to meet the enormous, challenging processes that can emerge from a drastic change of lifestyle. 'Unhappy stagnation', as we have called this arrestment in development, can happen any time throughout the lifespan, because the resource 'pool' can drain in any given set of circumstances. One reason for the relative predominance of conventionality in older age-groups is the accumulation of risks and the continuing possibilities of draining the 'pool'.

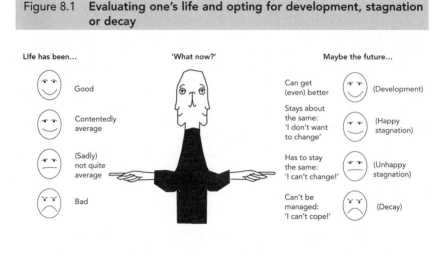

Figure 8.1   **Evaluating one's life and opting for development, stagnation or decay**

By contrast, those with enough resources and a negative evaluation of their present life will be challenged to consider possible changes. They are still young enough to begin a new education or a new career, to start a new family or another way of life, or to move to another town. People do not automatically stagnate with increasing age (and some never will). However, societies, which need and value stability to ensure continuity and social order (except at times of rapid societal shifts), often react negatively to this process. Within such cultures there are pressures towards making 'scapegoats' of people who have taken steps to try to alter their earlier life choices or who dare to make new choices. The social construction of 'mid-life crisis' for both men and women is one example of Western societies' attempts to mainstream their members and to create certain roles for their citizens. Protests against society's expectations are ridiculed and explained away with maturational shifts – whether they occur at the age of 'terrible three', in puberty or in mid-life. Dissatisfaction with life has nothing to do with one's biological age, but with the kind of life one is living.

From a cross-cultural perspective, research in the US (Chiriboga, 1997), India (Tikoo, 1996) and Hong Kong (Shek, 1996) gives no indication whatsoever of the existence of a common crisis or dissatisfaction with mid-life in any of these countries. On the contrary, the most frequently mentioned 'turning-point in life' experienced by American women between the ages of twenty and forty was 'growth' due to 'experiences in personal development' (Leonard and Burns, 1999). Additionally, what Stewart and Ostrove (1998) find to be the most common qualities in their sample of middle-aged American women is the sense of personal identity and confidence in self-efficacy, which does not derive from education, income or status, but rather from successfully handling life's difficulties. In a further US study, participants of all ages see mid-life as a time of increased stress, perhaps due to career pressures, and one with little leisure. At the same time, they consider mid-life to be a peak of competence, control and high productivity (Lachman *et al.*, 1994).

Psychological symptoms like depression and anxiety are often most predominant among people under thirty-five, but steadily decrease to the age of fifty-five (Pearlin and Mullan, 1992).

To summarize, the so-called mid-life crisis is a social construction, fuelled by the media. At the same time, there is a common prejudice held by society that middle adulthood is the time when individuals settle down and become staid and conventional. In reality, middle adulthood's challenges present the individual with the same opportunities and risks as challenges at any time in the lifespan – and there are almost as many ways to react to them as there are individuals.

Parenthood

As we have mentioned earlier, there is not a normative age in present-day Western societies at which it is 'appropriate' to become a parent. Particularly men, who are not biologically confined to certain reproductive ages, can start a second or third family, and become a father and a grandfather at the same time. However, we discuss the implications of parenthood here, although it can cover a broad age range, from mid-adolescence to late adulthood.

Irrespective of culture, one of the most significant events in an individual's life is parenthood. Becoming a parent involves the individual in a hierarchical social relationship from a position of power (the dia-metrically opposite position to that of the child). This event is no longer a normative shift for adults, but becoming a parent is still experienced by a large number of individuals in early to middle adulthood. What do parents have to learn, not only in relation to their child within the family setting, but also in relation to other micro-systems? The following are suggested tasks for new parents, that involve various interactions with others (see table 8.1).

Table 8.1 **Developmental tasks for new parents** (after Cusinato 1994: p.94)	
Relational adjustments	*Organizational adjustments*
With the new child	Change physical environment of the home
With partner	Share responsibility for the child
With the extended family	Housework and domestic duties
With friends	Working life
With work colleagues	Leisure time and 'free' time
With other adults (e.g. neighbours, doctor, district nurse, social worker)	Links with others outside the family, including social services

After the birth of a child, the renegotiation of family roles, and especially the arrangement of domestic tasks, is particularly important. Yet parent-hood in many families is still strongly marked by traditional gender roles. Even in countries with apparently high equality between the genders, like Norway, men do not participate in housework to any great extent, even if they opt for parental leave. The justification is that they are on parental leave to care for the child, not to do housework (Brandt and Kvande, 1998). Research in Denmark has shown that most equality in parental roles can be found in dual-career families and in families with self-employed mothers (Hestbæk, 1998). Furthermore, where there has previously been domestic role sharing, this pattern is more likely to continue after the birth of a baby. Most often, women perceive more 'personal' costs in having a child than men (Beckman, 1987). New fathers tend to demand the same priorities, though in modified form, as before the baby was born. They still want the same attention for themselves, a rich social life and freedom to pursue their own interests (Watson *et al.*, 1995), and tend to evaluate their marriage as less satisfactory after the birth of a child than before (Chalmers and Meyer, 1996).

One of the greatest difficulties for couples after the birth of the baby is a reduction in quality time with each other. Particularly where there is an accumulation of family problems (e.g. a child with colic, a death in family) for a couple with already limited resources, this build-up of stresses can lead to serious strains within the marriage (Schuchts and Witkin, 1989). As in any life phase, the timing and accumulation of challenges is crucial for their successful resolution. Given all these differences in resources and expectations, it is difficult to predict in what form or direction the challenge of parenthood will affect the partnership: 'Parenthood might enhance some marriages, undermine others and have little effect on still others' (Huston and Vangelisti, 1995: p.147).

In a longitudinal study covering the period of pregnancy to three years *postpartum*, Belsky and Rovine (1990) find that patterns of marital change are determined by multiple factors, including parental resources (e.g. education, length of marriage and age) and child characteristics (predictable temperament). However, though group means suggest a general deterioration in marital satisfaction after the birth of a child, a closer look at disaggregated sub-groups reveals that the pattern is more variable: some couples are happier, some remain unchanged, and some become distressed.

Parenting adolescents

Over the years, parents will be required to adapt and change the relationship with their growing children. This relationship gradually alters from a vertical one, in which the parents alone have authority, power and decision-making responsibilities, to an equal one, in which the growing teenager becomes a near-adult partner in the home. Hendry *et al.* (1993) have demonstrated how disagreements between parents and their adolescent offspring often revolve around daily issues such as the tidiness of teenage bedrooms, the volume of music, times of coming home from outings and parties and so on. More recently, Jackson, Cicogani and Charman (1996) have shown that the main arguments between parents and adolescent children centre on issues of mutual respect and partnership (e.g. who decides what TV programmes to watch), on the degree of independence granted to the adolescent, and on the amount of responsibility demanded by the parents. These daily issues between adolescents and their parents are similar in more traditional societies, such as Albania (Kloep and Tarifa, 1993b). Such cross-cultural findings leave the impression that adolescence is a period that is at least as difficult for parents as it is for teenage children! However, we need to know more about the middle years from a parental perspective, since our academic knowledge of this period is relatively sketchy (though for reviews, see Palkovitz, 1996; Seltzer and Ryff, 1994). It would also be useful to compare the experiences of middle-aged parents with childless couples, as this becomes an increasingly common feature of mid-life.

The empty-nest syndrome

Children in their late teens or early twenties will sometimes leave home, either to go to university or to start a job in another town before their parents have even reached older adulthood. This is a quasi-normative shift in Western societies, because it is fairly predictable and expected. With the uncertainties of the labour market, it takes place later and later in the young person's life. For example, over the last decade, the average age of leaving home in Britain has risen from seventeen to twenty-three (Coleman and Hendry, 1999).

Potential depressive reactions by parents to children leaving home have been labelled 'empty-nest syndrome'. Chiriboga (1991) describes the mothers' reactions as ranging from initial sadness and feelings of loss, to a perception of increased opportunities, and finally to a decrease in depression and an increase in happiness and pride. No such changes were found in men. Further, the 'empty-nest syndrome' appears to be a cohort effect for women of previous generations rather than for modern generations (see Adelman *et al.*'s 1989 US study). This may be due to the fact that leaving home has become a more normative event during the last decades, and also because modern Western women no longer define their personal or social value solely in relation to child-raising.

By contrast, when the experience of children leaving home is exacerbated by other crises, middle-aged men have been found to:

> experience stress, sometimes extreme stress, in reaction to crises such as divorce, drug and alcohol problems, and unemployment in their newly launched children's lives. Other work shows that middle-aged fathers' psychological distress is associated with their young adult children's perception that their relationships lack intimacy and emotional intensity [Thomas, 1994: p.201].

This differential coping of mothers and fathers may be due to a number of factors. Opportunities for new development may open up for mothers when the burden of child-caring is lifted, while for fathers, children leaving home might make it clear that they have missed, for ever, the chance to engage intimately as a parent in the family. (At the same time, the slow but inevitable approach of the age of retirement may signal to them how wrong the choice of 'career before family' was.)

Another aspect of the transition to an 'empty nest' is the possible influence and risk of marital disruption observed in many studies. Disharmony depends to some extent on the length of marriage, and risk decreases for those who have been married for more than 30 years (according to an US study by Hiedemann, Suhomlinova and O'Rand, 1998). One explanation for marital discord is that parents cannot cope with the many new challenges with which the 'empty nest' confronts them. For example, they have to find new tasks to fill the day, new topics to talk to each other about, and they have worries about their children's adjustments to their new independent lives. Of course, an alternative explanation could be that for many parents their children leaving is finally the chance to develop their own lives, and to pursue challenges and adventures that they might have been waiting for years to embark on. Some might do so together, but many wish to try this independently from marital restraints.

Parenthood in non-Western cultures

Becoming a parent in non-Western, traditional societies comprises quite different challenges, because many more children are planned for, being seen as help and support for old age and regarded as a resource for the whole family. Thus on the one hand, the whole extended family is engaged in the process of childcare, as Dybdahl and Hundeide (1998) describe from Somalia. On the other hand, weak economic resources and changes from rural economies to more industrial ones make child-raising a greater family burden than is justified by the 'pay-off' of care in old age (Jensen, 1998).

Furthermore, the death of a child, an event that can be regarded as highly non-normative in rich, industrial countries, may be seen as quasi-normative in poorer ones. In Angola, for example, 30 per cent of children die before they reach the age of five (UNICEF, 2000a). In Latin-American countries, tradition still demands that children are 'presented' in a special church ceremony when they reach the age of three – when they have demonstrated that they are likely to survive.

It would seem that the changes to traditional cultures created by globalization and market forces begin to undermine the structure of the life course, and evoke changes in the resource-management of these extended families. The move towards more Western styles of living removes the firm foundations of traditional ways of life. Again, the developmental challenge model provides an understanding of how such traditional life patterns can crumble in the light of relatively rapid societal shifts. Pillay (1988) gives an example of an Indian community in South Africa in which young people used to stay in the parental house even after marriage and the birth of their own children. With increasing acculturation and emancipation, however, a greater number of young people now leave their parental home. This means that their mothers have to face a new way of life. They suffer loneliness and are disappointed, because their lifetime expectation of growing old – circled by their children – is no longer being fulfilled.

Also within cultures, different parents tackle the challenges of child-rearing in a variety of ways. Hence, the dynamic interactions of 'linked lives' mean that no two children in the same family experience the same environments or develop identically. While this is true of all 'normal' families, in some cases the picture is even more complicated in non-normative parenthood.

Non-normative parenthood

Given the variety of challenges with which new parents are usually confronted, it is not surprising that additional challenges will tax individual resources. Extra complications can stem, for example, from non-normative off-time parenting, namely when it occurs during the teenage years instead of early or middle adulthood, as expected in most societies. Not only has the young adolescent mother to face many negative reactions from society, she is often also confronted with economic hardships and, perhaps, an unfinished education. At the same time, she has to deal with all the other normal tasks of adolescence. According to the developmental challenge model, she is at risk of being overwhelmed by more tasks than her resources allow her to cope with. For example, teenage mothers are more likely to drop out of school, to remain unemployed and dependent on state benefits, and to live in poor housing (Dennison and Coleman, 1998). In addition, rather than the father, she has most often to cope with the burden of single parenthood, with all its economic and social implications. Single mothers of all ages have been shown to be the group in society with the lowest life quality, because of economic problems and social isolation (UNICEF, 2000b; Wolvén, 1990). At the same time, single mothers with low educational qualifications perceive the situation of single parenthood as more stressful than others (Sander, 1993).

However, as Phoenix (1991) writes, the outlook for most of the teenage mothers in her study was already discouraging and bleak before the birth of their child, and the pregnancy was a consequence rather than the cause of their problems. Hence, recent research paints a complex, and in the main more positive picture of teenage parenthood. Many teenagers actually cope well with their role as a mother, often in spite of enormous difficulties (Phoenix, 1991). Further, in contrast to prejudices and stereo-typical views, many teenage fathers would actually like to be more involved in parenting (Voran, 1991). However, their actual contribution in economic and practical terms is relatively minor. Most teenage mothers get the support they really need from their own mothers, often staying in the parental home for the duration of their pregnancy and for at least the first few months of their child's life (Phoenix, 1991). The arrangement, however, can be a double-edged sword: the support might be needed and helpful, but it can also become an additional source of stress if perceived as intrusive and as restraining the teenage mother's independence from her own parents (Voran, 1991). Seen from the perspective of the grandmother, she too is 'pressed' into a role of non-normative parenting, being the mother of a teenage daughter as well as a grandmother. Several grandmothers in Dennison and Coleman's (1998) study describe the difficulties that arise from realizing that their daughter is 'only a teenager' herself, and therefore involved in a variety of roles. In this way the daughter needs time to go out and enjoy herself, to be involved in normal teenage activities, to be supported as a teenager and to be treated as a daughter and (adult) mother, all at the same time. Nevertheless, and in spite of the problems, the majority of the teenage mothers and their own mothers in the study evaluate their experiences as predominantly positive, thereby challenging the common view of teenage parenthood as a social catastrophe. Dennison and Coleman (1998) summarize their findings as follows:

> It is clear that simplistic negative images of young mothers are misplaced. Young mothers do not form a simple homogeneous group and the problems they face are often the same as those facing older mothers. Some women adjust well to their new role, others find it much more difficult or even impossible. Some women are able to be independent, others need to

rely heavily on the support of those around them. What is obvious, however, is that becoming a parent during the teenage years does not immediately condemn a young woman to a life of welfare dependence and her child to abuse and neglect as some politicians and some sections of the media would have us believe [p.29].

Once again, a risky and apparently negative life challenge has been shown to be capable of being transformed into an opportunity for development and growth, given the right circumstances and enough coping resources for the young mother and her immediate micro-system.

The same is true for another form of non-normative parenting, that of having a child with a mental handicap. Seltzer and Ryff (1994) review the few empirical studies that have investigated this particular challenge, describing parental reactions as initially resembling a crisis response. As years go by, however, most parents develop coping mechanisms that allow them to face the additional parenting challenges that are associated with the special needs of their child, often finding in the process an increase in family cohesion. The protective mechanisms that Seltzer and Ryff describe correspond well to some of the resources outlined in the developmental challenge model:

> adaptation in parents of a child with retardation is quite varied.... The protective mechanisms include strong and satisfying parental social networks, effective personal coping skills, and the quality and strength of the parental relationship with the child [p.18].

Career and unemployment

Another important aspect of middle adulthood is the role which work fulfils. Thus, in mid-life, many people in Western societies have pursued their career as far as possible and wish to retain (at least) their current occupational position. Consequently, work is mentioned as the major source of stress for many middle-aged men, but, in spite of the increasing number of those working, only for a fifth of women (e.g. Chiriboga, 1997). This may be the result of many women working part-time and/or in lower-paid jobs, because of their domestic circumstances or the biases of market economies. Because many women may have life values other than job achievement, another reason could be that few of them, and very few other than those from a middle-class background, have made inroads into key positions in industry, commerce or academic life. Findings from a cross-cultural study of male and female social-science students in 15 countries show that the higher the GNP of a country, the more likely the students are to consider that their personal occupational success is more salient for their self-esteem than the characteristics and quality of their family background. However, a significant gender difference influences this finding: only men from the more 'individualist' countries value 'family values' less than women (Watkins *et al.*, 1998).

The work situation, with its stresses, challenges and opportunities is not only an extremely important micro-system for the individual, it is also one of the most important exo-systems for other members of that individual's micro-system (Bronfenbrenner, 1979). Work affects children, spouses and friends. This can create positive or negative influences:

role conflicts, work overload and spillover effects from work have been observed as well as mutual role enhancement and satisfaction from the greater number of roles occupied (for a review, see Swanson, 1992). Whether the individual is happy or unhappy, stressed, challenged or bored at the workplace, works long or short hours or shifts, all sets the framework for other life sectors. Leisure time, the amount of energy left for engaging in family and the social network are affected and, over time, self-identity is shaped accordingly. Heavy work under unhealthy conditions can seriously tax people's life resources and contribute to early stagnation and even decay. Interesting, challenging and reinforcing work, on the other hand, can contribute to life satisfaction and further development, and thus make the individual a better parent, partner and friend.

Karasek and Theorell (1990) offer a model to predict what kind of work is most likely to produce strain and psychological and physical symptoms. They suggest that two characteristics in combination affect well-being dramatically: 'control', i.e. skill level and decision latitude at work, and 'work demands'. Jobs that make great demands on a highly skilled worker lead to learning and growth, to a more active leisure time, and to fewer stress symptoms. Undemanding jobs done by highly skilled workers cause least psycho-physical symptoms, but do not enable further development. Most significantly, great demands combined with low skill and low autonomy create most stress-related illnesses. Passive jobs, in which little control and few demands are experienced, lead to a gradual atrophying of skills and abilities, a more passive leisure time, and signs of depression. Over the years, Karasek and Theorell (1990) have compiled a great deal of empirical evidence from many different countries for their model, showing that high-demand/low-control jobs are most highly correlated with depression, exhaustion, pill consumption, coronary heart disease and job dissatisfaction.

As the reader might have observed, there are several similarities between Karasek and Theorell's work stress-model and the lifespan model of developmental challenge: whenever the goodness of fit between resources (here, work skills and autonomy) and challenges (here, work demands) are out of balance, there are serious consequences for development. Few demands lead to 'contented stagnation' (as in the high-control/low-demand group) or 'unhappy stagnation' (as in the low-control/low-demand group), while demands that by far exceed the individual's resources (high-demand/low-control) lead to illness and decay. Only high levels of challenge combined with a high degree of resource are associated with growth and development (though additionally with some positive stress).

Similarly, findings from research on personal attributes that char-acterize the 'successful' worker parallel the description of potential resources in the developmental challenge model: those who reveal personal initiative, an entrepreneurial orientation, have a self-motivating and proactive approach to work tasks, like to challenge role boundaries and change the work environment in the direction of growth. These are the individuals who are more likely to find a job and cope better with work stresses in modern societies (Frese, 2000). These types of worker can be contrasted to 'reactive' workers, who simply do what they are ordered to do, and stop when difficulties arise. According to Frese, these 'innovative' qualities stem from high self-efficacy, 'positive dissatisfaction' that leads to action, a high skill level and previous mastery experiences, aspirations to achievement and a positive-change orientation.

The challenge of unemployment

As we have shown, the challenges of work are important for self-identity and the expansion of resources. In that context, increasing unemployment rates create non-normative shifts for many adults. Present-day societies are characterized by a shrinking manufacturing sector and a predominant service sector. The post-industrial era has been characterized by a dramatic decline in the demand for unskilled labour. In the modern labour market, employment contexts are increasingly differentiated, with burgeoning competition for jobs. Unemployment is on the brink of becoming a normative experience. Those in work are constantly threatened by the possibility of losing their jobs, and those already unemployed have to cope with all the implications of this difficult situation. The stigma of not being 'normal' is, however, considerably lessened in areas or among sub-cultures in which unemployment has become a frequent event, particularly if economic problems are reduced by social security allowances or buffered by an extended family network. For instance, Näsström and Kloep (1994) could show that young men from a rural area in Sweden did not appear to suffer from the experience of unemployment, but instead enjoyed their free time with unemployed peers, hunting, fishing and skiing. Young women, on the other hand, lacking these leisure-time opportunities and the accompanying social networks, showed more signs of distress.

For older people, whose self-identity is strongly linked to their occupational role, unemployment may be psychologically harder than for young people (e.g. Jahoda, 1979; Kelvin, 1981). In an Israeli study, Kulik (2000) found that unemployed women over fifty are least likely to reject any new job offers, and that their health declined more sharply following unemployment than younger women. Furthermore, re-entry into the labourforce is less likely for unemployed people over forty, particularly if no new job is found within a year of redundancy. This leaves the older, long-term unemployed with feelings of resignation and uselessness (Henkens, Sprengers and Tazelaar, 1996). Mental distress (anxiety, depression, loss of confidence, reduction in self-esteem and happiness) is higher among the middle-aged unemployed than in younger and older groups (Theodossiou, 1998).

An earlier British study by Hendry and Raymond (1983) sheds some light on responses to the challenges of unemployment. The researchers attempted to identify various unemployed lifestyles, by reference to the perceived daily time structures devised by the young people within their research project.

Some young people who were not career-oriented, or who were without experience of a working existence (and the increased leisure spending-powers resulting from employment) found the unemployed lifestyle little different from the passive leisure they had been familiar with as school pupils. While a job might be welcome in the future, by seeing the experience as a 'vacation' from the constraints of work, and perhaps as an opportunity to contemplate their choice of future career, they had given their period of unemployment some positive meaning. Whilst not being active 'developers', some of them were using the time to plan and prepare for future achievement and advancement that would take them out of 'contented stagnation'.

Others recreated the male street-corner groups first notable in the 1930s (e.g. Jahoda, Lazarfield and Zeisel, 1933), and might be seen as 'unhappy stagnators', lacking the resources to seek out a fulfilling leisure existence or to find employment, though admittedly this was within a fairly adverse economic climate.

A further type of lifestyle could clearly be seen as 'unhappy stagnation', on the brink of 'decay'. These were a group of young people, mainly males, who spent their time indoors, watching TV and videos (in some cases up to 18 hours a day), seldom leaving the house or socializing with other people. They had given up all attempts to change their situation, and had retreated into a passive and solitary way of life. In general the majority of this group was totally negative in its attitudes towards the experience of unemployment. Rejected job applications, lack of day-to-day structure and continuing boredom had led to a feeling of apathy that affected any enthusiasm for tackling the situational challenges.

By contrast, the 'developers' (or 'entrepreneurs') in the sample could be identified by their willingness to use their social skills to seek out employment. They had the ability to access useful informal 'networks' as a precursor to gaining employment, to sign up for short-term training schemes, or to return for additional educational qualifications to enhance future employability. They attempted to set up alternative job opportunities, and took temporary part-time work, thus showing a desire to change their current circumstances, to gain experience and to seek further challenges and achievements.

Another finding was the 'hidden consequence' of unemployment in the emergence and reinforcement of traditional, stereotypical gender roles, as young people responded to the challenges of unemployment with its extended periods of 'free time'. Many young women turned to domestic chores, becoming the family's unpaid servant, while several young men used the rituals of 'signing on' and unsuccessful 'job-hunting' to go through the motions of a structured, organized day. This 'gendered' response to unemployment might have reversed somewhat in the inter-vening years in the UK. Walsh and Jackson (1995) found in their sample that only women use their time for self- and career development activities, while men report spending their time on hobbies and time-filling activities.

The question of why one individual is successful in coping with unemployment and developing through the experience, while another fails and drifts into despair, cannot be answered by referring to the length of time spent without work. Nor can it be answered by referring to a number of single psycho-social factors. Structure can be seen as supportive or stifling, families can be sympathetic or pressurizing, aspirations can be sustained or they can collapse, self-esteem can remain high in long-term unemployment or can plummet to the depths on a training scheme.

As with other developmental tasks we have discussed, a real under-standing of unemployment must not only take account of how all these factors interact, but also must try to gauge the individual's capacity to cope with positive and negative features of the process. These apparent paradoxes may be resolved by interpreting the experience of unemployment in terms of positive and negative 'trade-offs'. The reality of the process of unemployment can be viewed as a series of different psychological and social issues hitting the individual sequentially. Problems occur when several issues overlap. These factors, in combination, produce the elements around which coping strategies develop, or lead to a growing state of distress in the face of continuing unemployment. Thus, a number of negative factors – for example, low self-image, low aspirations and family pressures to find employment – would be likely to increase in long-term unemployment. In other cases, a supportive family, enjoyable leisure and a good time structure make it fairly easy for the individual to cope well even after a lengthy period without a job. Hence, like other life challenges, unemployment provides individuals with tasks, challenges, risks and 'steeling experiences', and produces differential, individual responses which can be interpreted as 'development', 'contented stagnation', or 'unhappy stagnation', dependent upon the potential resources in the individual's resource 'pool'.

Similarly, the effects of unemployment on the individual's micro-system vary with the circumstances and resources of significant others. For instance, unemployment for one partner can lead to increased arguments between the couple, less satisfaction with the quality of the partnership and even the risk of divorce – but only in marriages that were already distressed before the onset of unemployment (Liem and Liem, 1990).

As is so often the case, we do not know much about the antecedents and effects of unemployment in countries with extremely high unemployment rates, that is in the poorer nations of the world. Here the job market is so competitive that people often engage in legal or illegal activities that are not reported to the tax authorities (the so called 'informal economy' or 'grey market'), and thus they are not protected by labour laws or insurance. Such legal and illegal informal economies comprise between 15 per cent (US, Germany) and 60 per cent (Russia) of the economic activity of countries (Vaknin, 2000). In Brazil, the 13 million people employed by the informal economy equal the total number of workers in the public and industrial sectors combined (Neves, 1999). In addition, there are domestic workers, mainly women and often children, whose job is described as follows: 'A residue from slavery times, domestic workers…live in that limbo of coziness that often makes the employee a member of the family on one hand, depriving her of a just salary and benefits on the other' (Neves, http page).

Adding these domestic jobs to the rest of the legal informal economy, one can say that 32 per cent of Brazilians living in urban surroundings do not have legal, paid employment, while, in addition, around seven million do not have a job at all (Neves, 1999). In Mexico, the informal economy accounts for 13 per cent of the GNP and employs 28 per cent of the country's workers (*Mexico News*, 2000). Having a paid, steady, 'real' job is not the 'normative' experience of adults in many countries of the world.

The mid-life moratorium and the importance of leisure

At this period of the life course, there is the possibility for a 'moratorium' – a 'breathing space' – because there are no particular normative shifts looming for the individual. This moratorium gives the individual time for refining, generalizing and broadening skills, or for specializing in already acquired abilities in various life domains. Furthermore, the time can be used to learn 'chosen' skills, which are not absolutely necessary for present 'survival', but ones that can be improved in order to 'fill the "pool"' for future use: new experiences, hobbies, skills, areas of knowledge. As a preparation for the life stages to come, this life phase is as important to the life course as the psycho-social moratorium in adolescence described by Erikson (1968).

This is because there are few totally new sets of skills that *have to be* learned. However, in modern societies, the speed of technological development demands that the individual constantly adapts and elaborates on his or her skills in order to keep abreast of social change. Consider, for example, that in many European countries one now requires basic computer skills in order to buy a railway ticket! In less rapidly changing traditional cultures, individuals in mid-life usually have all the competencies needed to master their daily life and work, so there is no constant need to meet new challenges. A period of stability and 'happy' stagnation can be achieved. Yet in both types of culture, there is a risk in mid-life that the individual ceases to be alert to the possibilities and properties of change. Then, if societal shifts do occur and become part of the social fabric, this will leave the individual 'suddenly' de-skilled, feeling a loss of security, and at risk of 'unhappy' stagnation because they have opted out of any future considerations of learning about, and adapting to, these innovations.

We mentioned earlier that social life and career in a 'normal' life trajectory do not offer many radical life changes to the middle aged. Usually, family, residence and career are settled, and unless a person is dissatisfied with the status quo and opts for a new start in some or all these areas, certain routines might sneak into daily life. In this situation, many possibilities for new challenges and personal growth can be found within leisure time. Indeed, Havighurst (1972) chose the task of 'establishing meaningful leisure activities' as one of the most important developmental tasks of middle adulthood.

For instance, leisure can be seen as performing three different forms of social function:

- Independent leisure, in which one pursues a solitary hobby, such as collecting stamps.
- Parallel leisure, in which one meets people while carrying on with one's own activities or programme. Activities such as body-building, weight training or attending evening classes fit into this category.
- Collaborative leisure, in which one plays or performs with others, such as team sports or theatre groups.

These three types are reflections of the concept of adult development, since they balance social expectations and individual needs, affiliation and autonomy (Freysinger, 1995). Leisure can be an excellent opportunity for development, if it provides for learning and the refining of a variety of skills and the enhancement of one's social network (Mancini and Sandifer, 1995). Furthermore, as Freysinger (1995) concludes from an interview study of Americans between thirty-six and forty-three, leisure provides a means of self-expression, compensates for meaningless work, offers a chance to 'get away' from everyday living, facilitates performance of adult roles and provides opportunities to experiment with a change of roles:

> Leisure was a context wherein adults expressed both the relational and egocentric, expressive and instrumental sides of themselves. Leisure was part of the dialectic of self and other and whose synthesis has been identified as the goal of adult development [p.80].

We have argued throughout this book, that resources are not equally distributed, and neither are the opportunities to add new ones to the resource 'pool'. The differential possibilities to develop through leisure experiences are good examples of this:

- Firstly, leisure in itself is a feature of affluent societies: wherever it is difficult to sustain a family economically, all free time has to be used to create money or goods. In that context, gardening and sewing are not leisure-time pursuits, but rather necessary means of survival.
- Secondly, an increasing number of leisure-time activities have to be paid for and/or 'need' expensive equipment, thus excluding all those who cannot afford these expenses. (This is often used as an intentional social-class segregation policy.)
- Thirdly, the place where one lives has a strong influence on the kind of leisure and social activities one chooses. For instance, in towns in cold climates, one relies heavily on commercial activities in indoor clubs and restaurants; in cold rural areas, one can choose between outdoor activities like skiing or hunting, or church activities and home-based leisure. In urban areas in warmer countries, all social life proceeds on the main square, while in extreme rural regions the only lighted meeting-place for sitting and gossiping may be the roadside of the nearby highway.
- Finally, tradition, culture and law limit the free choice of activities for some groups.

To exemplify the last point, those under a certain age are prevented by law from visiting bars and discos – and the very old may voluntarily stop short of going to all-night raves. Bullfighting and public gambling are not allowed in many countries, and women of different religions are regarded as indecent if they wear bathing costumes or gymnastic leotards in public. In post-revolutionary Iran, for example, many leisure opportunities have been forbidden, most holidays declared mourning holidays, with commercial leisure venues closed, thereby leaving 'getting together with family and friends' as one of the few leisure opportunities available (Kousha and Mohseni, 1997). At any age, and in many cultures, women experience more constraints (economic, temporal, spatial and of opportunity) on their leisure activities than men. Already in their teenage years, girls to a large extent are encouraged to follow stereotypically graceful activities, such as skating, tennis and horse-riding. This is so even though these activities can embarrass many teenage girls because leisure fashions require that these sports reveal their developing physiques at a time when they are over-concerned about self-perceived inadequacies (Scraton, 1986). Then they are restricted in their use of leisure 'space' by their male peers (e.g. Griffin, 1993), and spend more time in obligatory activities (school and home chores) than boys (Alsaker and Flammer, 1999 in European countries and the US; Mohapatra, 2001 in India; Shaw, Kleiber and Caldwell, 1995 in Canada). The picture is precisely the same if one looks at adult leisure-time use: women spend more time doing housework than men (and consequently spend less time in leisure), whether they are employed or not (Firestone and Shelton, 1994). Thus, leisure can be constraining, because it reflects and reinforces gender stereotypes, but it can also have the opposite effect, such as offering opportunity for agency and proactivity (Shaw, 1994).

Shaw (1994) describes three different aspects of leisure – namely being constrained in pursuing leisure, leisure as being constraining, and leisure as resistance to constraints – to explain the meaning of leisure in women's lives. We want to broaden this viewpoint and argue that these three descriptions correspond to the characterization of developmental types provided by the lifespan model of developmental challenge outlined in chapter 3:

- Those who are restricted in their choice of leisure activities are most often those who lack resources in terms of money, time, skills, health or power. They have few possibilities to develop through their leisure, often using their free time for relatively passive pursuits: drinking beer, watching soap operas and sports on TV, and feeling bored. As such, they are examples of 'unhappy stagnators'.
- Next, we have the group who engages in leisure activities that are constraining, because they reinforce gender, class or cultural stereotypes and thus do not offer much of an opportunity for change and development. Individuals in this group might well be active, even developing their skills considerably in a narrow, specialized area. But they do not feel a need to change or try something new. Rather, they keep on doing what they have always done, and what seems to be appropriate for the group to which they belong. Men do gardening and repair and wash the car, women work in charity groups and attend aerobic classes; working-class members of this group go to Bingo or the cinema or the pub, middle- or upper-class ones go to the opera or dinner parties; Catholics support Celtic, Protestants Rangers. As such, these could be described as 'contented stagnators'.
- Finally, there are individuals who have both the resources and the will to try out new and atypical things, not caring too much about public opinion about which activities are appropriate and which are not. The boom in travel agencies offering adventure vacations to meet a growing demand, the increasing media exposure of women's soccer and men cooking, and the growing number of middle-aged and older people enrolling at university classes bear witness to their existence. For them, leisure provides a wide range of challenges and opportunities for growth. Thus, they are the 'developers'.

The point here is that there may be more to leisure in the middle years than has been considered and written about so far. Not only does it offer different (and in many cases the only) opportunities for further development during this life stage, it can, because of the significance it has for certain individuals, be the catalyst for further life changes. Kleiber (1999) emphasizes that leisure is one of the domains that offers voluntary engagement after the involuntary disengagement from many other areas of life in late adulthood, providing also possibilities for 'shared flow' with significant others. Thus, leisure choices and engagement in middle age might well provide a path for continued engagement and continued developmental challenges into old age. In other words, disengagements and re-engagements operate in dialectical concert to enhance development further.

Conclusions

The challenges of mid-life seem to revolve around career, relationships, family life and leisure. Many of these are to some extent self-initiated, because there are no normative shifts to contend with, and the individual has to reach out proactively to challenges or consider, as many do, settling for a conventional lifestyle. Wide acceptance of the status quo in mid-life adds stability to societies, which operate a certain amount of social control to allow only for gradual societal change. In the light of this stability, active steps have to be taken if the individual wishes to seek out new challenges. But it is important to stress that if people do not keep a watchful eye on the pattern of societal shifts, changes may come along with a rapidity that leaves them de-skilled and drained of resources into their future lives.

As one of the few quasi-normative shifts in adult life (occurring at different times from younger to older adulthood, and even as an 'off-time' challenge for some adolescents), we have described the trajectory of parenting from birth until the children leave home. Using the framework of the developmental challenge model, it becomes obvious that both 'normal' and 'non-normative' parenthood present a range of tasks and challenges to new parents and other members of their micro-system, which can turn into possibilities for developmental growth or risks. This depends on the amount and kind of resources that are available, and on other challenges that are concurrently present.

Because of the level of competence and achieved social status in mid-life, many people invest a great deal of time and effort in maintaining a career position, or indeed attempting to advance it. In this context, we discussed the non-normative event of unemployment and its implications for the individual, finding, once again, that negatively perceived events such as job loss can be important turning-points and opportunities for development, depending on the circumstances and the resources individuals can draw upon.

Middle adulthood can be a relatively quiet period of the lifespan, without too many changes and shifts, and may create a risk of (at least temporary) stagnation. One area that offers itself as a compensatory life zone is leisure. In leisure time, individuals can choose to try out new skills, to form new social relationships, and to break out of 'expected' social roles to do new and adventurous things – or they can stick to the usual, routine entertainment to which they have always adhered. Which of these leisure pathways is chosen depends on the number and amount of resources individuals possess, and on social restrictions on their leisure choices emanating from the macro- or micro-system. Hence, in mid-life, leisure choices and leisure involvement can be another step in the direction of either stagnation or development.

9 Late adulthood: back to the future?

Introduction

'Suddenly, overnight' the individual notices the almost imperceptible body changes that have actually been happening over the previous years, when there was no time in an apparently busy life for regular exercise. After many years of gradual physical changes, now is the time when a receding hairline, greying hair, a bulging stomach and many wrinkles just cannot be overlooked any longer, or hidden behind the various products of the fashion and cosmetic industry. Middle age is when your age shows round your middle, as Bob Hope reputedly said.

Bodily changes, such as decreasing physical powers or the inability to carry out tasks that could be dealt with easily and without any real exertion some years before, are no less significant than those that heralded the teenage years. When truly perceived and admitted, they embody a major maturational challenge to the individual. Moreover, what others say about one's changing physical shape may impinge significantly on one's self-esteem. The social impact and symbolic value of the ageing corpus may have more influence than the effects of the actual bodily changes during this maturational shift. It seems as if people can 'get by' with a less efficient body in older middle age, but not without the approbation of friends and peers.

Hence, in this chapter we look at four challenging aspects of older middle age – two normative maturational, one normative social and one quasi-normative shift – to illuminate the uses of the developmental challenge model in understanding development. More specifically, we cover the following four topics:

- the challenges associated with bodily changes
- the effects of the menopause
- the experiences of being a grandparent
- retirement from work.

Bodily changes

Beyond early adulthood, a number of changes occur in the body, and these are further affected by the generally sedentary lifestyle of those living in Western cultures. We said in the previous chapter that mid-life for many is a busy period that does not leave much time for leisure, and much less for exercise. Simultaneously, since many still feel strong and healthy, they are not especially susceptible to their GP's warnings that those who do not have time for exercise now will, some day, have to have time for illness.

We know from physiological research that muscle tissue does not contract as effectively as previously, and to some extent deteriorates. Put simply, people are not as strong, fast, powerful or blessed with physical endurance as they were in their youthful days. This process of bodily change happens over a relatively long period, although individuals may not necessarily be aware of it, since it is a gradual process. Occasionally, it comes to one's attention briefly. This can be, for example, when it is just a little more difficult to fasten a waist-band or belt; by looking at revealing holiday photos; or receiving the reactions of others (e.g. 'Putting on a bit of weight lately, hmm?' Or 'Your husband is jealous of you and me? But you could be my mother!').

One important aspect of the physical and metabolic changes of late adulthood is the influence that comes to the individual from wider society, which impinges on some of those in mid-life as the result of images in the press and the mass media. There is a 'myth of youth' abroad in Western cultures (e.g. Featherstone and Hepworth, 1991), and less age segregation in society (e.g. Maffesoli, 1996). These two factors combine to portray success, in business and in personal relations, in images of vitality, health, attractiveness and youthfulness. This has made many susceptible to the desire to approximate to these stereotypes. Such social pressures are no less powerful than they are on adolescents in terms of body image, which we discussed briefly in chapter 7. Lately, it even seems to affect non-Western cultures: Toledo de Paula *et al.*, (2000) report from Brazil that the concept of 'adultescence' (adult maturity in a youthful body) is popular among the middle aged.

How do older adults respond to these demanding images, and to medical advice to adopt a healthier lifestyle? Put another way, how do those in mid-life face the challenge of a changing body and altering metabolism? Some try to offset the process by exercising regularly, but, however worthwhile such a regimen might be in its own right, we know from physiological research that in mid-life, with a slower metabolism, more effort is needed for fewer fitness gains. Thus, the fitness challenge is relatively hard to achieve. Further, those who have wealth and material resources may turn to plastic and cosmetic surgery to lift sagging muscles, skin and fatty tissue, to remove adipose tissue, or replace a head of hair.

A worldwide industry has been created on the basis of this search for youth.

But this maturational shift cannot be halted, only slowed down and delayed. Featherstone and Hepworth (1993), amongst others, have discussed the different images of ageing in a societal context in terms of its social construction. On the one hand, the individual's subjective feelings are that 'inside' (i.e. their self-perceptions) they are as active and vital as before. On the other hand, wider society only perceives the 'mask' of gathering age, as Hepworth (1991) puts it.

In this situation there are risks on both sides. From the point of view of society, to dismiss the qualities of the individual on the basis of an ageing physique would be to lose the experience and wisdom of many in the workplace, in the context of leisure organizations, at home and in the local community. On the individual's side, a number of strategies can be pursued, some of which carry more risks than others. At one extreme, one could attempt to deny ageing and carry on exactly as before, with the risk of putting greater and greater strain on the resource 'pool', continually draining it. By contrast, one could take the physical and social changes as a challenge, and carry out a number of problem-solving attempts to consider the positive features in this maturational shift (for example, with age comes seniority, and more acceptance by and respect from others). From that stance, it would then be possible to move on, with a slightly differently functioning body, to new challenges of a different kind. The choice is simple: either to age gracefully or to be bitter about 'lost' youth – to develop or to stagnate.

The menopause

With the beginning of the menopause, the shift into older adulthood is even more marked for women than for men (though some male researchers try to convince their audience from time to time of the existence of an 'andropause'). What exactly is the menopause? In the first place, it is a maturational shift. Changes in the endocrine system, chiefly in the pituitary and hypothalamus glands and in the ovaries, cause the ovaries gradually to stop producing the hormones that control the menstrual cycle. This leads to the cessation of menstruation, sometimes quite abruptly, sometimes during the course of several years. Often, these hormonal changes are accompanied by bodily symptoms, such as 'hot flushes', night sweats, irregular menstrual cycles, fatigue, headaches and general irritability (Dan and Bernhard, 1989). Women display different symptoms with different degrees of severity. Porter *et al.* (1996), for example, have shown that only 57 per cent of the women in their Scottish sample had experienced one or more of 15 usual menopausal symptoms, and only 22 per cent found such symptoms a problem. This is one of several research findings that suggest menopausal symptoms have a strong psychosomatic component.

This leads to a second aspect of the menopause: its powerful socio-cultural symbolism. Apart from being a maturational shift, with possible bodily consequences, the menopause is seen in some (Western) cultures as if it were a non-normative event. It is regarded as a kind of female illness of which one should be ashamed, and one that can be treated with medicines and hormone-replacement therapy. In contrast, it has been suggested that the menopause is not a biological process at all, but rather a social construction (Palmlund 1997), or even an invention of the pharmaceutical industry, convincing women that they all suffer from an illness that has to be dealt with medically (Hepworth, 1995). Thus, the menopause consists of several challenges on several levels, psycho-social as well as medical. A woman's self-esteem, the attitudes of the members of her micro-systems, the roles ascribed to older women in a given culture, and the appropriate resources she can activate, all influence the way in which these challenges are resolved.

Finally, the menopause can also be seen as a marker of a more general life-course development, which is responded to with lifestyle changes and a search for new meanings in life (Greer, 1991; Jones, 1997). The influence of the macro-system, of the attitudes prevailing in society, and the roles assigned to women, become obvious if we look at cultural differences in the ways women tackle the challenges of the menopause. Kaiser's (1990) review shows that women in non-Western societies often enjoy enhanced status, political power and psychological well-being in conjunction with the menopause. This obtains for a variety of reasons: freedom from pollution taboos, seniority in the domestic setting, participation in the male domains of power, greater decision-making authority, respect and responsibility accorded to the elderly, and the fulfilment of the social duty to bear and raise children. In these cultures, the menopause is welcomed as a time of natural transition, a time to reward a woman's achievements and to accord her a new, socially valued role. Similar views were expressed by Korean women, who described the menopausal transition as one leading from suffering to comfort, from oppression to freedom, from being a wife to being a woman, from a productive life to a transformed one (Lee, 1997). Defey *et al.* (1996) recount how women in Uruguay stress the relevance of the menopause as a crisis-point in life, but laden with opportunities for self-accomplishment and greater autonomy. Not surprisingly, given the more positive social values of the menopause in many non-Western countries, Japanese women report fewer menopausal symptoms than women in the US and Canada (Lock, 1998).

In Western societies, findings are somewhat contradictory. While Wilbur, Miller and Montgomery (1995) report that the majority of women had neutral feelings towards menopause, Dan and Bernhard (1989) state that negative attitudes among women predominate. Both agree, however, that women who are undergoing the menopause and those in the post-menopausal state are most positive, mentioning personal freedom and the gaining of autonomy. Other researchers (e.g. Robinson, 1996, for a review) comment on the enormous differences among women in the experience of the menopause, in the same culture, and across cultures. For instance, lesbian women report fewer problems at the menopause than heterosexual women (Cole and Rothblum, 1990). These findings show that the influences of the macro-system can play an influential role in the way women cope with menopausal challenges.

As with other maturational shifts, the menopause is a process full of different challenges (which, as we have seen, vary largely with social values and cultural attitudes), and the number of individual resources available to meet them is significant. Like other challenges, the process of the climacteric for middle-aged women can be a trigger for further development. This seems particularly true for the majority of non-Western women, but is also valid for a growing number in the West (Jones, 1997). However, this process can become a risk when the concurrent goodness of fit between the available resources and the level of challenge does not match. This can be the case if the woman, in addition to the menopausal shift, is confronted with other demanding tasks, such as troublesome teenagers at home, new obligations at work or health problems. An 'off-time' menopause – for example one that happens too early by comparison with the social norm (i.e. at under the age of forty) – constitutes a particularly difficult challenge, and often drains a great deal of resources, particularly in relation to self-esteem (Singer and Hunter, 1999).

Being a grandparent

Shortly after their adult children have left home (and sometimes even before) another quasi-normative shift awaits the majority of those who are parents: they are 'converted' into grandparents. With the de-regulation of the life course, this can happen at almost any time in adulthood. Giarrusso, Silverstein and Bengtson (1996) found the range of grandparents' ages to run from 30 to 110 years! As with other quasi-normative shifts, however, it seems that this challenge is best coped with if it occurs 'on-time', which means at an age the particular society, or sub-culture, agrees upon as 'appropriate'. For instance, African-American women who became grandmothers between forty-one and sixty-five tend to value their grandchildren more, compared to those who were younger (thirty to forty-one) or older (sixty-six to eighty-two; Timberlake and Chipungu, 1992). Older grandmothers perceive themselves as more informed about and less frustrated by the role than younger ones, and as more successful in teaching their grandchildren (Watson, 1997).

What issues have to be coped with when a parent becomes a grandparent? To start with, becoming a grandparent may not be the only challenge individuals meet at this phase of the life course. Hansen and Jacob (1992), interviewing new parents and grandparents before and after delivery observed a conflict between the needs of the new parents and those of the grandparents. Grandparents were facing issues of retirement, health and general ageing, and needed their own children's support. The adult children, in turn, were occupied with their own, new-born children. In addition, matters of dependence and independence emerged. The young parents planned to do things differently from their parents, and did not want to turn to them for help immediately (which, *de facto*, many did shortly afterwards): 'The conflict between wanting to be needed and anxiety about being burdened, or even exploited, reported by many grandparents, also parallels the new parents' developmental issues' (p.476).

This finding is supported by other studies investigating grandparents' roles in the US (for a review, see Robertson, 1995). Grandparents seem to draw clear boundaries between parenting and grandparenting, and prefer voluntary, short-term baby-sitting to long-term arrangements, in order to ensure time for their own lives (Johnson, 1988). As we have seen in chapter 5, these expectations might well conflict with the expectations of the new parents, or they may clash with the occurrence of some non-normative event (such as the unexpected death of one of the young parents). Grandparents might find themselves cajoled or pressurized into a much more responsible parent-like role than they had wished for. People in late adulthood and into old age are often so occupied with work, hobbies, friends and other interests that they do not volunteer a great deal of their time to care-giving for the third generation. As a Norwegian grandmother put it:

> I have to admit that I am not so eager – well, I love my grandchildren very much, and we have good regular contact with them, but I think I am that active myself. So being available for every request such as baby-sitting, during the day, that I am not prepared to do. I think one has to be careful not to be exploited in one's old age, you know, by the other, the next generation [Kloep, 2000, unpublished].

However, the modern attitude of choosing to live one's own life into the latter years is mainly a phenomenon of Western cultures. Research among ethnic groups in the US, for instance, shows that the grandparent role is more significant for them, and family homes containing three generations are common. Additionally, it is usually the parents from the mother's side of the family who assume the role of mediator at times of crisis (Longino and Earle, 1996). Latino families tend to have larger families, stronger family bonds, and more interactions with and support from adult children than Anglo-Americans (McGreal, 1994). Grandparents occupy a central role in family activities and provide stability in times of disorientation, such as immigration, divorce or death. They identify strongly with their grandparent role, which typically involves child-rearing and family decision-making. However, this sometimes leads to conflicts between parents and grandparents, who are unable to reach consensus about their respective roles. It can also lead to divided loyalties among grandchildren (Burnette, 1999). For black families the extended kinship group is an important basis for inter-generational parenting and black grandparents do appear to play a more central role in family life than grandparents in white families. As a consequence, black children view their grandparents as extremely influential in teaching lessons about morality, education and faith (Hunter, 1997). Accordingly, African-American grandparents perceive themselves as more skilled in handling difficulties and managing frustration as a grandparent, and as playing a more parent-like role than their Anglo-American peers (Watson and Koblinsky, 1997). There also seems to be a higher centrality of the grand-father's role among older black men than white:

> While older whites were seen to place emphasis on the past and tend to hold themselves up as a model for the younger generation, older blacks were envisioned as emphasizing the future and, as a result, not pressing their customs and 'ways of doing things' on the young. This orientation was seen to contribute to more cohesion between generations [Kivett, 1991: p.256].

Grandparents everywhere have a multitude of roles to fulfil. They can be guards, surrogate parents and nurturers (Pruchno and Johnson's

1996 review in the US). They are also historians, telling stories from the past and transmitting heritage, mentors, sharing knowledge and influencing children's ideas about ageing, and role models (Kornhaber and Woodward, 1981). Grandparents can also be playmates, having more time to spend with children than other adults, and indulgent adults, 'spoiling' children. Then, they are partners, competitors; advisory counsellors and interfering know-alls for the parents. They can be the reason for marital disharmony, or they can play a compensatory role in times of trouble. In particular, adolescents report having meaningful relationships with their grandparents, deep personal conversations, companionship, intimacy and feelings of closeness (Hendry *et al.*, 1992; McGreal, 1994).

Risks associated with grandparenting

When grandparents choose the role of care-givers as the sole role in their lives, giving up other possibilities, they run the risk of losing all resources connected to a variety of options. Picture the situation in which grand-parents have moved in with their (employed) children in order to help them with childcare, often giving up their own social network and failing to develop alternative leisure-time activities after retirement. Years later, when the small grandchildren have grown into demanding adolescents, and their own health starts to weaken, they might find themselves more of a burden than a help to the family. Feeling drained of resources and bitter about the lack of gratitude, some become increasingly aggressive, nagging and demanding excessive care – which, reciprocally, may turn the whole family against them. This constellation can end in a catastrophe for the micro-system of the extended family, involving abuse and mutual hate.

As in other life stages, grandparents in ever-changing societies have a variety of roles to choose from, but few norms or role models to guide them. As Kornhaber and Woodward (1981) conclude from their study: 'They can also take advantage of the range of choices open to them by an increasingly age-irrelevant society....Under these evolving social circumstances, it is easy for grandparents to become confused over their emotional priorities' (p.179).

As we can see, the necessity of making life choices and adjusting to different roles has by no means become easier than it was in the adolescent years.

As the developmental challenge model predicts, how grandparents meet this new challenge in their lives depends on the range of resources they can mobilize, and on the number and degree of difficulty of concurrent challenges (see box above for risks associated with grandparenting). Research confirms this: Kornhaber and Woodward (1981) come to the conclusion that the way grandparents fulfil different, demanding roles depends on a variety of personal factors – their health, financial means, emotional histories and individual life goals. In their longitudinal study of over 800 grandparents from Iowa, King and Elder (1998) show that high levels of self-efficacy in grandparents are associated with a high level of involvement and high levels of responsibility towards their grandchildren. Grandparents who feel more efficacious are those who also get along best with their adult children. Efficacious beliefs promote higher involvement, and such involvement further promotes feelings of efficacy, so they become reciprocally related.

Becoming a grandparent is a challenge that most often leads to development and growth. However, as in all other life events, it can turn into a risk if dealing with the challenge drains too many resources. Thus, a vital task for grandparents is to select an 'appropriate' role or roles, allowing them to participate without interfering too much in the 'new' family, and leave time for them to pursue other activities in order to maintain their own social networks.

In most cases, however, grandparents do cope successfully with the challenge of adding a new member to their micro-system, and this can even be extended to the next generation. In a study of 12 different nationalities, Doka and Mertz (1988) show that over 90 per cent of their subjects experience great-grandparenthood as positive and emotionally fulfilling, describing it as 'life starting again in the family'. The majority though, chooses a rather 'remote' style of being a great-grandparent, preferring not to have too intense contact with the new generation of children – thus 'saving' their (possibly decreasing) resources to cope with the increasingly varied challenges of daily life.

Retirement from work

Most likely, the last normative shift the individual has to deal with is retirement from work, with its subsequent impact on lifestyle. This normative shift has usually been seen as the psycho-social marker for entry into genuine old age. Yet the exact age of mandatory retirement varies somewhat for different kinds of employment and between cultures, though generally there exists an upper age limit at which people are excluded from paid employment. Up to now, this upper limit for employment has been based solely on age, not on performance or capacity. By contrast, most industrialized countries now offer many individuals the possibility of retiring somewhat earlier than the legal retirement age, although that can have negative consequences for the retiral pension paid. In recent years, the growing number of retired people and the decreasing sums of national pension schemes have led to discussions in various Western parliaments about encouraging individuals to take out personal pension schemes, delaying retirement or defining a more flexible retirement age. There are, to date, few signs of a considerable number of older people – particularly in the middle classes – necessarily wanting to disappear entirely from the work scene.

Disengagement theory (Cumming and Henry, 1961) has sometimes been used in the past to defend the authoritarian and sometimes insensitive practice of pushing healthy, fully capable older employees out of the workforce against their wishes. The claim of this theory is that all people of a certain age actually want to disengage from society and productive, paid work, and to live out their old age quietly and in peace. This idea is still in vogue (see, for example, Henry, 1965, reprinted 1998) though it was contradicted by empirical findings shortly after it originally emerged. Havighurst, Neugarten and Tobin (1968) reasoned from their longitudinal study:

> We conclude that neither activity theory nor disengagement theory of optimal aging in itself is sufficient to account for what we regard as the more inclusive descriptions of these findings. (Old people) regret the drop of activity in their lives. At the same time, most older people accept this drop as an inevitable accompaniment of growing old; and they succeed in maintaining a sense of self-worth and satisfaction [p.171].

In other words, it seems to be true that with increasing age people are forced to be less active, though this is not necessarily a voluntary choice. It can be limitations in their physical abilities, social expectations or legal regulations that reduce activity in later life. What retired people do is thus a realistic adjustment of goals to objective facts, rather than a personal option. Accepting this, older people can regard these readjustments in their life as challenges and find a reasonable way to deal with them.

What are some of the tasks of retirement?

In the first place, of course, retirement means adjustments to days without going to one's previous place of employment. Rather like the unemployed, retired people have to learn to restructure their days and find satisfying things to do. It also means 'letting go', distancing oneself from the events still continuing at the workplace. If one loses contact with one's former work colleagues it means having to build up new social networks, unless that has already been accomplished. It might also mean adjustments in one's economic situation, which could imply moving to a smaller flat or giving up expensive hobbies. It can also have implications for marital relations: suddenly, a couple who might have rarely seen each other for the whole of their working lives will have to interact with each other 24 hours a day, find topics (other than work) to talk about, and reallocate the household tasks, or at least discuss the reallocation of household tasks.

Research has shown that gender equality does not increase considerably in older age. In a German sample of seventy to one-hundred-and-three-year-olds living with a partner, retirement was associated with spending less time on household tasks and having enhanced leisure time for men, whereas for women the reverse was observed (Klumb and Baltes, 1999). Additionally, it may be even more difficult to rearrange social and domestic roles within a marriage partnership if only one partner retires and suddenly has all the time in the world to travel and pursue hobbies, while the other is still involved in a working life. However, research evidence indicates that the outcome depends more on the earlier quality of the marriage than on the event of retirement itself (Bossé, 1998).

Observing people's adjustments to retirement, we find all kinds of solutions, reflecting different degrees of development or decay: for example, consider the successful politician or professional who, finally pressed to retire, loses all meaning in life and dies within a few months. Then, there are all those couples who bore each other at their golden-wedding party as they have done during the last decades, and whose only highlight in life is their weekly bingo session or bowling match. Then there are active, curious seniors who use their new freedom to do all the things they did not have time to do during their earlier life. Some even begin a completely new life in a house on the beach in Marbella or in a colonial flat in San Miguel de Allende. Given reasonable economic means and a certain standard of health, life after retirement can be as full of different options for further development as young adulthood was. In other words, if there is misery in old age, this is not an inevitable part of the ageing process. Rather, it is due to psycho-social circumstances often stemming from attitudes and values contained in the macro-system of a culture, the attitudes and resources of members of micro-systems, or the lack of individual resources such as health, money or skills. As with other life changes, retirement can become stressful if it happens 'off-time' and/or for reasons of health, if it coincides with other stressful events, or if it leads to a poor economic situation (Bossé, 1998).

How do older citizens themselves describe their life after retirement?
Often, the processes and experiences of retirement vary with the resources provided by social class, gender, type of previous employment, and economics and other background factors. In a longitudinal study of Norwegians between seventy-five and eighty-four years, Thorsen (1998) reports interesting social-class differences. Men with higher education, who regarded work as central to their self-identity, try for as long as possible to continue working in some form, to prove their special abilities in different ways; retired lower-grade administrators keep busy with all kinds of leisure-time tasks. Workers emphasize the freedom of retirement in old age, which they believe they merit. Women, who are much less oriented towards paid employment than men, are not particularly touched by retirement at all.

In our own interview study, with over 60 retired men and women in Trondheim, Norway (Kloep and Hendry, 1999b), it becomes clear that, like other life events, retirement has different meanings for different people, depending on circumstances, not least on the amount of resources available. We identified four different groups among our sample.

The first, and by far the biggest group, consists of still developing individuals. They are active, have an intensive social network, and cope easily with health problems, often perceived as minor ones. They have liked their job, but do not mind ending it in order to get time to try out other interests. For them, retirement is a growth experience. One seventy-one-year-old man, for instance, describes it in his own words:

> That I could let go of thinking of the work situation all the time meant that I could develop myself, have hobbies. Twice a week I am an instructor of a work-out group, and there we are on such fabulous terms. ... Because we developed through work and leisure, we gained a large number of new friends (apart from childhood friends) with whom we have contact. ... We are a gang, and we love to meet in the streets and take the last bus home! ... For us, the network grew, and I am happy about that, because you cannot rely on – we have these three daughters in town, you know – rely that they should support us at all times – they have their own family! ... Well, no, a family is what you have, but friends you should worship, take good care of! And so, so I have been lucky: my old dear is absolutely wonderful [laughs]. ... My health is good, I have nearly never been ill! In 1949, I had an accident on my bike and damaged my neck, that plagues me a bit, but I keep doing my exercises, so I have it under control. So, as

most people my age, I take some medicine against blood pressure and I have too 'thick' blood. But that's the only thing I have, if you want to call that illness, but it surely is not....I just came down when you arrived. I was in the attic, with some garden chairs, and I have to say, the last stairs were a bit tough on my breathing. But that you have to learn to live with, you just have to accept that you're not twenty-five anymore....But what we have most of, that is just time. So you just hurry slowly! Actually, all my life's been good. Maybe I was privileged....But I've become a bit crazy in my old age, now, because I have started to travel to the South, and that we have planned for next year, that we are looking forward to. Go down there and get some sun and warmth....No big plans, you can't have anymore. We have kind of a limitation on the time left to us, and we never know when that will be over. So, one takes one day at a time and is happy about each morning when one awakes with legs down and head up.

The second group consists exclusively of highly educated men in responsible positions. They have refused to retire completely, and have negotiated some way or other to continue work, which was possible in their high positions. For them, work is a way of life, and they dedicate most of their time to it. Some of them have a few hobbies apart from work, and a family life. But it is clear that work is absolutely central for them. They are highly satisfied with their life and have no complaints about old age at all. Nevertheless, we describe them as a 'contentedly stagnated' group, because they cling to the rather specialized, professional way of life they have always had, and do not develop further in other directions. They show many similarities to adolescents in the state of 'identity foreclosure' (Marcia, 1980). They can retain a perfectly satisfactory existence, if they are allowed to continue within a work setting. Let a seventy-five-year-old man, who is a typical member of this group, describe his situation:

Well, I finished that research project one and a half years before I reached 70. And then I worked with this project here, so that I could continue until I was 70. But I was far from ready, so I have been working here all the time, all the time up to now...I will still have an office...I love to be here, because I also do something that has nothing to do with the Institute, but with my subject discipline. An investigation on water resources. That I do totally on a voluntary basis....My wife has been a teacher. Now we are retired, both of us. Of course we can use our time totally as we want to. She likes to do outdoor sports, just now to go skiing. So, as a rule, I drive her to the skiing area, so that she can go on a cross-country tour, and I come here to my office.

In the third group we find people who have retired very recently, many of them unwillingly. Thus, they have not yet adjusted to this new phase of their life, and many are rather bitter about this abrupt shift, as they perceive it. Many had interesting jobs, which they liked, and they do not know how to make the adjustments to retirement. 'Free time' gives them time to think about the ageing process and to notice every little health problem that might occur to them. Perhaps they could be in another 'moratorium', exploring possibilities for identity formation even at this phase of their lifespan (Kroger, 2000). They keep draining their resources, and might, for the moment, be called 'unhappily stagnated'. However, time alone will tell if they can eventually mobilize sufficient resources to move on from this present crossroads between challenge and risk, find a 'turning-point' and continue to develop and grow, or if they will fall further into stagnation, bitterness and decay. This is what one of them, a sixty-seven-year-old man, retired for six months, has to say:

> But when you retire from your job, then you feel now you've joined the group of retired people, whom you always regarded as people who are a bit senile and who need help to get up from a chair and that kind of thing. ...And of course, that you are no longer part [of an organization], and that is an important thing. I have been in such a position for my entire career – I had a leading position. That perhaps made the transition more difficult than if I had been a joiner, then I could have continued doing a little bit of the same thing somehow. But in my occupation, that is somehow...I don't even have a dog to command now!...Each time something goes wrong, you check a little bit more, whether you feel something in your chest or whether your stomach troubles you a little more than usual. If you are at retirement age, you worry a bit more that it could be more serious than if you had a sore stomach when you were 25. You become quite occupied by these things. Moreover, I don't sleep as soundly!

The last group consists of a very small number with particular characteristics. They seem to have drained most of their resources some time ago, and retirement is simply another challenge that is too great for them. They often have serious health problems and lack social support in the form of a spouse or friends. They do not have many social interests or leisure pursuits, and in many cases they did not even like their previous job. They are possibly in a state of developmental decay – or 'identity diffusion', as Marcia (1980) would call it. This is what one member of this group, a sixty-two-year-old man, retired for two years, has to say:

> You see, my back gets worse, though I have stopped working. I thought it would be better, but it's worse. It is not long ago that my father died. My mother died first, but she was nearly blind for her last three years. So I've looked after myself since 1987. My father died last year, but he died at home. I lived with him, helped him the last years....It is so much harder if you are a bachelor. Well, if you are not married, then you don't have anyone...so you don't understand before you lose them, how good it is if your parents are there....I am a bachelor, I am not married. [long silence] Then, when I had to go to work, I had to go to bed early and get up early. Now I can stay up longer and sleep a little bit longer, I can visit relatives. I have one sister nearby with three boys, so I can have contact. And I have a brother in Canada: him I call. I had a hobby before, with horses. But I left that. Now, I don't have a hobby at all.

At this stage, we want to re-emphasize that most individuals do not perceive retirement as a negative life event. On the contrary, many view it as a positive challenge that gives them further opportunities for personal growth. The different activities and hobbies retired people take up and pursue with vigour and high competence reveal the range of skills, that many societies may lose by denying those who would like to remain in employment or in some other productive position after retirement age, to continue in some mutually beneficial way.

Conclusions

In this chapter on late adulthood, we have noted a number of significant changes and challenges. We began by looking at the bodily changes that gradually, but progressively over the years, create an awareness of lessening physical abilities and powers, and at the physical changes associated with personal appearance and attractiveness. These changes present challenges to the individual, and how they are dealt with has implications for the resource 'pool'. Entry into older adulthood can again be one of life's 'turning-points' that lead to either stagnation or to further development. We then looked at the evidence about the menopause as a significant maturational shift for women, concluding that if personal and social resources are high, this is a biological change involving only a small range of physical symptoms – if any – for the individual. The risks are that the menopause can occur at the same time as other life challenges, or that particular cultures create a social construction of the process that either 'medicalizes' it as an illness by indicating that it should be 'treated', or 'cosmeticizes' it and attempts to delay it as part of today's youth cult. By contrast, in more traditional societies the menopause seems to herald a growing acceptance of respect, seniority and the opportunity to face new challenges after the years of child-rearing.

Further, we were led into an exploration of the various aspects of becoming a grandparent. Again, important cultural differences were observed, both in the roles available to grandparents and in the different styles of grandparenting. These approaches have implications for the developing resources of the growing child and the parents, as well as for the grandparents themselves. Conflict points and ways of resolving them were discussed, and we were able to illustrate once more the idea of 'linked lives' in the individual life course.

Finally, we looked closely at how people in late adulthood react to reaching what is regarded as the social 'marker' of entry into old age, namely retirement. What we found was that the vast majority appreciates this shift as opening up the possibility of engaging in new challenges and development. A few refuse to disconnect from working life, and are perfectly happy as long as they are allowed to go on working in some way, but may turn bitter and feel useless if this possibility is taken away from them. Finally, a small minority that has been drained of resources somehow and sometime earlier in their life, regard retirement as yet another unwelcome event. They possess few resources to face up to this or other potential challenges in the future.

10 Old age: the ultimate challenge?

Introduction

It is rather pathetic, hearing all these middle-aged and older people claim at their birthday party: 'But I don't feel forty (or sixty, or eighty). I feel much younger!' 'Nonsense!' retorts O'Keefe: 'How do you know what it feels like to be that age? You have never been forty (or sixty, or eighty)! You think you know. That's ageism. You are just full of prejudices!' Research seems to prove O'Keefe right, as we will show in this chapter. Age is clearly not in the eye of the beholder: when asked at what age they would regard a person as 'being old', a sample of pupils in secondary schools in mid-Norway gave responses that ranged from thirty to ninety years (Kloep, 2000). There are no clear maturational markers, as in puberty, so that the normative shift to retirement is often used as a milestone to the last and, for some, the longest life phase. Nowadays, the de-standardization of the life course has altered this marker too. Retirement today can occur at any time between young adulthood and late old age. Thus, entry into this life phase is difficult to define.

In addition to the stigma associated with growing old in Western societies, it may be that accepting clear-cut signs of the ageing process is the hardest challenge for the individual to face during this life phase. The challenges of adjusting to declining physical abilities has both health and social implications. Furthermore, with progressing age there may be changes in the individual's social network. These may be due, in many cases, to the death of friends and family members. Bereavement, seen as a non-normative event in all earlier phases of the lifespan, becomes more and more normative with increasing age.

Old age is not without its psycho-social implications, as we will see in this chapter in examining the following developmental tasks:

- accepting the processes of ageing, and dealing with the social constructions of old age.
- learning to cope with bereavement and changes in one's social network.
- adjusting to diminishing physical abilities, and to a lower health status.

Finally, we discuss some strategies for successful ageing and for coping with the challenges of old age.

Accepting the ageing process and dealing with the social constructions of old age

The pressures in society to stay young, the lack of one's own experience of growing old, and the many myths associated with old age make people who are ageing but still feeling good believe that they must be the one exception to the rule. As Gibson (1992) says:

> When they get to a certain age, quite a number of people realize that the whole business of age-status is rather an illusion. All their lives they had expected to be 'old' when they reached a certain date on the calendar, but when they reached it they did not feel different. They realized that they were still 'young' in their inner being and perception of themselves. The viewer sees the externals, and because of his long conditioning by society's stereotypes of age, he cannot realize that many of these people feel just like he does in their inner selves [p.59].

Furthermore, some people need to deny their own ageing, since the stigma associated with old age in the West has a negative impact on their self-esteem (and thus on their life resources). Yet, one of the great freedoms of old age is that it releases individuals from the obligations of continuing to fulfill certain social roles and expectations (e.g. one no longer *needs to be* beautiful and sexy, or compete in every life domain).

Hogg and Abrams' (1988) theory of social identity, designed to explain the behaviour of low-status groups in society (e.g. the working class or ethnic minorities), can be usefully adapted to explain the coping strategies used by some older people. They employ these strategies in order to meet threats to their self-esteem and social identity, which stem from being defined as a member of a low-status group:

- One can question the mechanisms that define one's group as being of low status, gain political power and then attempt to change these attitudes and prejudices: this is called the strategy of 'social competition' (and we will return to this strategy later in the chapter).
- One can deny belonging to the group of 'the elderly' by clinging to membership of 'the younger generation' (i.e. 'social mobility'). This can be achieved (for a while) by measures ranging from simple denial ('I don't feel old') to spending large sums of money on cosmetic devices, such as make-up, hair colouring, wigs and anti-wrinkle creams, or even plastic surgery.

- One can cope by admitting to an age difference, but at the same time attaching special values to one's own age-group. This happens when older people demand, or are accorded, the status of 'being wise and knowing more' or 'meriting respect because of old age'.
- Finally, one can boost one's self-esteem by 'using' an even lower-status group, and emphasizing some social distance from them (i.e. 'social change'). This strategy is sometimes used by disillusioned elderly people, who turn their sarcasm towards 'the youth of today', announcing whenever possible that 'everything was better when I was young', and that 'we knew how to respect our elders'.

In the long run, these last three strategies are of doubtful efficacy in meeting the challenges of ageing and – contrary to what might be expected – are not very widespread among old people themselves. Usually, old people hold far more positive attitudes towards ageing than young ones do. In other words, they do not define themselves, or their age-peers, as belonging to a low-status out-group (e.g. Adams-Price, Henley and Hale, 1998). Uotinen (1998), for example, comparing different age-groups in a US and a Finnish sample, asking how old they would like to be, found that the ideal age of the groups over forty years differed only by between one and three years from their actual chronological age. The US sample reported a lower ideal age than the Finnish one (who also expressed more positive attitudes towards their current age). Similar results were obtained with a Norwegian sample ranging from sixteen to eighty-eight, in which ideal and chronological ages were highly correlated (r=.60, Kloep, 2000). These findings destroy the myth that everybody wants to be twenty for the rest of their lives! On the contrary, it is often younger people who wish to be older, are less positive about themselves, and worry about personal inadequacies (Dittman-Kohli, 1990; Montepare, 1991).

The denial of ageing is not as widespread or as necessary as cosmetic adverts would have us believe, nor is it very effective. It seems as if those who admit to themselves that they feel exactly as old as they actually are have greater life satisfaction, fewer negative expectations and less fear of ageing than those who report a greater discrepancy between actual and subjective age (Montepare and Lachman, 1989).

The fear of old age

So, where does the glorification of eternal youth and the fear of old age come from? Early in life, a socialization process is started that extends from the macro-system to the various micro-systems of a society and teaches the values, norms, expectations and dominating prejudices of the society to developing individuals. These values are internalized over time. Different cultures teach particular age-related expectations and, more often than not, individuals feel somewhat pressured to conform to these, in order not to lose social identity, social support and other potential resources. Thus, these values are powerful in influencing the individual's behaviour in different life phases.

In particular, industrial societies, in which values are closely related to being productive, continue to paint a pessimistic picture of old age:

> The persistence of the lifespan organization of the industrial society where children and adolescents are prepared for the labour market, where

ageing people are roughly excluded by retirement, has consequences on the experiences affecting later life. It is mainly responsible for the loss of role and social identity for retired people, and for the absence of meaning for later life [Henrard, 1996: p.677].

Old people's power and status are reduced, in the same way as children's and adolescents', because they are not productive. This is done, under the guise of patriarchal caring, in favour of the really productive (i.e. young and middle-aged adults: Hockey and James, 1995). This is clearly expressed in the metaphor of 'second childhood' when describing old age: 'There is a specific cultural repertoire of figurative language associated with ageing in Western contexts, which can be used to empower and emphasize independent adulthood at the expense of childhood and old age' (p.7).

This view has its consequences in social policies, in research practices and, most of all, in the general view of old age as decline, weakness, obsolescence, dependency and deterioration:

> Ageism generates and reinforces a fear and denigration of the ageing process, and stereotype presumptions regarding competence and the need for protection. In particular, ageism legitimates the use of chronological age to mark out classes of people who are systematically denied resources and opportunities that others enjoy, and who suffer the consequence of such denigration, ranging from well-meaning patronage to unambiguous vilification [Bytheway, 1995: p.14].

Old people are also the only minority group that can be ridiculed publicly without eliciting strong protests from civil-rights groups. Even in a country that boasts of civic equalities, such as Norway, the newspaper cartoon shown in figure 10.1 created no critical reaction whatsoever. In fact, the situation of powerlessness in which many old people find themselves is even worse than that of children. The neglect of children can lead to them growing up into dangerous, socially destructive adolescents and adults, which is why this has to be prevented. No such argument exists against the neglect of the elderly (Hareven, 1995). Furthermore, childhood has the positive feature of being a period in which powerlessness will one day give way to empowerment, while the same cannot be said of old age. Consequently, what the elderly fear most in ageing is an increase in dependency, a loss of autonomy, and becoming a burden, particularly to their own children, as Dittman-Kohli (1990), for example, could show in her German sample.

Ageism is widespread, and has for a long time also haunted research. Usual themes in research include the identification of risk factors and characteristics explaining diseases in old age (Seeman, 1994). But research samples have often been biased, selected from institutionalized old people, or people with conditions like Parkinson's or Alzheimer's diseases. However, results have sometimes been generalized to the whole population of elderly people. By contrast, Mayer *et al.* (1996) have shown that the number of old people in Berlin who live permanently in institutions is lower than 10 per cent (9 per cent, for instance, of over seventies), making them an unrepresentative sample. Biased research of this kind can be compared to the work of a researcher who draws far-reaching conclusions about the life of all adolescents by observing a sample of institutionalized teenagers suffering from anorexia.

Figure 10.1 **An example of ageism: newspaper cartoon from Norway**

'Didn't there use to be a steering wheel here?'
(from *Byavisa Trondheim*, 29 April 1998, p.2; with kind permission of Kjetil Strand)

Normative and quasi-normative challenges

The use of chronological age to judge people's abilities and performance has led to the existence of several normative and quasi-normative demands in society. For instance, it is extremely difficult for unemployed people over the age of fifty to find a new job. For nearly all professions there is an age of compulsory retirement, in spite of all the evidence showing that there is little relationship between age and job performance (Salthouse and Maurer, 1997). Among the few exceptions to this, however, is the post of President of the US, and those of most parliamentarians in the Western world! Moreover, in some countries, there are increasing demands that the driving licence be automatically withdrawn from drivers at a certain age, thus assuming, without exception, that performance is inevitably linked to chronological age. These social constructions of ageing, having their origins solely in social prejudices, create normative challenges for older citizens. Unlike prejudices against most other groups, ageism is one which all of us will have to suffer ourselves some day. We will all eventually become a member of that 'out-group'. The more negative our expectations are about old age, the more difficult it will be to face this challenge when it appears:

> The public policies of compassionate ageism and the scientific parameters of gerontology, no less than outright age discrimination in industry and professions and the social exclusion of older people from the mainstream of the community, have reinforced the terror of age: the weak, catastrophic, victim face of age [Friedan, 1993: p.75].

Widespread ageism is itself one of the hardest challenges to overcome during the ageing process. Prejudices and myths around decay and meaninglessness can become self-fulfilling prophecies. Levy (1996) shows experimentally that exposing older people to subliminal words expressing negative descriptions of older persons can effectively cause deterioration in their achievement on cognitive tests. No such deterioration happens to older people getting positive subliminal words, or for a group of younger people. These results show how cognitive achievements can be impaired by negative self-images derived from general stereotypes of ageing.

Earlier, we mentioned that one possibility in coping with the challenges of ageism is the adaptation of a 'social competition' strategy, as used by other low-status groups (see Hogg and Abrams, 1988). This involves questioning the mechanisms that define one's group as being of lower status, gaining a noticeable degree of political power, and attempting to alter the attitudes and mechanisms that operate. Of course, for individuals to defy the predominant attitudes in a society, a range of resources is needed. We saw in previous chapters that 'swimming against the tide' requires courage, and thus a general feeling of security, of having support or sufficient resources, is vital. So it is unlikely that people who are in a state of 'unhappy stagnation' will be able to fight against these prevailing attitudes. They are more likely to deny the ageing process (as did the 'identity assimilators' within the Whitbourne, Sneed and Skultety, 2001, model discussed in chapter 3). Nor will those who build most of their resources on the security created by belonging to and conforming with a particular group be able to resist. They have been effectively and conventionally socialized into their society, and will conform to the stereotype of the elderly (like Whitbourne, Sneed and Skultety's 'identity accommodators'). In other words, just as a relatively mindless and continuing conformity to the standards of youth culture can prohibit further development towards the end of adolescence, so, later in life, it can lead to conformity to the 'victim-decline' model of old age (Friedan, 1993).

Recent societal changes may alter this gloomy picture. This is particularly true in prosperous Western societies, in which demographic shifts may work in favour of old people. Never before have they been so numerous by comparison to the young, and never before have they been so healthy, economically comfortable, independent, free to choose their life options and potentially politically powerful. This picture is, of course, complicated by differences in social class and nationality. Few worn-out former mine workers in Wales, or ageing widows living with their unemployed grown-up children in a two-room apartment in Dresden, would recognize themselves in this new scenario.

Again, it is the amount and kind of potential resources that predestine people to meet challenges successfully, and these resources are not equally distributed among individuals. But, given these resources, and given the demographic shifts in many Western countries, which in several ways now empower older people personally and politically, it is no longer necessary for them to subscribe to a decline model of old age. Rather, they can substitute that paradigm with a model of development and growth. In fact, the greater the number of elderly peoples following a new trajectory, the less non-normative this style of living becomes, and therefore the more socially accepted.

Changes in social networks

Another alteration that can be expected with increasing age is that old friends and relatives die, and new friends may be difficult to find. Thus, in this section we concentrate on the following questions: how does the individual's social network actually change with increasing age? Is loneliness a normative event? How do old people cope with loneliness and with bereavement?

One surprising answer that research findings give us is that our expectations regarding old age are far too negative. Very old people (i.e. eighty-five to one-hundred-and-four) in the Berlin Ageing Study did report that they had fewer members in their social networks than younger ones (i.e. seventy to eighty-four), but, the number of very close friends or partners did not differ between the two age-groups (Lang and Carstensen, 1994). Thus, the social world of very old people is still characterized by a high density of contacts with emotionally meaningful friends. Only the number of their more distant social contacts decreases. In old age, meaningful social support continues to be an important resource for the individual. Field (1999), in her US sample of seventy-four to ninety-three-year-olds, could not find any changes in their perceived ability to make new friends, to keep old ones, or in the amount of contact with friends over a period of 14 years. Contact with closest friends remains stable over time, while the usefulness of, and the contact with, casual friends seems to decline with age.

Social support has a significant effect on well-being, as in younger years (see e.g. Hendry and Reid, 2000). The presence of close family members, though not necessarily one's children, seems to be a particularly strong resource in meeting daily challenges in old age. Parental status seems to be unrelated to well-being (e.g. McMullin and Marshall, 1996), but siblings play a special and specific role, as the following studies from Sweden, the US and Canada demonstrate. The support of siblings contributes to life satisfaction more than either friends' or children's support. Additionally, one's feelings about one's siblings enhances life satisfaction more strongly than how often one meets them (McMamish-Svensson *et al.*, 1999). The quality, rather than the quantity, of support seems to be the characteristic that enhances the older person's resource 'pool'. In particular, older people without a spouse or children appear to gain from the emotional support and care they receive from their siblings. Simply perceiving that sibling support would be available if needed promotes well-being, and presumably ensures greater resources in the 'pool' (Connidis, 1994; Vaillant, 1994). Hendry (1985) also theorized that in old age many people return to organized social and leisure activities mainly as venues for making new friends, extending social networks, meeting new partners and developing new interests in the wake of possible partner and friendship losses.

Bereavement

In spite of the fact that older people are not as lonely as often believed, with increasing age they do have to face up to the possible loss of friends and relatives, a difficult challenge to overcome. Unexpected bereavement is similar to other non-normative events that occur at various times through the lifespan, and for which the individual has not had time to prepare. An unexpected death appears to be particularly difficult to cope with (Ingebretsen and Solem, 1998), while having been able to say farewell seems to lead to a better process of coping with bereavement (Niebor, 1997). If, for instance, the death of a spouse is 'expected', and if there is time to discuss economics and other matters, the negative affects in widowhood can be somewhat ameliorated (O'Bryant, 1991; Niebor, 1997), though long-term adjustment is unaffected by the circumstances of death (Stroebe and Stroebe, 1993). Thus, bereavement is a multi-dimensional process, affecting the person psychologically, physically, socially, economically and spiritually.

Perhaps because death becomes a more normative event with increasing age, older widowers and widows seem to adjust better and to suffer less depression than younger ones (Zisook *et al.*, 1993). They have more peer role models to observe and copy, with whom to discuss matters, and from whom to receive support. However, death always leads to changes in family roles and expectations, and the particular situation depends upon whether it is a child, a sibling or a partner who dies. Because men generally tend to marry somewhat younger women, and statistically have a shorter life expectancy, it is mainly older women who have to experience the loss of their marriage partner.

However, even an event as sad as the loss of a loved one does not have to be unbearable in the long run. A longitudinal study in the US showed that for most people neither bereavement nor the subsequent burden of widowhood has an appreciable long-term effect on psycho-social functioning (McCrae and Costa, 1993). In most studies, depression and psychological problems increase immediately after the death, but decrease over time (usually a period of between one and two years) to a normal level (Gallagher-Thompson *et al.*, 1993; Thompson *et al.*, 1998). This is not true, however, for grief and feelings of loss: here, slow recovery rates of up to one or two decades have been reported (Wortman, Silver and Kessler, 1993). The experience of grief is described as being similar to a rollercoaster ride, with many ups and downs and a slow and gradual improvement over time (Lund *et al.*, 1993).

As Salahu-Din (1996) found in a study of black and white widows in the US, for some people widowhood can actually lead to positive growth experiences, even if the partner's death is initially devastating. Lieberman (1992) reports that 20 per cent of the women studied in his sample reconstitute a totally new social network after the death of their husband, and many show excellent adaptation and experience personal growth. Widows appear to undergo a process of compensation for the loss of a spouse by seeking out other widows and establishing fairly intensive ties with them (Ferraro and Farmer, 1995). For men who are little involved in social activities, and who describe their deceased spouse as having been their only confederate, coping with widowhood seems to be extremely difficult, even putting their own lives at risk (Gallagher-Thompson *et al.*, 1993). Because of women's ability to benefit from relationships with friends and relatives, House, Landis and Umberson (1988) propose that it is more beneficial to men's health to be married, and more detrimental to their health to be widowed, than it is for women.

Perhaps because of this, and in contrast to their attitudes to marriage in early adulthood, widowers in old age may often seek new brides after a relatively short period of mourning, whereas widows generally seem less interested in new live-in partners. In Sweden, for instance, more and more elderly widows choose to have 'living-together-apart-relationships' with new partners, insisting in keeping their own flat for themselves – and refusing to act as the cleaning lady for his (Borell and Karlsson, 2000). Pickard (1994) reports that elderly widows in Wales are very reluctant to remarry, not wanting to give up the freedom they have finally gained through widowhood, and not daring to risk their good relations with other family members by introducing a new man into the house-hold. In comparing the well-being of Dutch widows and widowers, Stevens (1995) found that widowed women report higher well-being than widowed men, even when gender-related variables like income, education and health (of which men had more) and the number of social networks (of which women had more) are held constant. In addition, Lubben's (1988) study suggests that older widows not only feel better than widowers, they also feel better than married women of the same age: they report considerably fewer health troubles (such as pains, sleeping problems, nervousness and anxiety), and have a more extensive social network. Nearly half the married women did not have even one close friend!

On the other hand, women who defined their whole life in terms of being a wife and mother may have greater difficulties in finding a new role in widowhood than those who had a variety of social roles throughout life. Their situation is similar to that of the men we discussed earlier, who had devoted their life to their work and cannot find anything meaningful to do after retirement. This may explain why women over sixty-five who have been single all their lives are healthier and more satisfied than divorcees or widows (Newton and Keith, 1997).

It is at such 'turning-points' in life where the disadvantages of 'con-tented stagnation', of 'having put all one's eggs in one basket' becomes evident. Whether the loss of a significant other in old age leads to either growth or to a further draining of resources is, of course, dependent on how other resources are affected. It will be strongly influenced by economics, social class, social stigma, culture, inheritance rights and social attitudes. The experience of widowhood has been different at different periods of history, particularly for women (Blom, 1991), and it is surely different in different cultures today. The picture becomes even more complicated if cross-cultural mobility is taken into account: in Turkey, for example, widows depend largely on support from their sons. Many young males, however, emigrate to other European countries for jobs. There, they and their wives often adopt different cultural values and the feeling of obligation to ageing parents decreases, a fact that particularly affects poorly educated rural widows (Lopata, 1996).

In general, the developmental challenge model predicts that bereave-ment and widowhood, as other major events in life, presents the individual with a series of challenges, and that it is the number and severity of these challenges in interaction with the individual's resource 'pool' that in the end leads to further development, stagnation or decay. Besides loneliness, widows and widowers report that lack of skills to cope with daily problems (household activities for men; house repairs, financial and legal issues for women) is one of the greatest difficulties that they have to face after the death of their spouse (Lund *et al.*, 1993). The third problem they complain about is the dilemma of reconciling living their new lives as they want to, and the expectations of others. They mention, for example, problems of deciding what to do with the deceased partner's pet that they have never liked, or remarrying in the face of opposition from grown-up children (Lund *et al.*, 1993).

Because of the interaction of various benign or harmful factors accompanying widowhood, and the different resources individuals can activate, it is not surprising that Lund *et al.* (1993) find considerable diversity in the adjustment process, both among and within bereaved spouses. They find that people simultaneously experience a wide range of contradictory feelings and behaviours: being angry, guilty and lonely, and at the same time deriving personal strength and pride through coping. After 12 years of studying bereavement, they conclude that being competent in social, interpersonal, instrumental and resource-identification skills leads to more favourable adjustment and to the learning of new skills, which in turn enhances self-esteem and well-being:

> We do not believe that simply the passage of time by itself brings about successful adjustments. Time is important because the many difficulties require time to emerge, be identified, develop strategies, and achieve some degree of successful adjustment or resolution. A passive strategy of waiting for time to heal a wound will not lead to satisfactory bereavement adjustments [Lund *et al.*, 1993: p.252].

In other words, if bereavement leads to active coping, the learning of new skills and a strengthening of personal resources, it can lead to growth and development, in spite of the grief that may remain.

Health

'When you are over 70 and you wake up in the morning without pain, you are dead!' says a recent newspaper headline. Can the deterioration of health in old age possibly be regarded as an opportunity for development? In line with the prejudices of ageism, old age is often regarded as being synonymous with poor health. However, illness and death are not caused by age in itself, but are influenced by other factors such as biological disposition, environment and lifestyle (see, for example, research reviews by Coplan and Strawbridge, 1994; Rowe and Kahn, 1997). During the last decades, cultural and social forces, together with medical advances, at least in industrialized countries, have been able to offset many of the weaknesses inherent in the biological lifespan architecture of many old people (Smith and Baltes, 1999). It is not a normative maturational shift necessarily to suffer deteriorating health with growing age. There are simply more people with impaired health the further we progress along the life course. This is because the risk of exposure to illness and injury accumulates over the years, so that in any subsequent age-group, a greater number are not completely healthy. But old age is not a disease in itself. Thus, the number of people with one or more serious or chronic illnesses simply increases through the lifespan by statistical accumulation. In the Berlin ageing study, Baltes and his colleagues (Mayer *et al.*, 1996) point out that by age seventy or older, 33 per cent of the sample suffer from at least one serious disease, while 98 per cent experience some kind of illness. Nevertheless, almost 30 per cent judge their health 'good' or 'very good'.

From this we can conclude that by age seventy, a large number of people will have faced the tasks of coping with an illness of some kind. In fact, older people report having more daily health troubles and, more-over, perceive their problems as less malleable than younger ones (Folkman *et al.*, 1987). Younger and middle-aged individuals have to deal primarily with episodic stresses such as particular problems at work or in the family, influenza, industrial injuries and so on. Health problems in later life, on the other hand, tend to be chronic, and have to be dealt with on a daily basis (Aldwin *et al.*, 1996). Hence, the chronically ill have to face the same challenges over and over again. This might not be easy, but it can still be a task with developmental potential, as Aldwin (1991) states: 'Health problems may not be perceived as controllable, but nonetheless they might be manageable, and the process of managing the problem may give rise to feelings of efficacy' (p.179).

As Grand *et al.* (1988) found in a French study, functioning after disease can, in part, result from other compensatory (non-physical) factors such as feelings of usefulness and social activities. As with other life challenges, the presence of various resources helps individuals to deal with poor health. In the Amsterdam Longitudinal Aging Study (Penninx, *et al.*, 1997a, 1998), the presence of a partner, many close social relationships and, particularly, personal coping characteristics, such as self-competence, self-esteem and persistence in the face of adversity, were identified as being specially valuable for chronically ill older people. Here the interdependence of different resources becomes obvious: good health, for example, helps in overcoming the loss of a spouse, while the presence of a spouse helps the individual to deal with illness. Therefore, it is easy to understand why coping with multiple problems is so difficult, and often in the end completely drains resources.

Subjective perceptions of health

Clearly, health and illness have a strong impact on life satisfactions. A healthy, capable body is one of the strongest potential resources we have, whereas health impairments make us more and more vulnerable in meeting other challenges. However, it is not the objective quality of health that is most crucial, but how healthy individuals perceive and feel themselves to be, that has the greatest impact on how well they cope. Perceived health status also predicts successful ageing and longevity more strongly than health assessments by medical doctors (Mayer *et al.*, 1996 in Germany; McMamish-Svensson *et al.*, 1999 in Sweden; Mossey and Shapiro, 1982 in the US; Pijls, Feskens and Kromhout, 1993 in the Netherlands; Roos and Havens, 1991 in Canada). Self-efficacy beliefs regarding the ability to perform various activities in daily life predict higher self-reported levels of physical and social functioning (Seeman *et al.*, 1999). Further, in a representative, non-institutionalized sample of

US adults over sixty, most report that their health does not limit their activities at all, and only 15 per cent state that their health constrains them 'a great deal'. Despite the fact that 62 per cent of the total sample actually suffer from one or more chronic conditions, only 6 per cent report that they are 'not very,' or 'not at all' satisfied with their lives (Herzog, 1991).

The myth of a steady deterioration of health and fitness in old age is, to some extent, a misconception originating from an artefact of group statistics in cross-sectional research. Since, in any age-group, there will be some people who are about to die, the higher up the age scale we go, inevitably, the more such cases there will be. These will distort the arithmetical average for the group. In reality, for most people, a steady plateau of health–life satisfaction is maintained for a fair span of years before they eventually die.

In fact, a number of research studies have shown that for most elderly people there is no evidence that getting older reduces their happiness and self-perceived health, provided that they have sufficient factors in their lives that maintain their morale. Given an adequately satisfying emotional life, they will adapt to adverse conditions, such as the stiffening of the joints with arthritis, and continue to lead as full lives as before (Gibson, 1992).

Newer insights and more recent research findings defy the idea of an inevitable destiny of ill health and decay into old age. Rather, they supply evidence that deteriorating health can be a challenge that stimulates growth:

> States of deficit and limitations are powerful catalysts for cultural progress and new forms of mastery or cultural innovation. By accepting this challenge, it may be possible not only to learn more and more about the reserve capacities of old age, but also about the conditions of a 'culture of old age' whose primary commitment is the conquest of the deficits of biological aging and the creating of conditions facilitative of high levels of subjective well-being, agency, and a sense of personal control [Baltes and Graf, 1996: p.436].

Cognitive functioning

There is a similar story to tell about cognitive functioning. For years, it had been an accepted myth that cognitive abilities decline with increasing age. This assumption was based mainly on cross-sectional studies showing that older people have lower scores than younger ones on intelligence tests. However, these results again prove to be products of methodological artefacts. Researchers neglected to consider that older cohorts had fewer years of schooling than younger ones and, in addition, that the older samples often consisted of people living in institutions. Even the validity of intelligence tests themselves, originally constructed for a white middle-aged population, has been questioned when used with older people. This is similar to misconceptions about differences in IQ scores between Westerners and traditional tribespeople, or to the underestimation of children's intellectual capacities as a consequence of the uncritical use of the same measurement instrument across different populations, which we discussed in chapter 6.

Labouvie-Vief (1982) put forward the hypothesis that ageing brings qualitative changes in thinking that may mimic decrements in ability, but in fact signal a higher level of structural organization, a new set of more autonomous thinking strategies to meet the new demands this life phase. In other words, a different way of tackling cognitive challenges in old age.

Moreover, even studies of potential changes in the brain due to the ageing process have been questioned. There is a considerable variety in the structural changes in the brain, and the brain of one ageing individual varies appreciably from that of another (Scheibel, 1997). Recent findings suggest that decay as well as growth can characterize brain changes at any age, and that brain ageing is a highly specific process, rather than a global deterioration (for a review, see van der Molen and Ridderinkhof, 1998).

The faculties that seem to be mainly affected are the speed and accuracy of information processing, sometimes called 'fluid intelligence', whereas 'crystallized' intelligence, reflected in culture-based knowledge, shows a stable developmental pattern at least into the eighth decade (Baltes, 1997; Schaie, 1996). Scheibel (1997) gives an illustrative example of this:

> One has only to compare the behavior of the average 18-year-old driver behind the wheel with that of a 60- or 70-year-old to conclude that information-processing speeds decrease with age. By the same token, every parent or grandparent knows how much more expensive it will be to provide insurance coverage for the teenage driver than for himself. That lifelong accumulation of experience that we call judgement, or perhaps wisdom, may well make up for the age-related slowing of cerebral processing and recall. In fact … it may be just that extra processing time that allows the distillates of previous experience to be retrieved and integrated into the final decision [p.123].

While Smith and Baltes (1999) suggest that this decline is biologically determined, and therefore inevitable at some point in one's later life phase, some studies suggest that environmental stimulation can have beneficial effects on the brain at any age (for a review, see Diamond, 1991), and evidence has been found that the 'use-it-or-lose-it' principle might also apply to the brain (Swaab, 1991). For instance, Shimamura *et al.* (1995) could show that elderly professors from Berkeley University did not reveal the same decline on memory measures as are usually observed in standard groups of individuals of the same age. Clearly science has not yet pronounced its last word on this issue, but again, research evidence presents a much more optimistic picture of functioning in old age than has been proposed previously.

There is a broad variation in functioning for different individuals in old age, when it becomes particularly clear how resources interact, and how possessing some leads to obtaining others. This is a phenomenon that we call positive accumulation – a modern version of the biblical parable of the talents? A repeated loss of resources can lead to the opposite phenomenon, a cumulative downward spiral. In Penninx *et al.*'s (1997b) Amsterdam longitudinal study, old people were more likely to die than others if they had been suffering for some time from loneliness and low mastery feelings (i.e. poor self-efficacy). The researchers explain this as follows: 'A lack of coping resources causes individuals to judge events or situations in life as more stressful, which may directly increase mortality risk through influencing neurologic, hormonal and immunologic control systems' (p.518).

In another longitudinal study, House *et al.* (1994), demonstrate that the various elements comprising socio-economic status moderate the relationship between age and health. Individuals in upper socio-economic positions approach the ideal of relatively low levels of morbidity and functional limitations until quite late in life, whereas at lower socio-economic levels, morbidity and functional limitations rise steadily throughout middle and old age. This relationship is, however, further mediated by differential exposure to risk factors. The higher socio-economic groups exhibit better health behaviours, lower levels of stress, greater mastery and self-esteem through the lifespan. Thus they possess a whole range of potentially better psycho-social resources than others to cope with the challenges of old age. Baltes and Lang (1997) found a similar kind of relationship between different individual resources and an active, varied life in old age, and propose the following:

> This is not to say that individuals rich in resources will not experience functional loss at all, but they will begin with loss experiences at higher levels of functioning. In other words, the aging process might reflect the same slope of differences or decline in functioning, but functional deterioration will manifest itself later because still-available resources may be used to compensate and optimize with or select from in the face of real or anticipated losses [p.433].

Finally, if we examine the resources and risks of those in very advanced old age we find an interesting range of interacting factors, namely self-perceptions and social and biological elements, which determine progress, maintenance or decay. The relative effectiveness of psychological, social, material and cultural interventions, which may compensate for biological losses, decreases in old age. At the same time, age-associated losses in biological potential increase, bringing individuals to the very limits of their adaptive capacity: 'Psychologically speaking, advanced old age appears to be a situation of great challenge and a period characterized by chronic stress. Advanced old age, the fourth age, is a kind of testing-the-limits situation for psychological resilience' (Smith and Baltes, 1999: p.67).

Furthermore, Crimmins, Hayward and Saito (1996) suggest that the percentage of dysfunctional, inactive time of the remaining lifetime is 20 per cent for seventy-year-olds, whereas for ninety-year-olds it is close to 60 per cent. In the end, it seems as if the number and nature of challenges confronting very old people will eventually drain the resources of even the most resourceful individuals, though it may take many years to do so.

In this state, and at that age, one of the most dreaded shifts of the lifespan can occur: loss of independence. This may start off with the loss of one's driving licence and end with the loss of one's home, and the move to a nursing home, leaving individuals with the task of coping with shrinking autonomy and reduced mastery (Pearlin and Mullan, 1992). Nevertheless, *de facto*, institutionalization only happens to a small percentage of very old people in Western societies, and increasing amenities, such as ambulatory nursing, and 'meals-on-wheels' services allow a growing number to remain in their own home if they so wish.

Aspects of the challenges of old age

In an attempt to account for both losses and gains in old age, Baltes and Baltes (1990) offer a model that includes the ideas of 'selective optimization with compensation'. Within the framework of this model, 'success' is defined as goal achievement, and 'successful ageing' as the minimization of losses and the maximization of gains. The strategies for successful ageing are presented as follows:

- Selection. This involves directionality, goals or outcomes. In advanced old age, and faced with increasingly drained resources, individuals can evaluate their choice of goals and drop some of them in favour of other more important ones (as they see them). Thus, they can channel their energy into a few projects and in this way maximize them. Deterioration in hearing, sight or memory, for example, needs increasing compensatory efforts, which can lead to the difficulty of trying to do too many things at the same time. This may lower stress tolerance, because too many stimuli can easily become overwhelming. In an experimental study, Li *et al.* (2001) offer evidence that older people presented with a dual task (e.g. memorizing while walking on a narrow track), choose to concentrate on walking at the cost of memorizing. Lang and Carstensen (1994) demonstrate a similar selection strategy used by older people in their retention of friendships: with increasing age, many people reduce the number of friends in their 'outer' (i.e. more casual) social network in order to be able to devote their diminishing energies to socializing with their really close friends.
- Optimization. This involves the means of achieving desired outcomes. For instance, the time and energy saved by selecting only a few targets is now freed up to be concentrated on the remaining goals (e.g. having more time to dedicate to training). B.F. Skinner (1983), some years before his death, wrote an essay about his own efforts to cope with the ongoing memory problems that he suffered from the age of eighty onwards. He described how he devised practical ways of using memory aids, such as keeping notes, executing a task before he forgot it, and using thematic prompts. He even developed social strategies to hide the problem, such as having his wife pretend that she already knew the person to whom he could not introduce her because he had forgotten the person's name.
- Compensation. This denotes a response to a loss in resources used to maintain desired outcomes by counterbalancing them with other resources. Staudinger and Freund (1998) give an example of this strategy from their research in Germany. Those seventy to one-hundred-year-olds who described themselves as having a variety of different roles despite deteriorating health displayed higher subjective well-being, than those who offered a narrower self-description: losses in one area (e.g. health) can be compensated for by a variety of alternatives. Interestingly, this relationship between health and role

variation did not exist in high-income groups in Staudinger and Freund's study, perhaps because high income-groups can compensate for certain losses in physical functioning by their economic resources (e.g.using taxis). Another finding was that, in accord with Baltes and Baltes' (1980) model, investing energy in too many different areas was associated with lower subjective well-being. It seems better to concentrate energy selectively when resources are relatively depleted than to distribute it over many areas.

Baltes and Baltes (1980) explain how ageing individuals, faced with a loss of resources, and with a high number of challenges to meet (mainly in deteriorating health), use a range of strategies to rearrange a goodness of fit between these daily challenges and the resources they can mobilize. Translated into the terminology of the developmental challenge model, these strategies comprise mainly an intentional reduction in the tasks to be coped with, so that resources can be concentrated on highly valued or necessary tasks.

Brandtstädter and his colleagues (1995) focus their research on old people's use of this strategy. They argue that in old age the investment of physical and temporal resources on the right goals is critical, and that the adaptation of personal goals and ambitions to given constrained circumstances is absolutely unavoidable (Brandtstädter and Wentura, 1995). In this process, they distinguish two kinds of strategies: 'assimilative' strategies and 'accommodative' ones. Assimilative strategies are those that alter or modify the course of personal development in accordance with one's aspirations (e.g. we try harder to succeed). Accommodative strategies, on the other hand, are aimed at adjusting one's goals and standards to realistic possibilities and to the constraints of development. Over time, one mode can be transformed into the other. For example, the goal of retaining a youthful appearance can be attained for a while by using anti-wrinkle cream, dying one's hair or combing it over any balding patches (i.e. an assimilative approach). After a while, however, these efforts will be less and less successful, and one opts for an accommodative approach, such as changing one's looks into a 'fashionable' or 'interesting' look for one's age. Though Brandtstädter and his colleagues adopt a positive view of ageing, Carstensen and Freund (1994) comment that the concepts of loss and coping are still too dominant in their theory. They point out that certain goals are changed rather than blocked in old age, this being due not to stresses but rather to other factors, such as new life opportunities.

When resources decline, assimilative activities may no longer be possible – clinging to goals that have become unrealistic will lead to repeated failure, wasted time and diminished self-esteem. Lowering or changing one's goals can keep a sense of personal control intact:

> Processes such as disengagement from blocked goals or the lowering of aspirations have usually been looked upon in the psychological literature with slight contempt, and have often been associated with notions of resignation and loss of control. The theoretical stance taken here suggests on the contrary that in the transition toward old age, such processes gain importance for maintaining a positive self-view and a sense of personal continuity [Brandtstädter and Wentura, 1995: p.91f].

Adjusting goals and readjusting ambitions seem strategies that are highly effective in attaining a maintenance of self-efficacy and a boosting of life satisfaction. They might well be among the most important strategies in coping with the functional losses of old age. Qualitative and quantitative empirical evidence collected by Brandtstädter, Rothermund and Schmitz (1997) suggests that adaptations to the problems of old age depend a great deal on the interplay between active-assimilative modes of fighting losses and accommodative modes of coping. This involves an adjustment of personal goals to situational constraints, and is also one of the reasons that in empirical studies, a decline in self-esteem has not been found with increasing age:

> Successful ageing, however defined, involves processes that mutually adjust the individual's conceptions of the actual, desirable, and potential courses of personal development in such ways that problems of self-esteem, identity deficits, and depression are avoided [Brandtstädter and Greve, 1992, 1994: p.72].

Conclusions

In this chapter we have demonstrated that there will always be many older people who have sufficient resources, interests and pursuits, and who are not too concerned about deteriorating health. They will perceive themselves as lively and active. As long as they possess sufficient resources to meet challenges, development can and will continue. In this context, even the disappearance of certain resources can be seen as a challenge in itself, and a sound, perceived health status and self-esteem can be maintained, at least until, finally, most resources are drained, and the ability to cope with daily tasks is radically weakened. Towards the end of the chapter, we looked more closely at the processes and mechanisms involved in overcoming physical impairment and other possible limitations, and in meeting the challenges of advanced age. In the next chapter, we look at the characteristics of successful living through the entire lifespan and at the key themes in lifespan development.

11 Emerging themes of lifespan development

Introduction

As we have seen throughout this book, development can be understood as a series of dynamic interactions between the individual and the multiple levels of social systems, institutions and contexts. A lifespan perspective, then, is linked to a concern with issues about the relationships between cultural evolution and individual development. It has also to do with the role individuals themselves play in their own development, and with life-course continuity and discontinuity in relation to resources, challenges and risks. As Lerner (1998) argues:

> The changing match, congruence, or goodness-of-fit between the developmental characteristics of the person and of his or her context provides a basis for consonance or dissonance in the ecological milieu of the individual. The dynamic nature of this interaction constitutes a source of variation in positive or negative outcomes of developmental change [p.14].

This accumulation of the specific roles and events an individual experiences across the lifespan – involving maturational, normative, quasi-normative and non-normative events – alter the person's developmental trajectories in ways that would not have occurred had another set of roles and experiences been undergone. Further, apart from the different social systems (i.e. micro-, meso-, exo- and macro-systems), time and historical change also create diversity within the ecological systems affecting the individual's development.

Hence, in this chapter we consider some of the themes and ideas we have addressed throughout the book. We begin our review by studying some of the qualities and characteristics that seem to enable the life course to be a process of continuous challenge. We then extend our focus and re-examine the developmental challenge model as a vehicle for understanding the challenges, resources and risks involved in lifespan development and offer two varying case studies to demonstrate its use in interpreting 'real life' situations in terms of development, stagnation or decay. The chapter concludes with a summary of the model's values and usefulness. Hence, the chapter examines:

- the process of continuous challenge
- the developmental challenge model
- key features of the developmental challenge model.

The life course as a process of continuous challenge

Brandtstädter and Greve (1992, 1994) claim that assimilative activities take place mostly during middle adulthood, while accommodative processes take place toward late adulthood and old age. This leaves the impression of an age-related readiness for certain coping strategies that we have seen throughout the book need not necessarily be true. We would claim rather that assimilative strategies are used as long as there are enough resources available to ensure a reasonable probability of success. Accommodative strategies only take over whenever it becomes clear that individual resources will not be adequate, or sufficient, to obtain the desired goals (see box below for examples).

Examples of accommodative strategies at different points in the lifespan

Compare two individuals. Nicky is a slightly knock-kneed teenager. He might do better to forget his ambitions about a professional football career and concentrate on his outstanding talents for percussion instead. (He can still play for his school team, and in an amateur soccer league after he leaves school). In the same way, Robbie will finally have to give up trying to impress the bikini-clad girls at the swimming pool with acrobatic dives when he's well into his sixties. Now it is time for him to use his energies to charm the ladies at the bridge club, to retain his golf handicap, or even start a new career as golf-club secretary or captain.

This can happen at any stage of the lifespan, and is dependent upon what the goals are, what normative and non-normative constraints prevent the individual from meeting them, and what resources are available to support intended goal attainment. Greve (2000), for example, defines 'high flexibility' as the ability to perceive the gain inherent in losses, and thereby the possibility to reframe and 'produce' reality. He finds that those exhibiting high flexibility are more careful in their movements in older age. This is a realistic adaptation to reduced functioning, so that intentional adaptation does not lower self-esteem. However, a high-flexibility coping strategy is not restricted to the elderly: Greve also gives examples of how this kind of strategy enables young offenders serving a prison sentence to be resilient and maintain their self-esteem. Actually, this principle is observable from very early in the lifespan. Vereijken and Thelen (1997) demonstrate its use in infants learning to walk. They observe no less than 22 different variations of belly crawling, while the variability of performance in early walkers is much lower. They interpret their findings as follows:

> Belly crawlers are free to discover multiple solutions for moving and there is no reason for infants to settle on a stable solution. In contrast, hands-and-knees crawling has more stringent constraints on balance control and there is risk from falling. The confluence of both factors may lead a stable, less variable diagonal gait pattern. In sideways cruising, balance constraints are even more serious than in hands-and-knees crawling. There is risk of losing control over reactive forces and falling from an upright position. Thus, beginning cruisers may clamp down on degrees of freedom, showing little variability in performance [Vereijken and Thelen, 1997: p.144].

It seems quite obvious that children younger than one year old can already apply the accommodative strategy of selective optimization.

Furthermore, pursuing goals whose attainment one is uncertain about can lead to an accumulating negative cycle in the individual's appraisal assessments of projects yet to be attempted, with related behavioural and emotional outcomes. Consequently, the pursuit of realistic goals is a strategy that adds to resources, while trying to attain uncertain outcomes causes a continuing draining of resources. Uncertainty leads to unsatisfactory outcomes and lowered well-being, which again increases subsequent uncertainty, as Salmela-Aro and Nurmi (1996) show in their study of female Finnish students. In turn, the evaluation of projects in terms of high-outcome expectations and low stress is associated with good health, psychological well-being, life satisfaction, lack of hypochondria, low anxiety and low levels of depression.

In other words, readjusting goals to match one's resources is an effective strategy not only in the transition to old age, but whenever there are insufficient resources available to reach a goal or attain a desired outcome. In describing the developmental concerns through the challenging adolescent years, Coleman (1974; Coleman and Hendry, 1999) identifies the fact that adolescents often consciously select and tackle only one issue at a time from the range of tasks that may be concerning them. In this way they appear to have a reasonably successful transitional process towards adulthood. Dealing with more than one focal issue at a time would exceed their resources, so that they – in a similar way to elderly people – select the most important targets on which to concentrate their resources. Hence, the selection of goals seems actually not to be very different for different phases of the life course.

Redefining goals in order to obtain a better goodness of fit between one's resources and one's aspirations is an effective strategy throughout life. Admittedly, in old age there might be a larger number of individuals who come to the limits of their available resources than in any other life phase, but that does not turn accommodative activities into *the* strategy for old age. It is relevant and valid across the lifespan.

The same is true for the strategies of optimization and compensation: during the lifespan, whenever there is a loss or lack of resources they can be compensated for by utilizing new resources (such as the supporting arm of someone in learning to walk or when walking has become impaired, or when the ground is slippery), applying new strategies (such as leaving home earlier to reach the bus stop in time, if one can't walk quickly) or by mobilizing other resources (such as paying for a taxi). Such strategies can be used to enhance success in the goals we finally choose. Ongoing assessment of goals, resources and expected outcomes is an important meta-skill in this context (see box below for examples). Many different resource areas are needed if it should be necessary to compensate one for the other:

> Sensori-motor, cognitive, personality, and social resources have imminent importance for successful ageing because they facilitate the interplay between three adaptive processes: selection, compensation, and optimization: the more resources a person has, the easier it is to anticipate, confront, and adapt to ageing losses [Baltes and Lang, 1997: p.433].

But this is not only applicable to ageing losses. We would add that it applies to all kinds of losses and changes across the lifespan, as Baltes and Graf (1996) also admit: 'To prevent a possible misunderstanding, we emphasize that selective optimization with compensation is not specific to old age; we assume that it is a process that operates in all phases of life' (p.453).

With that comment, we have returned to the major point we made at the beginning of this chapter: there is nothing to be said about successful ageing that would not at the same time be a description and prescription of successful living at any age.

Lifespan examples of goal assessment

During the whole lifespan it is advantageous to employ goal assessment and re-assessment as well as cost–benefit analysis: How much is one willing to sacrifice for a major life goal? Is it worthwhile to drain other resources, at least for a time, to attain this one goal and thereby to miss out on other chances, on other skills or social support? Does it pay off in the long run to sacrifice one's family for a career – or a career for a family? Should one sacrifice most of one's time and effort to become a slalom or gymnastic teenage superstar, or is it better to rehearse and practise the psycho-social skills of the 'normal' teenager? How much time, money and effort should one spend to keep on looking five years younger? To name but a few…

Meta-skills as important resources

In the developmental challenge model, selection, optimization and compensation would be categorized as resources, which are made up of 'meta-skills'. As we have mentioned previously, but briefly (see chapter 6), these are generalizable skills that can be used to ensure success in a variety of situations. Other skills that belong in this group are, for instance, learning strategies, self-evaluation, creative, innovative actions, and planning skills (Kloep and Hendry, 1999a). Vygotsky (1930) called the various psychological tools and strategies that people use to aid their thinking and behaviour 'signs', and he argued that we cannot understand human thinking without examining the different 'signs' that the various cultures provide. Rutter (1987) points out that in enabling vulnerable individuals, it is necessary to focus on protective processes that bring about changes in life trajectories from risk to adaptation and development. He includes:

- those that reduce the risk impact
- those that reduce the possibilities of negative chain reactions
- those that promote self-esteem and self-efficacy
- those that open up opportunities.

Among these meta-skills, much attention has been given to the skills of 'learning to learn'. With the rapid development of technology, far too much knowledge has been accumulated by mankind than can be learned and understood by single individuals. In the times of Leonardo da Vinci, it was still possible for scholars to take part in most aspects of existing knowledge. Nowadays, textbooks have hardly left the publishing house before they are obsolescent, at least in part (so read on quickly!). No teacher or university professor can accurately predict what curriculum will best prepare pupils for the demands of their future lives. Hence, in the tradition of Bacon, Leibnitz, Pestalozzi and Dewey, many pedagogues in the Western world intensify and subscribe to an ancient claim. That is, that to enable students to learn whatever skill or knowledge they need, we should teach them learning strategies instead of cramming them with facts (e.g. Bjørgen, 1993, 1995; Fürntratt and Möller, 1982; Nisbet and Shucksmith, 1984). The box below gives examples of some of these learning skills.

Some examples of meta-skills

1. Learning skills:
   - self-assessment
   - task-planning
   - perspective-taking
   - versatility in seeking solutions
   - evaluating solutions
   - refining
   - modifying
   - finding and selecting information, including accessing 'virtual' sources
   - mind-mapping
   - memorizing
   - rehearsing
   - seeking innovative settings for the trying out of new skills
   - using skills in a variety of situations in order to ensure their general applicability.

2. Strategies of a 'scientific approach to life':
   - critical thinking
   - testing hypotheses and assumptions
   - questioning evidence
   - logical induction and deduction
   - analysis and synthesis of information.
3. Planning skills:
   - goal-setting
   - finding pathways to attain goals
   - identifying barriers in goal-achieving and removing them
   - actively enhancing the probability of success by keeping different possible solutions viable
   - having persistence and perseverance.

Though learning strategies are mainly discussed in the context of formal schooling, they play an important role throughout the lifespan, as long as learning continues. So, we would answer the allegorical question: 'Can one can teach an old dog new tricks?' by answering: 'Yes, one can – provided the dog has previously learned the art of learning throughout its life'.

Very similar to these learning skills, and equally important, are the skills we would call 'taking a scientific approach to life' (see box above). All these are extremely important for facing the information 'explosion' that is already occurring, for example on the Internet. Individuals need to be enabled to sift through the available information on the Web and come to independent conclusions as to its relative worth, based on valid and appropriate criteria: the whole face of education may change crucially in the very near future. Young people and adults need to be presented with a set of learning styles entirely different to the current emphasis on recall and 'facts'.

Another important set of meta-skills is planning skills (see box above). For example, instead of passively waiting until that dream job turns up, or until the knight in shining armour on the white horse passes by, the individual can take active steps to achieve goals over the longer term. This can involve such simple tasks as checking adverts in newspapers and the Internet, taking some extra education classes, or joining the local riding club (just in case the knight goes there to ride his white horse). This is a shorthand way of saying that it is important always to have alternative plans in case the original one does not work out. More often than not, 'happy coincidences' are the result of long-term planning and careful preparation work. Quinton and Rutter (1988), for instance, find that the possession of life planning skills is the most important characteristic distinguishing young women who overcame the disadvantages of having been institutionalized as children from those who did not.

Recently, Staudinger and Baltes (1996; Staudinger, 1999; Baltes and Staudinger 2000) have begun to describe a number of skills that they believe coalesce into the concept of 'wisdom'. They consider that the following, amongst others, are essential resources for the 'art of life':

- rich factual and procedural knowledge
- lifespan contextualism
- value relativism
- recognition and management of uncertainty.

They have also found that in the ages between twenty and seventy-five there is not an age-related increase in 'wisdom', as defined above, but rather stability in this quality. Perhaps this stability is a feature of the variability in the array of skills inherent within the collective wisdom 'package'. In other words, at certain periods of life some qualities of wisdom blossom, only to lessen in salience at some other (later) life phase, to be replaced, however temporarily, by other necessary skills included in the collection of wisdom competencies. In our terms, this would be the enhancement of the resource 'pool' in the accomplishment of certain tasks, so that later demands could be met from other 'interacting' aspects of the individual's resource 'pool'.

Throughout this book we have emphasized yet another important ability, namely resilience and endurance in the face of failure. A common saying among adolescents is: 'Things that don't kill me, just make me strong!' We have to admit there is a grain of truth in this. Rutter (1996) stresses the importance of 'steeling experiences' for the development of resilience in times of trouble, quoting the results of a study with hospitalized children (Stacey *et al.*, 1970). Those children who had spent nights away from home before, coped much better with hospitalization than those who had not. The advantage of such 'steeling experiences' is, of course, not limited to childhood. Palinkas (1992) reports another example: staff from 'winter-over crews' at Antarctic stations suffer from isolation, confinement, conflict, lack of privacy, high altitude, darkness, low humidity and extreme cold, leading to rising depression rates and other psychological symptoms. However, a follow-up of some of these groups after their return home revealed that these groups (in total) experienced 20 per cent fewer first hospital admissions than a large control group during the next six years. Palinkas (1992) concludes that short-term health risks can lead to long-term health benefits: a process of adaptation takes place, in that some people learn new strategies from stressful experiences or develop new resources to cope with subsequent stressful experiences. What they learn is a combination of compromise and control, and the ability to utilize coping strategies and resources developed in one particular context in a wide variety of future contexts. Similarly, Rowe and Kahn (1997) conclude from their review of successful ageing that most people who do age successfully have been through daily hassles and experienced amounts of stress occasionally, and that resilience in recovering from such stressful episodes is essential. In other words, the best way of preparing for challenges is to experience challenges, as we have shown with various examples from each period of the lifespan in previous chapters.

Consideration of the developmental challenge model

Trying out a variety of tasks and learning a great diversity of skills – being a generalist rather than a specialist – appears to have sound survival values and is a useful way of ensuring that the resource 'pool' contains many interacting elements throughout the lifespan. For instance, if we consider the animal world for a moment, by comparison with the other animals, human beings are not particularly competent at any one activity. Even the best of us cannot run as fast as a cheetah, swim as elegantly as a dolphin, rip up trees as powerfully as a gorilla, jump as high as a flea, and we cannot even fly unaided. Yet human beings would almost always win in an animal decathlon. We can carry out nearly all these physical feats with some degree of competence. But, in addition, we have the intelligence to compensate for the lack of physical ability and meet challenges by eventually inventing necessary external aids. If we could fly unaided we might not have invented flying machines. Shortcomings are also challenges for development.

Further, we can communicate our ideas and the accumulated knowledge from the past to others in a variety of sensory modes, such as speech, the written word, visual imagery and telecommunications. We do not simply employ imitation, guidance and role-modelling, as other animals do, but we teach our young in a planned, multifaceted way. Given this versatility, we are primed for both learning and change.

An example from the animal world

After some discussion of Bronfenbrenner's (1979) ideas in chapter 2, we claimed that the developmental challenge model is an ecological model of human development. Hence, if we continue with this analogy of human beings and other animals, it is now important to think about eco-systems, and relate these ideas back to the model.

Animals survive within an ecological system that allows them to develop various specialized skills necessary for the continuance of the species. This involves a close interaction between the members of a particular species and the physical environment. For instance, the mountain gorillas of Uganda live in the lush rainforests, in which there is plenty of vegetation to be foraged for. They consume vast quantities of bamboo shoots and foliage daily, and are, thus, specialist eaters, staying in hierarchical family groups, each of which is headed by a relatively old and experienced male 'silver-back'. Certain challenges, for example in the form of an impending drought, can be coped with by preparatory eating, followed by a period of living off body fat, or travelling enormous distances to find food. But if the changes in the eco-system prevail for a lengthy period, it is not possible for the gorillas to adapt their diet. Life is even more precarious for some birds, which can only eat one type of grub or only nest in one kind of tree.

Hence, the environmental shifts that occur in nature or are caused by deforestation of the rainforests, can have devastating effects on those creatures not versatile enough to meet challenges by utilizing different aspects of their resource 'pool'. For them, it is possible to go on in contented stagnation only as long as there are few alterations to their eco-system. When radical shifts are demanded of them, they do not have the qualities of adaptation. So the resources that enable them to survive in relatively unchanging environmental circumstances cannot be called into play when rapid changes occur, and they cannot 'dip into' their resource 'pool' for alternative behaviours and practices, nor can they alter or reduce their goals. Further, we can note that even in the jungle no challenge is a risk by itself, but is an interaction with dynamic, ever-changing resources and shifts in the eco-system.

Looking now at security, we become aware that when the vegetation is lush and green, each gorilla has a relatively full resource 'pool', feels secure and is presumably happy with life. In that phase, they are individually in a position to seek challenges and develop. Without security, there is little possibility of development. When there is a great deal of environmental change, insecurities develop and challenges become over-taxing. Over time, then, decay, with its remorseless draining of resources, is the outcome, rather than development.

Like the mountain gorilla, we have to face tasks, which can be either a myriad of daily hassles or more complex life events. Life's challenges are made up of many smaller tasks and processes as well as major issues, all of which are challenges to be faced. Importantly, these tasks are encompassed by the macro-system of particular societies. The macro-system (and our historical time) dictate the different tasks that will be faced, the different customs, laws and social values that will act as filters to our decision-making processes. For example, it is possible to speculate that more normative, traditional societies, in which the challenges of the life course may be seen to be similar for most people in particular age phases, influence them to become more alike in expectations, behaviour and in social or age-related roles. The traditional type of macro-system seems to create security, stability and contented stagnation (as long as there are few societal shifts).

By comparison, individualistic societies with several non-normative shifts and rapid technological and social changes present their citizens with a greater variety of different challenges, a wider range of experiences, but the consequence of this is less security for many. These societies demand that their citizens face up to a wider range of challenges and shifts, less security if these present difficulties, and thereby create greater chances for individual development, but also for individual decay. However, with increasing globalization, more and more traditional cultures are experiencing greater and more varied societal shifts. As we have repeated throughout the book, the mechanisms of development in operation cross-culturally will be the same in terms of challenges, risks, resources, stagnation, development or drained decay, even though the outcomes may differ widely.

Qvortrup (1994) suggests that young people are seen by adults as 'human becomings', not human beings. In his writings, he stresses that they are in fact competent social actors in their own right and should be treated fairly as such within modern societies. In connection with this, Csikszentmihalyi and Rathunde (1998) stress the importance of seeing development from the perspective of young people as active agents in their own ontogeny:

Individuals have to *want* to develop and become more complex. And they will want to do so only if they enjoy it. If they do not, development becomes alienated, because the child as well as the adult will learn and grow primarily for extrinsic reasons. The child will study to graduate from school, the adult will work to get a pay check and be promoted, and both will endure their present conditions listlessly, in anticipation of a more pleasant future. This is not the kind of developmental trajectory that leads to complexity, or to a desirable old age. By contrast, development is intrinsic if a person feels that every moment of life is worth experiencing for its own sake....And complex development is intrinsic if a person learns to enjoy learning, meeting new challenges, overcoming obstacles, unfolding potentialities for being that are not naturally easy to use. When a child can enjoy both quiet and adventure, solitude and gregariousness, discipline and spontaneity, cognitive convergence and divergence, then he or she will *want* to become more complex. Whatever we can do to facilitate that kind of development will benefit the community as well as the child who is about to become a person on its stage [p.667].

All aspects of life and living – 'becoming', 'being' and 'having been' – are essential parts of our existence, as well as being important for development, for in their own right they make up our unique identity at any age. Where we come from, where we are going and, perhaps especially, where we *are* at present in our life course are all necessary components of our existential being and of our developmental trajectories. The lifespan model of developmental challenge takes into consideration that the developmental process across the life course is based on the past (i.e. our previous actual and potential resources), the present (i.e. the tasks, challenges and risks we face, and our current actual and potential resources) and the future (i.e. our development, stagnation or decay). Hence, at the same time as life requires us to focus on the 'here and now', we are also in the process of 'becoming' at all stages of the life course. The child is becoming an adult, the young adult is becoming middle aged, the adult in mid-life is becoming elderly. Importantly, we carry both the remnants of our 'having beens' and the foundations of our 'becomings' across all life phases (e.g. *we* have 'old Leo' or 'ageing Marion' with us now as we write).

The developmental challenge model and the analysis of development

In this chapter we began to look at various aspects of the developmental challenge model from a slightly different perspective. Within the model's framework we considered humans and members of the animal kingdom. Now we turn our attention more specifically to the values of the developmental challenge model for analyzing development on the micro- and macro-level.

At the beginning of this book, we promised that the model would facilitate the creation of a theoretical framework for answering questions about human behaviour and development through the lifespan. In order to illustrate this, we outline two case-studies, one describing a whole community (see box below), and one depicting a small fraction of a single learner's newly developed psycho-motor skills (see second box below), in order to show how the developmental challenge model can help us to analyze and theoretically understand both situations more clearly.

A sample analysis of Chamulan Indian culture using the developmental challenge model

Imagine that you are a social scientist on holiday, and you happen to visit a very different culture. Let us suppose you come to the Indian village of Chamula in southern Mexico. As a tourist you observe the following things: the Chamula are an indigenous tribe of Mayan descent, who have managed to preserve their traditions and lifestyle into modern times. Every day they dress in their colourful, traditional costumes and follow a set of strict rules in their daily living (though some of these rules deviate considerably from general Mexican laws). Men work in the fields and make pottery; women embroider clothes and prepare meals (which it is forbidden for men to do). No-one outside the Chamula tribe is allowed to live in their village, and recently there have been bloody incidents, when families who had converted from a mixture of paganism and Catholicism to a Protestant faith have been driven out of their houses and the community. The Chamula exist with economic difficulties, trying to make a living by selling their handicrafts to tourists in the nearby city of San Cristóbal. As they all produce exactly the same items and sell them in the same manner, the city is flooded with far more embroidered bracelets than there are tourists to buy them. The goods are often sold by children, who assist their parents in the trade instead of going to school. As a result, many of them lack basic education. Many Chamulan fathers have an alcohol problem, so that the burden of maintaining and sustaining the family often lies with the women and older children. Family cohesion is high, and each family member supports the other.

As an interested tourist from a different culture, we guess you would ask yourself a range of questions about the Chamulan lifestyle, such as:

- Why does a minority group like the Chamula not keep peace amongst themselves instead of chasing those of a slightly different faith out of the community, thus depleting an already small tribe?
- How could some of their traditions survive into the present, in spite of globalization's influence on Mexican society generally, with increasing international tourism and a strong Spanish-Mexican cultural influence around the region?
- Why do they all sell the same objects, instead of offering a variety of goods and finding new niches in the local market?
- Why do so few of them try to get higher educational qualifications and find well-paid jobs elsewhere?

Applying the developmental challenge model along with the ecological theory of Bronfenbrenner (1979), you can find some of the answers to these and other questions for yourself before reading the suggested answers below, where the developmental challenge model is used to interpret the cultural situation of the Chamulans.

- Keeping traditions, and belonging to an 'in-group' creates security, and for a time that coherence helped the Chamula tribe to survive. Given few resources, in present times of change, when they cannot survive on small-scale farming and handicrafts, this situation has become 'unhappy stagnation'. Signs of that are that traditional rules and compliance with them have to be enforced. Any change is too powerful a challenge for such a group to meet, and thus it creates anxiety. All tendencies towards change have to be fought, and not even slight variations in faith can be tolerated in the community.
- The entrepreneurial skills of finding a market niche need a relatively full resource 'pool'. Selling bracelets has proved to be relatively successful in the past, so it appears risk-free becoming a bracelet-vendor. There seem to be no adaptable resources whatsoever to react to the challenge of an overcrowded market. Without assets, putting resources into a new venture, such as producing and selling, for example, embroidered napkins or tablecloths, is too high a risk – there are no ways for them to test whether such a product would actually sell better than the traditional products. So, the stagnated choice is to do what has been reasonably successful in the past rather than to take a (perceived) high-risk course. (By the way, one also finds indications of this way of thinking in much less remote circumstances. For example, why do most Italian restaurants in Europe – apart from those in Italy itself – have much the same menu?)
- Not having attended primary school as children, it would be a challenge that largely exceeds the resources of most Chamulans to find education or employment elsewhere. In any case, what kind of employment would that be? Probably a badly paid job in a factory in a town far away from the home village, without the resources an extended family can provide. So massive a change might destroy the securities of tradition without necessarily replacing them with worthwhile alternatives. Not even if you, as a tourist with a soft heart, could offer a scholarship and financial support to that little girl who keeps begging for food and pesos on the main square, could she accept. How could she abandon her care of three smaller siblings and her mother to go to a school that cannot promise her or her family a better, more financially secure, future? Lives are so linked and micro-systems so interwoven that no simple external measure can be applied without disrupting the whole eco-system.

Having looked at an example of the developmental challenge model's abilities to analyze a complex macro-cultural setting, we now turn our attention to observations on a micro-individual level, in order to test the 'strength' of the model in providing insights into the interaction of resources and challenges during the acquisition of a relatively simple psycho-motor task.

Suggested analysis of learning a psycho-motor skill using the developmental challenge model

Consider with us a good swimmer trying to improve his crawl. The coach starts by giving instructions on how to bend the front arm when drawing it out of water to begin the arm recovery phase. The trainee tries this out immediately, and gets the movement right after a few tries. Now he gets some new coaching instructions: 'In your leg kick, keep your heels under the surface. Don't move them too fast, and reach out farther with your hand before it enters the water.' When the swimmer tries this for the first time, something rather surprising happens. He has suddenly forgotten how to co-ordinate his movements and even how to breathe. He swallows water and ends the practice coming up coughing. However, after some seconds of recovery, he tries again and again...

If you use the developmental challenge model to understand his behaviour, it should be fairly easy to analyze this learning sequence:

- Being a good swimmer, knowing how to breathe and how to co-ordinate arm and leg movements, this trainee has enough resources to cope with the challenge of a single change in his learned movements.
- He does not yet, however, have sufficient skills to internalize a number of added instructions, including the overload of too many new ones at once (i.e. bad coaching).
- The skilled sequences of movements breaks down, even the already acquired sequences. He falls temporarily back on earlier psycho-motor patterns, seeking the security of known movements – a time when he did not know how to breathe 'correctly', and swam with his head up out of the water. Now his whole present movement system is disturbed to a degree that he does not succeed, and has to give up the practice.
- But this continues only for a while, given the skills level, experience and high self-esteem that he has as a swimmer. He feels secure enough to try again, in spite of his failure, and with practice succeeds eventually.
- On the other hand, relative beginners might well have been completely put off swimming by such an experience, because they would panic in a similar situation: they have not yet developed sufficient aquatic skills (i.e. resources), so that any demand at this stage immediately overloads their resource 'pool', and they do not have enough positive past experiences of their competency level to feel sufficiently secure to try again. Failure at this stage may drain their 'swimming resources' to such a degree that a near-phobic reaction towards the activity and the context develops.

By this stage we hope it is evident that the developmental challenge model is capable of being used to analyze and interpret tasks and challenges from the individual micro-level up to the level of cultural analysis.

The developmental challenge model and the prediction of development

These case studies show how the developmental challenge model can be used to explain behavioural changes (or their absence) in normal and unusual situations, at both the individual and the macro-system levels. But can it also be used to predict development?

The answer is both negative and affirmative. Science claims to be able to predict events if all determining variables are known. For instance, if one knows the exact temperature and humidity in a room, and the amount of water in a glass placed there, it is possible to predict how much time it will take for the water to evaporate. But if temperature and humidity are not stable, and now and then some water is spilled from the glass, predictions will become fairly inaccurate. In the case of human development, there are far too many interactive variables involved than could ever be measured. Therefore, individual predictions can never be much more than sophisticated guesses.

However, that is the fate of every science outside of the controlled walls of the laboratory. Medical science cannot predict for a single individual how long he or she will live, even after thorough investigation. All it can do is offer some 'rules of thumb' or blueprints and guidelines as to what most often influences health and longevity positively and negatively – no guarantees are offered. We claim that a similar level of predictability can be derived from the developmental challenge model, and that it can be improved further, once research has discovered more about potential resources, lifetime challenges, and their interaction with each other and the individual's different psycho-social systems. However, exact predictions will never be possible, because: 'developmental phenomena represent an open-systems process in which the exact predictability of outcomes is impossible, because these outcomes are constructed over time in the process of organism–environment transaction' (Valsiner, 1997: p.315).

The proposed values of the developmental challenge model

As Lewin (1943) is often cited as stating that there is nothing as practical as a good theory, we now proceed to examine the practical values of the developmental challenge model. The majority of theorists in the world tend to regard development as defined by age, physical growth and social transitions. However, this kind of definition has some remarkable weaknesses. It implies that a human being does not develop much after adolescence, and especially not in the latter phases of the lifespan. So development, with few exceptions, is regarded as synonymous with child and adolescent psychology. Furthermore, many describe development as happening in distinct stages.

Consistent with the ideas presented in the developmental challenge model, Bee (1998), in applying the ideas of Levinson (1978, 1996) and Loevinger (1984), comes to the conclusion that development does not occur in stages. Rather it occurs in sequences of experience, which are shared by many individuals in a given culture, all following similar – but different – pathways. Such a description fits well with our views of shifts through the lifespan.

The second linked concept Bee offers is that of alternating periods of stability and transition, and she sees these as neither fixed to age stages nor universal. These can be explained in terms of the processes involved in our concepts of challenges and attendant risks through the lifespan, in which the achievement of a desired goal can lead to a period of 'dynamic security', with skills being consolidated and resources developed. Across the lifespan, individual biological and social 'clocks' can create patterns of stability and change for each of us, though these can vary as a result of different physiological, cultural and cohort 'triggers'. Bee (1998) sums up the style of development or stagnation that can occur when one of life's challenges is faced:

> In each of these transitions, I think there is an opportunity for growth because the transition may call the internal models into question or force you to face new issues. Puberty triggers a whole new set of questions about independence and autonomy, marriage forces each of us to deal with the habits and internal models we bring to relationships, middle age may cause you to question that most unexamined assumption, the feeling of invincibility or immortality. People living through crisis or transition sometimes say, 'I am beside myself'. It is a revealing phrase, reflecting perhaps, their sense of being momentarily outside of one's normal frame. There may well be pain involved, a sense of dislocation and loss, but there may also be an opportunity to change the frame, to reshape the internal models. ... Not everyone takes that opportunity. Many of us come to and through these points of transition without re-examining our assumptions or taking up new tasks. But growth at some deeper level seems especially possible at these transitional points. ... For some, a transition results in depression, alcoholism, or perhaps even regression to earlier forms of coping. For others, the disequilibrium is followed by a return to the previous status quo. But there is an opportunity for change and growth at each turn of the spiral [p.538].

By combining the concepts of 'sequences' and 'stability and change', but without the assumption that everyone will necessarily experience transitions at the same time or in the same way, it is possible to see that the potential sequences of change during the lifespan will be different for different individuals. Hence, developmental 'pathways' will be varied: not everyone will follow them to the same extent, and some sequences involved will be the processes of non-normative shifts. Individual differences will mean that the timing of these changes will be idiosyncratic and the results varied, as we could predict from the developmental challenge model. As a consequence, it is obvious to note the similarities of babies to each other in appearance and behaviour (despite the claims of doting parents). Already by the teenage years, individuals differ remarkably in behaviour, looks and interests. By old age, finally, the biological, psychological and social variations among the elderly are great.

Thus, one advantage of the developmental challenge model is that it makes no assumptions about stages and sequences, but rather considers transitions and pathways through the life course in relation to the individual's potential resources in the face of challenges at any time during the lifespan.

Another aspect to be taken into account is the prevailing ethnocentricity of many current developmental theories. Little can be generalized from these to provide an understanding of human development in different parts of the world, though Western theories have been used, and continue to be used, with little thought to cross-cultural differences. As Cahan *et al.* (1993) put it:

> If childhood is not everywhere and everyplace the same – and the anthropologists and social historians have been amply demonstrating to us that it is not – then the meaning and object of all forms of psychological research have to be reconsidered [p.210].

Similarly, many theories fail to take account of wider macro-social shifts and changes, and the influences of historical time in their descriptions of development. Thus, more inventively, developmental theories should become less value-laden, containing less implicit assumptions about universals of development, and less static and culture-bound, if they are effectively to take account of the ever-increasing pace of social and technological change and its influence on individual development. The developmental challenge model describes the mechanisms of development in ways that are applicable to all cultures and at all times in history.

The critical reader might argue that we have used mainly research examples from the Western industrialized world to illuminate the model's explanatory power. However, this is due to the shortcomings of empirical research from other cultures. What is clearly needed is more research on the developmental shifts in various countries of the world, and on the mechanisms that direct adaptation processes. Are normative shifts different in less individualistic societies? Are the processes implied in transitions like retirement, parenthood or divorce equal or different? Are there other more important challenges in the lives of people in more traditional cultures than we consider from our rather narrow theoretical (i.e. Western) perspective? For example, what does the experience of oppression, poverty, war or persecution mean for the individual's development? What resources are necessary to face the challenges of life in the Third World? More cross-cultural findings would strengthen the universality – and the understanding – of developmental processes (see, for example, box below).

'Healthy nutrition' as a resource defined by cross-cultural relativity

The powerful influence of the macro-system on creating cultural differences in challenges and risks, as well as in individual resources can be illustrated with the example of so-called healthy nutrition.

Cultural values influence what is regarded as an 'attractive body' and 'health food':

- People with 'ideal weight' according to European standards would be regarded as 'undernourished' in some African cultures.
- The significance and symbolic value of food in a social context, as an expression of status, as a leisure pursuit, as a cultural representation or as means to gain health and well-being is different in different cultures.

- Even what is regarded as a 'satisfying' meal is not the same in different cultures: Germans would regard a Norwegian lunch as a snack (because it consists of open sandwiches), while Scots (used to having porridge, bacon, egg and beans for breakfast) would not regard the Italian toast with marmalade and cappuccino as anything more than a side dish…

Macro-social resources influence problems associated with nutrition differently:

- Some regions cannot afford to offer the minimum amount of food to their inhabitants, so under-nourishment is the consequence.
- Rich countries have problems educating their inhabitants to eat less, with consequent increasing rates of obesity.
- The power of the multinational junk-food industry, together with the desperate wish of some cultures to imitate and adopt the American way of life as perceived progress, destroys traditional eating habits even in poor countries (e.g. Argentina: Dardo, Marra and Tavormina, 2001), with resulting unbalanced nutrition. One of the most cherished symbols of freedom and democracy in Tirana (Albania) after the fall of communism, for example, was the establishment of a fake McDonald's in the city centre – the 'real one' had not shown a commercial interest at that point.

It seems clear that attitudes, behaviours and even more obvious symbolic features such as 'the body' and 'healthy food' represent such cross-cultural relativity that it is impossible to examine these features only through Western eyes, applying Western theoretical models to the interpretation and formation of policies.

In the light of this, we want once again to emphasize that the developmental tasks individuals may meet during their lifetime will vary greatly across time and culture, but that the underlying mechanisms of development remain the same.

The strength of what we are presenting here is that the underlying mechanisms of development are universal, and that the individual is acknowledged as an effective social agent. Additionally, the model can also be used in conjunction with other modern theoretical frameworks, some of which have been referred to in the text, in order to enhance understanding or to extend illumination of the many interacting and inter-locking systems that go to make up the ecology of human development.

But while providing this framework for analyzing, understanding and interpreting the mechanisms of development, there is a limitation that needs to be pointed out: because of the variety of tasks individuals meet, the timing of these within their particular life course, and the interactions of various psycho-social systems, there is no one model that can adequately explain the totality of individual development – there would have to be as many models as there are individuals. Extensive variability exists among people because genotypes and environments vary. No two people have the same fusion of genes and contexts in their lives. Individual differences within and across all levels of human ecology are of core significance in understanding the developmental process.

The developmental challenge model illustrates development as an accumulation of abilities and resources derived from meeting challenges successfully throughout the lifespan. At the same time, it makes us alert to the vast array of interacting variables that affect our lives and create a myriad of different pathways to development, stagnation and decay. The developmental challenge model offers a general framework of analysis and interpretation that can subsequently be tailored to fit the life course of each single individual. Most significantly, for self and for society, the model can help to empower individuals:

- by providing strategies to analyze the mechanisms and processes of challenge and risk through the lifespan
- continually to take steps to strengthen resources of all kinds
- to help plan their own life course
- to take action in implementing change
- to consider the influence their actions have on lives 'linked' to theirs.

Thus individuals themselves can initiate a positive spiral of development and move towards competent self-agency and control over life, and the achievement of successful living for themselves and others.

R eferences

Adams-Price, C.E., T.B. Henley and M. Hale (1998) 'Phenomenology and the meaning of aging for young and old adults', *International Journal of Aging and Human Development*, 47 (4), 263–277.

Adelman, P.K., T.C. Antonucci, S.E. Crohan and L.M. Coleman (1989) 'Empty nest, cohort, and employment in the well-being of midlife women', *Sex Roles*, 20 (3/4), 173–188.

Adolph, K.E. (1997) 'Learning in the development of infant locomotion', *Monographs of the Society for Research in Child Development*, 56 (3, serial no. 251).

— (2001) personal communication.

Ainsworth, M. (1979) 'Attachment as related to mother–infant interaction', in *Advances in the Study of Behavior*, 9 (eds J.S. Rosenblad, R.A. Hinde, C. Beer and M. Busnel), Academic Press, New York, NY.

Alapack, R.J. (1991) 'Adolescent first kiss', *The Humanistic Psychologist*, 19 (1), 48–67.

— (1999) 'Jealousy in first love: unwitting disclosure', in *Invitations to dialogue: the legacy of Sidney M. Jourard*, (eds A.C. Richards and T. Schumrum), Kendall/Hunt, New York, NY, 91–106.

Aldwin, C.M. (1991) 'Does age affect the stress and coping processes? Implications of age differences in perceived control', *Journals of Gerontology, Psychological and Social Sciences*, 46B (4), 174–180.

— (1992) 'Aging, coping, and efficacy: theoretical framework for examining coping in life-span developmental context', in *Stress and Health among the Elderly* (eds M.L. Wykle and J. Kowal), Springer, New York, NY, 96–113.

Aldwin, C.M., K.J. Sutton, G. Chiara and A. Spiro (1996) 'Age differences in stress, coping, and appraisal: findings from the normative aging study', *Journals of Gerontology, Psychological and Social Sciences*, 51B (4), 179–188.

Alsaker, F.D. and A. Flammer (1999) 'Time use in an international perspective, II: the case of necessary activities', in *The Adolescent Experience: European and American Adolescents in the 1990s* (eds F.D. Alsaker and A. Flammer), Lawrence Erlbaum Associates, Hillsdale, NJ, 61–83.

Andersson, B.E. (1995) 'Does school stimulate young people's development?' in *Studies on Youth and Schooling in Sweden* (ed. B. Jonsson), Stockholm Institute of Education Press, Stockholm.

Argyle, M. (1967) *The Psychology of Interpersonal Behaviour*, Penguin Books, Harmondsworth.

Arnett, J. (1998) 'The young and the reckless', in *Developmental Psychology: A Reader* (eds D. Messer and J. Dockrell), Arnold, London.

Baltes, P.B. (1987) 'Theoretical propositions of life-span developmental psychology: on the dynamics between growth and decline', *Developmental Psychology*, 23, 611–626.

— (1997) 'On the incomplete architecture of human ontogenesis: selection, optimization, and compensation as foundations of developmental theory', *American Psychologist*, 52, 366–381.

Baltes, P.B. and M.M. (1980) 'Plasticity and variability in psychological aging', in *Determining the Effects of Aging on the Central Nervous System* (ed. G.E. Girslo), Sohering, Berlin, 41–66.

— (1990) 'Psychological perspectives of successful aging: the model of selective optimization with compensation', in *Successful Aging: Perspectives from the Behavioral Sciences* (eds P.B. and M.M. Baltes), Cambridge University Press, New York, NY, 1–34.

Baltes, P.B. and L.R. Goulet (1970) 'Status and issues of a life-span developmental psychology', in *Life-span Developmental Psychology: Research and Therapy* (eds L.R. Goulet and P.B. Baltes), Academic Press, New York, NY, 4–21.

Baltes, P.B. and P. Graf (1996) 'Psychological aspects of aging: facts and frontiers', in *The Life-span Development of Individuals: Behavioural, Neurobiological and Psychosocial Perspectives* (ed. D. Magnusson), Cambridge University Press, Cambridge, 427–460.

Baltes, P.B., U. Lindenberger and U.M. Staudinger (1997) 'Life-span theory in developmental psychology', in *Handbook of Child Psychology*, 5th ed., vol. 1 (eds W. Damon and R.M. Lerner), Wiley, New York, NY, 1029–1143.

Baltes, P.B., H.W. Reese and L.P. Lipsitt (1980) 'Life-span developmental psychology', *Annual Review of Psychology*, 31, 65–110.

Baltes, P.B. and U.M. Staudinger (2000) 'Wisdom – a metaheuristic (pragmatic) to orchestrate mind and virtue toward excellence', *American Psychologist*, 55 (1), 122–135.

Baltes, M.M. and F.R. Lang (1997) 'Everyday functioning and successful aging: the impact of resources', *Psychology and Aging*, 12 (3), 433–443.

Bandura, A. (1977) *Social Learning Theory*, Prentice Hall, Englewood Cliffs.

— (1986) *Social Foundations of Thought and Action: A Social Cognitive Theory*, Prentice Hall, Englewood Cliffs.

Barnet, H.S. (1990) 'Divorce stress and adjustment model: locus of control and demographic predictors', *Journal of Divorce*, 13 (3), 93–109.

Barnombudsmannen (1997) *Barndom sätter spår, Rapport från barnens myndighet*, Barnombudsmannen, Stockholm.

Barr, R.G. (1998) 'Crying in the first year of life: good news in the midst of distress', *Child Care Health and Development*, 24 (5), 425–439.

Baumrind, D. (1996) 'The discipline controversy revisited', *Family Relations*, 45, 405–414.

Beck, U. (1992) *Risk Society: Towards a New Modernity*, Sage, London.

Beckman, L.J. (1987) 'Changes in motivation for parenthood among young married couples', *Population and Environment*, 9 (2), 96–110.

Bee, H. (1998) *Lifespan Development*, 2nd ed., Longman, London.

Bell, R.Q. (1968) 'A reinterpretation of the direction of effects in studies of socialization', *Psychological Review*, 75, 81–95.

Belsky, J. and M. Rovine (1990) 'Patterns of marital change across the transition to parenthood: pregnancy to three years postpartum', *Journal of Marriage and the Family*, 52, 5–19.

Bierbrauer, G. (1994) 'Towards an understanding of legal culture: variations in individualism and collectivism between Kurds, Lebanese and Germans', *Law & Society Review*, 28 (2), 243–264.

Bjørgen, I. (1993) 'The truncated and the intact concept of learning', *Revista Portuguesa de Educação*, 6, 23–54.

— (1995) *Ansvar for Egen Læring*, Tapir, Trondheim.

Blom, I. (1991) 'The history of widowhood', *Journal of Family History*, 16 (2), 191–210.

Bolognini, M., B. Plancherel and O. Halfton (1996) 'Life events and daily hassles: what impact on mental health in early adolescence?' in *Conflict and Development in Adolescence* (eds L. Verhofstadt-Denève, I. Kienhorst and C. Braet), DSWO Press, Leiden, 35–45.

Borell, K. and S.G. Karlsson (2000) 'Ældre kjæresetfolk – hver for sig', *Gerontologi og samfund*, 16 (4), 85–87.

Bossé, R. (1998) 'Retirement and retirement planning in old age', in *Clinical Gerontopsychology* (eds I.H. Nordhus, G.R. Vanden Bos, S. Berg and P. Fromholt), Cappelen, Oslo.

Bourdieu, P. (1973) 'Cultural reproduction and social reproduction', in *Knowledge, Education and Cultural Change* (ed. R. Brown), Tavistock, London, 71–113.

Bourdillon, M. (2001) 'Child labor and tea in Zimbabwe', paper presented at 'Children and young people in a changing world' conference, Agrigento, Italy, 9–16 June.

Bowlby, J. (1969) *Attachment and Loss*, Basic Books, New York, NY.

Brandt, B. and E. Kvande (1998) 'Masculinity and child care: the reconstruction of fathering', *Sociological Review*, 46 (2), 293–313.

Brandtstädter, J. and W. Greve (1992) 'Das Selbst im Alter: Adaptive und protektive Mechanismen', *Zeitschrift für Entwicklungspsychologie und Pädagogische Psychologie*, 24 (4), 269–297, English translation: 'The aging self: stabilizing and protective processes', *Developmental Review* (1994), 14 (1), 52–80.

Brandtstädter, J. and D. Wentura (1995) 'Adjustment to shifting possibility frontiers in later life: complementary adaptive modes', in *Compensating for Psychological Deficits and Declines: Managing Losses and Promoting Gains* (eds R.A. Dixon and L. Bäckman), Lawrence Erlbaum Associates, Hillsdale, NJ, 83–106.

Brandtstädter, J., K. Rothermund and U. Schmitz (1997) 'Coping resources in later life', *European Review of Applied Psychology*, 47 (2), 107–114.

Bril, B. (1997) 'Culture et premières acquisitions motrices: enfants d'Europe, d'Asie, d'Afrique', *Journal de Pédiatrie et Puériculture*, 5, 302–314.

Bril, B., M. Zack and E. Nkounkou-Hombessa (1989) 'Ethnotheories of development and education: a view from different cultures', *European Journal of Psychology of Education*, 4 (2), 307–318.

Bronfenbrenner, U. (1979) *The Ecology of Human Development: Experiments by Nature and Design*, Harvard University Press, Cambridge, MA.

Bronfenbrenner, U. and P.A. Morris (1998) 'The ecology of the developmental process', in *Handbook of Child Psychology*, 5th ed., vol. 1 (eds W. Damon and R.M. Lerner), Wiley, New York, NY, 993–1028.

Buchmann, M. (1989) *The Script of Life in Modern Society*, University of Chicago Press, Chicago, IL.

Burnette, D. (1998) 'Grandparents raising grandchildren: a school-based small group intervention', *Research on Social Work*, 8 (1), 10–27.

— (1999) 'Social relationships of Latino grandparent care-givers: a role theory perspective', *The Gerontologist*, 39 (1), 49–58.

Büchner, P. (1990) 'Aufwachsen in den 80er Jahren', in *Kindheit und Jugend im interkulturellen Vergleich* (eds H.H. Krüger and L. Chisholm), Leske und Budrich, Opladen, 79–123.

Bytheway, B. (1995) *Ageism*, Open University Press, Buckingham.

Cahan, E., J. Mechling, B. Sutton-Smith and S.H. White (1993) 'The elusive child: Ways of knowing the child of history and psychology', in *Children in Time and Place: Developmental and Historical Insight* (eds G.H. Elder, J. Modell and R.D. Parke), Cambridge University Press, New York, NY, 192–223.

Campbell, M. (1995) 'Divorce at mid-life: intergenerational issues', *Journal of Divorce and Remarriage*, 23 (1/2), 185–202.

Carstensen, L.L. and A.M. Freund (1994) 'The resilience of the aging self', *Developmental Review*, 14, 81–92.

Cashmore, E.E. (1984) *No Future*, Heinemann, London.

Chalmers, B. and D. Meyer (1996) 'What men say about pregnancy, birth and parenthood', *Journal of Psychosomatic Obstetrics and Gynecology*, 17, 47–52.

Chase-Lansdale, P. and E.M. Hetherington (1990) 'The impact of divorce on life-span development: short and long term effects', in *Life-span Development and Behavior*, vol. 10 (eds P.B. Baltes, D.L. Featherman and R.M. Lerner), Lawrence Erlbaum Associates, Hillsdale, NJ, 105–150.

Chiriboga, D.A. (1991) 'Risk factors in divorce: a life course perspective', in *Divorce: Crisis, Challenge or Relief?* (eds D.A. Chiriboga and L.S. Catron), New York University Press, New York, NY, 280–292.

— (1997) 'Crisis, Challenge, and Stability in the Middle Years', in *Multiple Paths of Midlife Development* (eds M.E. Lachman and J.B. James), University of Chicago Press, Chicago, IL, 293–322.

Chisholm, L. and M. Du-Bois Reymond (1993) 'Youth transitions, gender and social change', *Sociology*, 27, 259–279.

Christie, N. and K. Bruun (1996) 'Den gode fiende: Narkotikapolitikk i Norden', Universitetsforlaget, Oslo, 2nd ed.

Colburn, K. Jr, P.L. Lin and M.C. Moore (1992) 'Gender and the divorce experience', *Journal of Divorce and Remarriage*, 18, 213–218.

Cole, E. and E. Rothblum (1990) 'Commentary on sexuality and the midlife woman', *Psychology of Women Quarterly*, 14, 509–512.

Coleman, J.C. (1974) *Relationships in Adolescence*, Routledge, London.

Coleman, J.C and L.B. Hendry (1999) *The Nature of Adolescence*, 3rd ed., Routledge, London.

Coleman, J.S. (1988) 'Social capital in the creation of human capital', *American Journal of Sociology*, 94 (Supplement), 95–120.

Coles, B. (1995) *Youth and Social Policy: Youth, Citizenship and Young Careers*, University College of London Press, London.

Connidis, I.A. (1994) 'Sibling Support in Older Age', *Journals of Gerontology, Psychological and Social Sciences*, 49B (6), 309–317.

Coplan, G.A. and W.J. Strawbridge (1994) 'Behavioral and social factors in healthy aging', in *Aging and Quality of Life* (eds R.P. Abeles, H.C. Gift and M.G. Ory), Springer, New York, NY, 57–78.

Costa, P. and R. McCrae (1988) 'The NEO-PI/FFI manual supplement', *Psychological Assessment Resources*, Odessa.

Crimmins, E.M., M.D. Hayward and Y. Saito (1996) 'Differentials in active life expectancy in the older population of the United States', *Journals of Gerontology, Psychological and Social Sciences*, 51B, 111–120.

Csikszentmihalyi, M. (1975) *Beyond Boredom and Anxiety*, Jossey–Bass, San Francisco, CA.

— (1990) *Flow: The Psychology of Optimal Experience*, Harper Perennial, New York, NY.

— (1997) *Finding Flow: The Psychology of Engagement with Everyday Life*, Basic Books, New York, NY.

Csikszentmihalyi, M. and K. Rathunde (1998) 'The development of the person: An experimental perspective on the ontogenesis of psychological complexity', in *Handbook of Child Psychology*, 5th ed., vol. 1 (eds W. Damon and R.M. Lerner), Wiley, New York, NY, 635–684.

Cumming, E. and W.E. Henry (1961) *Growing Old*, Basic Books, New York, NY.

Cusinato, M. (1994) 'Parenting over the life cycle', in *Handbook of Developmental Family Psychology and Psychopathology* (ed. L.L'Abate), John Wiley, New York, NY.

Dan, A.J. and L.A. Bernhard (1989) 'Menopause and other health issues for midlife women', in *Midlife Myths: Issues, Findings, and Practice Implications* (eds S. Hunter and M. Sundel), Sage, Newbury Park, CA, 51–66.

Dardo, A., G. Marra and S. Tavormina (2001) 'From la Mona to McDonalds: changes in eating habits of children and young people in the 90s in Buenos Aires', paper presented at 'Children and young people in a changing world' conference, Agrigento, Italy, 9–16 June.

Davis, J. (1990) *Youth and the Condition of Britain: Images of Adolescent Conflict*, Athlone Press, London.

Defey, D., E. Storch, S. Cardozo, O. Díaz and G. Fernández (1996) 'The menopause: women's psychology and health care', *Social Science Medicine*, 42 (10), 1447–1456.

Dennison, C.D. and J.C. Coleman (1998) 'Teenage motherhood: experiences and relationships', in *Pregnancy and Childbirth* (ed. S. Clement), Churchill Livingston, Edinburgh.

Diamond, M.C. (1991) 'Environmental influences on the young brain', in *Brain Maturation and Cognitive Development* (eds K.R. Gibson and A.C. Peterson), Aldine de Gruyter, New York, NY, 107–124.

Dittman-Kohli, F. (1990) 'The construction of meaning in old age: Possibilities and constraints', *Ageing and Society*, 10, 279–294.

Doka, K.J. and M.E. Mertz (1988) 'Meaning and significance of great-grand-parenthood', *The Gerontologist*, 28 (2), 192–197.

Donaldson, M. (1978) *Children's Minds*, Collins, London.

Durkheim, E. (1893, 1964) *The Divison of Labour in Society*, Free Press, New York, NY.

Dybdahl, R. and K. Hundeide (1998) 'Childhood in the Somali context: mothers' and children's ideas about childhood and parenthood', *Psychology and Developing Societies*, 10 (2), 131–145.

Elder, G.H. Jr (1974) *Children of the Great Depression: Social Change in Life Experience*, University of Chicago Press, Chicago, IL.

— (1975) 'Adolescence in the life cycle: an introduction', in *Adolescence in the Life-cycle* (eds S.E. Dragastin and G.H. Elder Jr), John Wiley, New York, NY, 1–22.

— (1986) 'Military times and turning points in men's lives', *Developmental Psychology*, 22, 233–245.

— (1987) 'War mobilization and the life course: A cohort of World War II veterans', *Sociological Forum*, 2, 449–472.

— (1997) 'The life course and human development', in *Handbook of Child Psychology*, 4th edition, vol. 1 (eds W. Damon and R.M. Lerner), Wiley, New York, NY, 939–991.

— (1998) 'The life course as developmental theory', *Child Development*, 69 (1), 1–12.

Elder, G.H. Jr, R.D. Conger, E.M. Foster and M. Ardelt (1992) 'Families under economic pressure', *Journal of Family Issues*, 13, 5–37.

Elder, G.H. Jr, T. Van Nguyen and A. Caspi (1985) 'Linking family hardship to children's lives', *Child Development*, 56, 361–375.

Emick, M.A. and B. Hayslip (1996) 'Custodial grandparenting: New roles for middle-aged and older adults', *International Journal of Aging and Human Development*, 43 (2), 135–154.

Erikson, E.H. (1959) 'Identity and the life cycle', *Psychological Issues*, Monograph 1, International Universities Press, New York, NY.

— (1968) *Identity: Youth and Crisis*, Faber and Faber, London.

Eysenck, H.J. and M.W. (1985) *Personality and Individual Differences: A Natural Science Approach*, Plenum Press, New York, NY.

Fagot, B.I. and K. Kavanagh (1990) 'The prediction of antisocial behavior from avoidant attachment classifications', *Child Development*, 61, 864–628.

Farnsworth, J., M.A. Pett and D.A. Lund (1989) 'Predictors of loss management and well being in later widowhood and divorce', *Journal of Family Issues*, 10 (1), 102–121.

Farrington, D.P. (1989) 'Long-term prediction of offending and other life outcomes', *in Criminal Behavior and the Justice System* (eds H. Wegener, F. Loesel, and J. Haisch), Springer, New York, NY, 26–39.

Featherstone, M. and M. Hepworth (1991) 'The mask of ageing and the postmodern life course', in *The Body, Social Process and Cultural Theory* (eds M. Featherstone, M. Hepworth and B. Turner), Sage, London, 371–389.

— (1993) 'Images of ageing', in *Ageing in Society* (eds J. Bond, P. Coleman and S. Peace), Sage, London, 304–332.

Ferraro, K.F. and M.M. Farmer (1995) 'Social compensation in adulthood and later life', in *Compensating for Psychological Deficits and Declines* (eds R. A. Dixon and L. Bäckman), Lawrence Erlbaum Associates, Hillsdale, NJ, 127–145.

Field, D. (1999) 'Continuity and change in friendships in advanced old age: Findings from the Berkeley older generation study', *International Journal of Aging and Human Development*, 48 (4), 325–346.

Firestone, J. and B.A. Shelton (1994) 'A comparison of women's and men's leisure time: Subtle effects of the double day', *Leisure Sciences*, 16 (1), 45–60.

Fiske, M. and D. Chiriboga (1991) *Change and Continuity in Adult Life*, Jossey Bass, San Francisco, CA.

Flanagan, C.A. (1990) 'Families and schools in hard times', *New Directions in Child Development*, 46, 7–26.

Folkman, S., R.S. Lazarus, S. Pimley and J. Novacek (1987) 'Age differences in stress and coping processes', *Psychology and Aging*, 2 (2), 171–184.

Frese, M. (2000) 'Innovation and initiative', paper presented at the XXVII International Congress of Psychology, Stockholm 23–28 July.

Freud, S. (1905, 1938) 'Three contributions to the theory of sex', in *The Basic Writings of Sigmund Freud* (ed. A.A. Brill), Random House, New York, NY.

Freysinger, V.G. (1995) 'The dialectics of leisure and development for women and men in mid-life: An interpretative study', *Journal of Leisure Research*, 27 (1), 61–84.

Friedan, B. (1993) *The Fountain of Age*, Simon & Schuster, New York, NY.

Fuller-Thompson, E., M. Minkler and D. Driver (1997) 'A profile of grandparents raising grandchildren in the United States', *The Gerontologist*, 37 (3), 406–411.

Furlong, A. and F. Cartmel (1997) *Young People and Social Change: Individualisation and Risk in Late Modernity*, Open University Press, Buckingham.

Furlong, V.J. (1991) 'Disaffected pupils: Reconstructing the sociological perspective', *British Journal of Sociology of Education*, 12 (3), 293–307.

Fürntratt, E. (1974) *Angst und Instrumentelle Aggression*, Weinheim, Beltz.

Fürntratt, E. and C. Möller (1982) *Lernprinzip Erfolg*, vol. 1, Peter Lang, Frankfurt.

Gallagher-Thompson, D., A. Futterman, N. Farberow, L.A. Thompson and J. Petterson (1993) 'The impact of spousal bereavement on older widows and widowers', in *Handbook of Bereavement: Theory, Research and Intervention* (eds M.S. Stroebe, W. Stroebe and R.O. Hansson), Cambridge University Press, Cambridge, 227–239.

Gander, A.M. (1991) 'After the divorce: Familial factors that predict well-being for older and younger persons', *Journal of Divorce and Remarriage*, 15 (1/2), 175–192.

Garvin, V., N. Kalter and J. Hansell (1993) 'Divorced women: Factors contributing to resiliency and vulnerability', *Journal of Divorce and Remarriage*, 21, (1/2), 21–39.

Giarrusso, R., M. Silverstein and V.L. Bengtson (1996) 'Family complexity and grandparent role', *Generations*, 20 (1), 17–23.

Gibson, E.J. (1991) *An Odyssey in Learning and Perception*, MIT Press, Cambridge, MA.

Gibson, H.B. (1992) *The Emotional and Sexual Life of Older People*, Chapman and Hall, London.

Glick, J. (1975) 'Cognitive development in cross-cultural perspective', in *Review of Child Development Research*, vol. 4 (ed. F.G. Horowitz), University of Chicago Press, Chicago, IL.

Goldscheider, F. and C. (1994) 'Leaving and returning home in 20th century America', *Population Bulletin*, 48 (4), 2–35.

Goldscheider, F., A. Thornton and L. Young-DeMarco (1993) 'A portrait of the nest-leaving process in early adulthood', *Demography*, 30 (4), 683–699.

Golombok, S. and R. Fivush (1994) *Gender Development*, Cambridge University Press, New York, NY.

Gore, S. and J. Eckenrode (1996) 'Context and process in research on risk and resilience', in *Stress, Risk and Resilience in Children and Adolescents* (eds R.J. Haggerty, L.R. Sherrod, N. Garmezy and M. Rutter), Cambridge University Press, Cambridge, 19–63.

Grand, A., P. Grosclaude, H. Boucquet, J. Pous and J.L. Albarede (1988) 'Predictive value of life events, psychosocial factors and self-rated health on disability in an elderly rural French population', *Social Science and Medicine*, 27, 1337–1342.

Gray, C.A. and S.M. Geron (1995) 'The other sorrow of divorce: The effects on grandparents when their adult children divorce', *Journal of Gerontological Social Work*, 23 (3/4), 139–159.

Greer, G. (1991) *The Change: Women, Ageing and the Menopause*, Hamish Hamilton, London.

Greve, W. (2000) 'Sources of resilience: Positive response to crime and punishment', paper presented at the XXVII International Congress of Psychology, Stockholm 23–28 July.

Griffin, C. (1993) *Representations of Youth*, Polity, London.

Gurko, T.A. (1997) 'Parenthood in changing sociocultural conditions', *Russian Education and Society*, 39 (10), 39–53.

Hall, C.S. (1954) *A Primer of Freudian Psychology*, World, New York, NY.

Hamilton, S.F. and N. Darling (1989) 'Mentors in adolescents' lives', in *The Social World of Adolescents* (eds K. Hurrelmann and U. Engel), de Gruyter, New York, NY, 121–141.

Hansen, L.B. and L.B. Jacob (1992) 'Intergenerational support during the transition to parenthood: Issues for new parents and grandparents', *Families in Society: The Journal of Contemporary Human Services*, 73 (8), 471–479.

Hareven, T.K. (1995) 'Changing images of aging and the social construction of the life course', in *Images of Aging* (eds M. Featherstone and A. Wernick), Routledge, London.

Harlow, H.F. and M.K. (1966) 'Learning to love', *American Scientist*, 54, 244–272.

Harlow, H.F. and R.R. Zimmerman (1959) 'Affectional responses in the infant monkey', *Science*, 130, 421–432.

Havighurst, R.J. (1972) *Developmental Tasks and Education*, 3rd edition, McKay, New York, NY.

Havighurst, R.J., B.L. Neugarten and S.S. Tobin (1968) 'Disengagement and patterns of aging', in *Middle Age and Aging: A Reader in Social Psychology* (ed. B.L. Neugarten), University of Chicago Press, Chicago, IL, 161–177.

Hays, B.C. (1994) 'One marriage – two divorces: International comparison of gender differences in attitudes', *International Journal of Public Opinion Research*, 6 (1), 13–34.

Heelas, P., S. Lash and P. Morris (eds) (1996) *Detraditionalization: Critical Reflections on Authority and Identity*, Blackwell, Cambridge.

Hendry, L.B. (1983) *Growing Up and Going Out*, Pergamon, London.

— (1985) 'Young people, school and leisure: Developing metacognitive skills?' Keynote address, Proceedings of the Leisure Studies Association Conference: 'Youth and Leisure', Ilkley, Yorkshire, April 12–14, 21–49.

Hendry, L.B., A. Glendinning, M. Reid and S. Wood (1998) 'Lifestyles, health and health concerns of rural youth: 1996–1998', Report to the Department of Health, Scottish Office, Edinburgh.

Hendry, L.B. and M. Kloep (1996) 'Is there life beyond "flow"?' Proceedings of 5th Biennial Conference of the EARA, University of Liege, May 1996.

Hendry, L.B., M. Kloep and S. Olsson (1998) 'Youth, lifestyles and society', *Childhood*, 5 (2), 133–150.

Hendry, L.B. and M. Raymond (1983) 'Youth unemployment: Leisure and lifestyles', *Scottish Educational Review*, 15 (1), 28–40.

Hendry, L.B. and M. Reid (2000) 'Social relationships and health: The meaning of social "connectedness" and how it relates to health concerns for rural Scottish adolescents', *Journal of Adolescence*, 23 (6), 705–719.

Hendry, L.B., W. Roberts, A. Glendinning and J.C. Coleman (1992) 'Adolescents' perceptions of significant individuals in their lives', *Journal of Adolescence*, 15, 3, 255–270.

Hendry, L.B., J.S. Shucksmith, J. Love and A. Glendinning (1993) *Young People's Leisure and Lifestyles*, Routledge, London.

Hendry, L.B., J.S. Shucksmith and K.L. Philip (1995) *Educating for Health: School and Community Approaches*, Cassell, London.

Henkens, K., M. Sprengers and F. Tazelaar (1996) 'Unemployment and the older worker in The Netherlands: Re-entry into the labour force or resignation', *Ageing and Society*, 16, 561–578.

Henrard, J.C. (1996) 'Cultural problems of ageing especially regarding gender and intergenerational equity', *Social Sciences and Medicine*, 43 (5), 667–680.

Henry, W.E. (1965, 1998) 'Engagement and disengagement: Toward a theory of adult development', in *Essential Papers of Aging* (eds M.P. Lawton and T.A. Salthouse), New York University Press, New York, NY, 56–67.

Hepworth, M. (1991) 'Positive ageing and the mask of age', *Journal of Educational Gerontology*, 6.2, 93–101.

— (1995) 'Change and crisis in mid-life', in *Birth to Old Age: Health in Transition* (ed. B. Davey), Open University Press, Ballmore, 143–154.

Herzog, R. (1991) 'Measurement of vitality in the American's changing live study', *Proceedings of the International Symposium on Aging*, series 5, no. 6, DHHS Publication no. 91-1482, US Department of Health and Human Services, Hyattsville.

Hestbæk, A.D. (1998) 'Parenthood in the 1990s: Tradition and modernity in the parenthood of dual-earner couples with different lifemodes', *Childhood*, 5 (4), 473–491.

Hetherington, E.M. (1989) 'Coping with family transitions: Winners, losers, and survivors', *Child Development*, 60, 1–14.

Hetherington, E.M., T.C. Law and T.G. O'Connor (1997) 'Divorce: Challenges, changes, and new chances', in *Family in Transition* (eds A.S. Skolnick and J.H. Skolnick), 9th edition, Harper Collins, New York, NY, 176–185.

Hiedemann, B., O. Suhomlinova and A.M. O'Rand (1998) 'Economic independence, economic status, and empty nest in midlife marital disruption', *Journal of Marriage and the Family*, 60, 219–231.

Hockey, J. and A. James (1993) *Growing Up and Growing Old*, Sage, London.

— (1995) 'Back to our futures: Imaging second childhood', in *Images of Aging* (eds M. Featherstone and A. Wernick), Routledge, London.

Hogg, M.A. and D. Abrams (1988) *Social Identifications*, Routledge, London.

House, J.S., K.R. Landis and D. Umberson (1988) 'Social relationships and health', *Science*, 241 (4865), 540–545.

House, J.S., J.M. Lepkowski, A.M. Kinney, R.P. Mero, R.C. Kessler and R. Herzog (1994) 'The social stratification of aging and health', *Journal of Health and Social Behavior*, 35, 213–234.

Hunter, A.G. (1997) 'Counting on grandmothers: Black mothers' and fathers' reliance on grandmothers for parenting support', *Journal of Family Issues*, 18 (3), 251–269.

Huston, T.L. and A.L. Vangelisti (1995) 'How parenthood affects marriage', in

Explaining Family Interactions (eds M.A. Fitzpatrick and A.L. Vangelisti), Sage, Newbury Park, CA, 147–176.

Ingebretsen, R. and P.E. Solem (1998) 'Death, dying and bereavement', in *Clinical Geropsychology* (eds I.H. Nordhus, G.R. Vandenos, S. Berg and P. Fromholt), American Psychological Association, 177–181.

International Labour Organisation (1998), 'Statistics on working children and hazardous child labour in brief', Bureau of Statistics, http://www.ilo.org/public/english/comp/child/stat/stats.htm, downloaded 23 January 2001.

Isaacs, M.B. and G.H. Leon (1987) 'Social networks, divorce, and adjustment: A tale of three generations', *Journal of Divorce*, 9 (4), 1–16.

Jackson, S., E. Cicogani and L. Charman (1996) 'The measurement of conflict in parent–adolescent relationships', in *Conflict and Development in Adolescence* (eds L. Verhofstadt-Denève, I. Kienhorst and C. Braet), Psychological Studies, 26, DSWO Press, Leiden.

Jahoda, M. (1979) 'The impact of unemployment in the 1920s and 1970s', CS Myers Lecture, 2, 44–62.

Jahoda, M., P.F. Lazarfield and H. Zeisel (1933) *Marienbad: The Sociography of an Unemployed Community*, Tavistock, London.

Jendrek, M.P. (1994) 'Grandparents who parent their children: circumstances and decisions', *The Gerontological Society of America*, 34 (2), 206–216.

Jensen, A.M. (1994) 'The feminization of childhood', in *Childhood Matters* (eds J. Qvortrup, M. Bardy, G. Sgritta and H. Wintersberger), Aldershot, Avebury.

— (1998) 'Parenthood and childhood in the Scandinavian countries: Challenges of responsibility', *Childhood*, 5 (1), 55–67.

Johnson, K. (1988) 'Active and latent functions of grandparenting during the divorce process', *Gerontologist*, 28, 185–191.

Jones, G. and C. Wallace (1990) 'Jenseits von Individualisierungstendenzen', in *Kindheit und Jugend im Interkulturellen Vergleich* (eds H.H. Krüger and L. Chisholm), Leske and Budrich, Opladen, 125–145.

Jones, J.B. (1997) 'Representations of menopause and their health care implications: A qualitative study', *American Journal of Preventive Medicine*, 13 (1), 58–65.

Kaiser, K. (1990) 'Cross-cultural perspectives on menopause', *Annals of the New York Academy of Sciences*, 592, 430–432.

Karasek, R. and T. Theorell (1990) *Healthy Work: Stress, Productivity, and the Reconstruction of Working Life*, Basic Books, New York, NY.

Kelvin, P. (1981) 'Work as a source of identity: The implications of unemployment', *British Journal of Guidance and Counselling*, 9, 2–11.

King, V. and G.H. Elder Jr (1998) 'Perceived self-efficacy and grandparenting', *The Journals of Gerontology, Psychological and Social Sciences*, 53B (5), 249–257.

Kivett, V.R. (1991) 'Centrality of the grandfather role among older rural black and white men', *The Journals of Gerontology, Psychological and Social Sciences*, 46B (5), 220–258.

Kleiber, D.A. (1999) *Leisure Experience and Human Development: A Dialectical Interpretation*, Basic Books, New York, NY.

Kloep, M. (1982) *Zur Psychologie der Aufgabenschwierigkeit*, Peter Lang, Frankfurt.

— (1994) 'When parents discuss the price of bread', in *Troubling Children* (ed. J. Best), Aldine de Gruyter, New York, NY, 47–65.

— (1998) *Att Vara Ung i Jämtland*, Uddeholt, Österåsen.

— (1999) 'Love is all you need? Focusing on adolescents' life concerns from an ecological point of view', *Journal of Adolescence*, 22, 49–63.

— (2000) 'The Trondheim lifespan study', unpublished document, Norwegian University of Science and Technology (NTNU), Trondheim.

— (2001) 'Young people, school and organized leisure: Over- or underprotected contexts?' Invited lecture at the European Conference about 'Unprotected time. Risks and opportunities for young people (aged 10–15) in the European Union', Alma Mater Foundation, Bologna, 25–27 October.

Kloep, M. and L.B. Hendry (1997) 'In three years we'll be just like Sweden! – Anomie, Albania and university students', *Young*, 5, 2–19.

— (1999a) 'Challenges, risks and coping in adolescence', in *Exploring Developmental Psychology* (eds D. Messer and S. Millar), Arnold, London.

— (1999b) 'Old dog – new tricks? Development in the last phase of life', paper presented at the IXth European Conference on Developmental Psychology, 1–5 September, Spetses, Greece.

Kloep, M., L.B. Hendry, A. Glendinning, J.E. Ingebrigtsen and G.A. Espnes (2001) 'Young people in "drinking societies"? Norwegian, Scottish and Swedish adolescents' perceptions of alcohol use', *Health Education Research*, 16 (3), 279–291.

Kloep, M. and A. Nauni (1994) 'Girls' rebellion against patriarchal society: value change in Albania', in *Youth in a Changing World* (ed. M. Kloep), Report 1994:20, Mitthögskolan, Östersund.

Kloep, M. and F. Tarifa (1992) 'The impact of social support and parental educational style on the depression test scores of Albanian children', paper presented at the 22nd Congress of The European Association of Cognitive and Behaviour Therapy, Coimbra, Portugal.

— (1993a) 'Linking economic hardship to families' lives and children's psychological well-being', *Childhood*, 1, 125–133.

— (1993b) 'Albanian children in the winds of change', in *Human Resource Development* (ed. L.E. Wolvén.), Report 1993: 6, Högskolan i Östersund, 85–116.

Klohnen, E.C., E.A. Vandewater and A. Young (1996) 'Negotiating the middle years: Ego-resiliency and successful midlife adjustment in women', *Psychology and Aging*, 11 (3), 431–442.

Klumb, P.L. and M.M. Baltes (1999) 'Time use of old and very old Berliners: Productive and consumptive activities as functions of resources', *The Journals of Gerontology, Psychological and Social Sciences*, 54B (5), 271–278.

Knudsen, K. and K. Wærness (1996) 'Er ekteskapet som institusjon på vei ut i Skandinavia?' *Tidsskrift for Samfunnsforskning*, 37 (3), 299–327.

Kornhaber, A. and K.L. Woodward (1981) *Grandparents/Grandchildren: The Vital Connection*, Transaction Books, New Brunswick, NJ.

Kousha, M. and N. Mohseni (1997) 'Predictors of life satisfaction among urban Iranian women: An exploratory analysis', *Social Indicators Research*, 40, 329–357.

Kraft, P., S. Breivik, I. Holsen and E. Roysamb (2000) 'Body image and depression: a longitudinal study of adolescents aged 13–18', paper presented at the XXVII International Congress of Psychology, Stockholm, 23–28 July.

Kroger, J. (2000) *Identity Development: Adolescence Through Adulthood*, Sage, London.

Kulik, L. (2000) 'Women face unemployment: A comparative analysis of age groups', *Journal of Career Development*, 27 (1), 15–33.

Labouvie-Vief, G. (1982) 'Dynamic development and mature autonomy', *Human Development*, 25, 186–193.

Lachman, M.E., C. Lewkowicz, A. Marcus and Y. Peng (1994) 'Images of midlife development among young, middle-aged, and older adults', *Journal of Adult Development*, 1 (4), 201–211.

Lang, F.R. and L.L. Carstensen (1994) 'Close emotional relationships in late life: Further support for proactive aging in the social domain', *Psychology and Aging*, 9 (2), 315–324.

Lazarus, R.S. (1993) 'Coping theory and research: Past, present, and future', *Psychosomatic Medicine*, 55, 234–247.

Lee, K.H. (1997) 'Korean women's experience of menopause: New life', *Health Care for Women International*, 18, 139–148.

Lempers, J.D., D. Clark-Lempers and R.L. Simons (1989) 'Economic hardship, parenting, and distress in adolescence', *Child Development*, 60, 25–39.

Leonard, R. and A. Burns (1999) 'Turning points in the lives of midlife and older women', *Australian Psychologist*, 34 (2), 87–93.

Lerner, R.M. (1998) 'Theories of human development', in *Handbook of Child Psychology*, 5th ed., vol. 1 (eds W. Damon and R.M. Lerner), Wiley, New York, NY, 1–24.

Levinson, D.J., with C.N. Darrow, E.B. Klein, M.H. Levinson and B. McKee (1978) *The Seasons of a Man's Life*, Knopf, New York, NY.

Levinson, D.J. (1996) *The Seasons of a Woman's Life*, New York, NY.

Levy, B. (1996) 'Improving memory in old age through implicit self-stereotyping', *Journal of Personality and Social Psychology*, 71, 1092–1106.

Lewin, K. (1943) 'Psychology and the process of group living', *Journal of Social Psychology*, 17, 113–131.

Li, K.Z.H., U. Lindenberger, A.M. Freund and P.B. Baltes (2001) 'Walking while memorizing: Age-related differences in compensatory behaviour', *Psychological Science*, 12 (3), 230–237.

Liao, C. and T.B. Heaton (1992) 'Divorce trends and differentials in China', *Journal of Comparative Family Studies*, 23 (3), 413–429.

Lieberman, M.A. (1992) 'Limitations of psychological stress model: Studies of widowhood', in *Stress and Health Among the Elderly* (eds M.L. Wykle, E. Kahara and J. Kowal), Springer, New York, NY, 133–150.

Liem, J.H. and G.R. (1990) 'Understanding the individual and family effects of unemployment', in *Stress Between Work and Family* (eds J. Eckenrode and S. Gore), Plenum Press, New York, NY, 175–204.

Lock, M. (1998) 'Menopause: Lessons from anthropology', *Psychosomatic Medicine*, 60, 410–419.

Loeber, R. (1985) 'Patterns and development of antisocial child behavior', *Annals of Child Development*, 2, 77–116.

Loevinger, J. (1984) 'On the self and predicting behaviour', in *Personality and the Prediction of Behaviour* (eds R.A. Zucker, J. Aronoff and A.I. Rabin), Academic Press, New York, NY, 43–68.

Longino, C.F. Jr and J.R. Earle (1996) 'Who are the grandparents at century's end?' *Generations*, 20 (1), 13–16.

Lopata, H.Z. (1996) *Current Widowhood: Myths and Realities*, Sage, Thousand Oaks, CA.

Lorenz, F.O., R.L. Simons, R.D. Conger, G.H. Elder Jr, C. Johnson and W. Chao

(1997) 'Married and recently divorced mothers' stressful events and distress: Tracing change across time', *Journal of Marriage and the Family*, 59, 219–232.

Lubben, J.E. (1988) 'Gender differences in the relationship of widowhood and psychological well-being among low income elderly', *Women and Health*, 14 (3), 161–189.

Lund, D.A., M.S. Caserta and M.F. Dimond (1993) 'The course of spousal bereavement in later life', in *Handbook of Bereavement: Theory, Research and Intervention* (eds M.S. Stroebe, W. Stroebe and R.O. Hansson), Cambridge University Press, Cambridge, 240–254.

Løkken, G. (2000) 'Toddler peer culture', Doctoral thesis, Norwegian University of Science and Technology (NTNU), Trondheim.

MacDonald, R. (1997) 'Dangerous youth and the dangerous class', in *Youth, the Underclass and Social Exclusion* (ed R. MacDonald), Routledge, London.

Madison, L.S., J.K. Madison and S.A. Adubato (1986) 'Infant behavior and development in relation to fetal movement and habituation', *Child Development*, 57, 1475–1482.

Maffesoli, M. (1996) *The Time of the Tribes*, Sage, London.

Magnusson, D. and H. Stattin (1998) 'Person-context theories', in *Handbook of Child Psychology*, 5th edition, vol. 1 (eds W. Damon and R.M. Lerner), Wiley, New York, NY.

Mancini, J.A. and, D.M. Sandifer (1995) 'Family dynamics and the leisure experience of older adults: Theoretical viewpoints', in *Handbook of Aging and the Family* (eds R. Bliesznev and V.H. Bedford), Greenwood Press, Westport, CT, 132–147.

Marcia, J.E. (1980) 'Identity in adolescence', in *Handbook of Adolescent Psychology* (ed J. Adelson), Wiley, New York, NY.

— (1996) 'The importance of conflict for adolescent and lifespan development', in *Conflict and Development in Adolescence* (eds L. Verhofstadt-Denève, I. Kienhorst and C. Braet), DSWO Press, Leiden, 13–19.

— (2000) 'Some directions for research on identity in adulthood', paper presented at the XXVII International Congress of Psychology, Stockholm, 23–28 July.

Martin, K.A. (1996) *Puberty, Sexuality, and the Self*, Routledge, London.

Maslow, A.H. (1970) *Motivation and Personality*, 2nd edition, Harper and Row, New York, NY.

Matre, S. (2000) 'Samtaler mellom barn: Om utforskning', *Formidling og Leik i Dialoger*, Det Norske Samlaget, Oslo.

Mayer, K.U., P.B. Baltes, M.M. Baltes, M. Borchelt, J. Delius, H. Helmchen, M. Linden, J. Smith, U.M. Staudinger, E. Steinhagen-Thiessen and M. Wagner (1996) 'Wissen über das Alter(n): Eine Zwischenbilanz der Berliner Altersstudie', in *Die Berliner Altersstudie* (eds K.U. Mayer and P.B. Baltes), Akademie Verlag, Berlin.

McClelland, D.C., J.W. Atkinson, R.A. Clark and E.L. Lowell (1953) *The Achievement Motive*, Appleton-Century-Crofts, New York, NY.

McCrae, R.R. and P.T. Costa Jr (1993) 'Psychological resilience among widowed men and women: A 10-year follow-up of a national sample', in *Handbook of Bereavement* (eds M.S. Stroebe, W. Stroebe and R.O. Hansson), Cambridge University Press, Cambridge, 196–207.

McGreal, C.E. (1994) 'The family across generations: Grandparenthood', in *Family Psychology and Psychopathology* (ed. L. L'Abate), John Wiley, New York, NY, 116–131.

McKenry, P.C. and S.J. Price (1991) 'Alternatives for support: Life after divorce: A literature review', *Journal of Divorce and Remarriage*, 15 (3/4), 1–19.

McMamish-Svensson, C., G. Samuelson, B. Hagberg, T. Svensson and O. Dehlin (1999) 'Social relationships and health as predictors of life satisfaction in advanced old age: Results from a Swedish longitudinal study', *International Journal of Aging and Human Development*, 48 (4), 301–324.

McMullin, J.A. and V.W. Marshall (1996) 'Family, stress and well-being: Does childlessness make a difference?' *Canadian Journal of Aging*, 15 (3), 355–373.

McRobbie, A. (1994) *Postmodernism and Popular Culture*, Routledge, London.

Mead, G. (1934) *Mind, Self and Society*, Chicago University Press, Chicago, IL.

Mexico News (2000) 'Tax evasion in Mexico's informal economy totals 7.75 billion dollars', 28 October, http://www.quespasa.com, downloaded 16 January 2001.

Miletti, M.A. (1984) *Voices of Experience: 1500 Retired People Talk About Retirement*, TIAA, New York, NY.

Moen, P., E.L. Kain and G.H. Elder Jr (1983) 'Economic conditions and family life: Contemporary and historical perspectives', in *American Families and the Economy* (eds R.N. Nelson and F. Skidmore), National Academy Press, Washington, DC, 213–254.

Mohapatra, M. (2001) 'Childhood and gender bias in India: A comparative perspective over time and space', paper presented at 'Children and young people in a changing world' conference, Agrigento, Italy, 9–16 June.

Montepare, J.M. (1991) 'Characteristics and psychological correlates of young adult men's and women's subjective age', *Sex Roles*, 24 (5/6), 323–333.

Montepare, J.M. and M.E. Lachman (1989) '"You're only as old as you feel": Self-perceptions of age, fear of aging, and life satisfaction from adolescence to old age', *Psychology and Aging*, 4 (1), 73–78.

Morgan, L. (1989) 'Economic well-being following marital termination', *Journal of Family Issues*, 10 (1), 86–101.

Morrow-Kondos, D., J.A. Weber, K. Cooper, and J.L. Hesser, (1997) 'Becoming parents again: Grandparents raising grandchildren', *Journal of Gerontological Social Work*, 28 (1–2), 35–46.

Mossey, J.M. and E. Shapiro (1982) 'Self-rated health: a predictor of mortality among the elderly', *American Journal of Public Health*, 72, 800–808.

Myers, J.E. and N. Perrin (1993) 'Grandparents affected by parental divorce: A population at risk', *Journal of Counseling and Development*, 72, 62–66.

Nauni, A.P. (1999) 'Migration, identity and adaptation: The case of Kosova Albanian youths and their parents in Oslo', unpublished thesis, University of Oslo, Department for Sociology and Social Geography, Oslo.

Näsström, C. and M. Kloep (1994) 'The effect of job practising on the psychological well-being of unemployed youth', in *Young People and Work* (eds M.F. Gamberale and T. Hagström), Arbete och hälsa, 33, Arbetsmiljöinstituttet, Solna.

Neugarten, B.L. (1968) 'Adult personality: Toward a psychology of the life cycle', in *Middle Age and Aging: A Reader in Social Psychology* (ed. B.L. Neugarten), University of Chicago Press, Chicago, IL, 137–147.

Neves, F. (1999) 'Making do', Brazzil, June, http://www.brazzil.com/cvr-jun99.htm, downloaded 16 January 2001.

Newton, R.L. and P.M. Keith (1997) 'Single women in later life', in *Handbook on Women and Aging* (ed J.M. Coyle), Greenwood Press, Westport, CT, 385–399.

Niebor, A.P. (1997) 'Life-events and well-being: A prospective study on changes in well-being of elderly people due to a serious illness event or death of the spouse', Thesis Publishers, Amsterdam.

Nisbet, J. and J. Shucksmith (1984) *Learning Strategies*, Routledge and Kegan Paul, London.

O'Bryant, S.L. (1991) 'Forewarning of a husband's death: Does it make a difference for older widows?' *Omega*, 22 (3), 227–239.

Oldman, D. (1994) 'Adult–child relations as class-relations', in *Childhood Matters* (eds J. Qvortrup, M. Bardy, G. Sgritta and H. Winterberger), Aldershot, Avebury.

Palinkas, L.A. (1992) 'Going to extremes: The cultural context of stress, illness and coping in Antarctica', *Social Science and Medicine*, 35 (5), 651–664.

Palkovitz, R. (1996) 'Parenting as a generator for adult development: Conceptual issues and implications', *Journal of Social and Personal Relationships*, 13 (4), 571–592.

Palmlund, I. (1997) 'The social construction of menopause as risk', *Journal of Psychosomatic Obstetrics and Gynecology*, 18, 87–94.

Papastefanou, C. (1999) 'Adult daughters' relationships with their parents and their leaving home in three different countries', paper presented at the IXth European Conference on Developmental Psychology, 1–5 September, Spetses, Greece.

Pape, H. and T. Hammer (1996) 'Sober adolescence – Predictor of psychosocial maladjustment in young adulthood?' *Scandinavian Journal of Psychology*, 37, 4, 362–377.

Parker, H., J. Aldridge and F. Measham (1998) *Illegal Leisure*, Routledge, London.

Parten, M.B. (1932) 'Social participation among pre-school children', *Journal of Abnormal and Social Psychology*, 27, 243–269.

Patterson, G.R. (1996) 'Some characteristics of a developmental theory of early-onset delinquency', in *Frontiers of Developmental Psychopathology* (eds M.F. Lenzenweger and J.J. Haugaard), Oxford University Press, New York, NY, 81–124.

Pavis, S., S. Cunningham-Burley and A. Amos (1997) 'Alcohol consumption and young people', *Health Education Research*, 12, 311–322.

Pearlin, L.I. and J.T. Mullan (1992) 'Loss and stress in aging', in *Stress and Health Among the Elderly* (eds M. L. Wykle, E. Kahara and J. Kowal), Springer, New York, NY, 117–132.

Penninx, B.W.J.H., T. van Tilburg, A.J.P. Boeke, D.J.H. Deeg, D.M.W. Kriegsman and T.M. van Eijk (1998) 'Effects of social support and coping resources on depressive symptoms: Different for various chronic diseases?' *Health Psychology*, 17, 551–558.

Penninx, B.W.J.H., T. van Tilburg, D.J.H. Deeg, D.M.W. Kriegsman, A.J.P. Boeke, and J.T.M. van Eijk (1997a) 'Direct and buffer effects of social support and personal coping resources in individuals with arthritis', *Social Sciences and Medicine*, 44, 393–402.

— (1997b) 'Effects of social support and personal coping resources on mortality in older age: The longitudinal aging study Amsterdam', *American Journal of Epidemiology*, 146 (6), 510–519.

Philip, K. and L.B. Hendry (1996) 'Young people and mentoring – towards a typology', *Journal of Adolescence*, 19, 189–201.

— (2000) 'Making sense of mentoring or mentoring making sense? Reflections on the mentoring process by adult mentors with young people', *Journal of Community and Applied Psychology*, 10, 211–223.

Phoenix, A. (1991) *Young Mothers*, Polity, London.

Piaget, J. (1964) 'Development and learning', in *Piaget Rediscovered* (eds R. Ripple and V. Rockcastle), Cornell University Press, Ithaca, NY.

— (1970) 'Piaget's theory', in *Handbook of Child Psychology*, 4th edition, (ed. P.H. Mussen), Wiley, New York, NY.

Pickard, S. (1994) 'Life after a death: The experience of bereavement in South Wales', *Ageing and Society*, 14, 191–217.

Pijls, L.T.J., E.J.M. Feskens and D. Kromhout (1993) 'Self-rated health, mortality, and chronic diseases in elderly men. The Zutphen Study, 1985–1990', *American Journal of Epidemiology*, 138 (10), 840–848.

Pillay, A.L. (1988) 'Midlife depression and the empty nest syndrome in Indian women', *Psychological Reports*, 63 (2), 591–594.

Pledge, D.S. (1992) 'Marital separation/divorce: A review of individual responses to a major life stressor', *Journal of Divorce and Remarriage*, 17 (3/4), 151–181.

Porter, M., G.C. Penney, D. Russell, E. Russell and A. Templeton (1996) 'A population based survey of women's experience of the menopause', *British Journal of Obstetrics and Gynaecology*, 103, 1025–1028.

Pruchno, R. (1999) 'Raising grandchildren: The experience of black and white grandmothers', *The Gerontologist*, 39 (2), 209–221.

Pruchno, R.A. and K.W. Johnson (1996) 'Research on grandparenting: Review of current studies and future needs', *Generations*, 20 (1), 65–70.

Quinton, D. and M. Rutter (1988) *Parenting Breakdown: The Making and Breaking of Intergenerational Links*, Avebury, Aldershot.

Qvortrup, J. (1994) 'Childhood matters: An introduction', in *Childhood Matters* (eds J. Qvortrup, M. Bardy, G. Sgritta and H. Wintersberger), Aldershot, Avebury, 1–23.

— (2000) 'Macroanalysis of childhood', in *Research with Children: Perspectives and Practices* (eds P. Christensen and A. James), Falmer Press, London, 77–97.

— (2001, forthcoming) 'Sociology of childhood: Conceptual liberation of children', in *Childhood and Children's Culture* (eds F. Mauritsen and J. Qvortrup), Odense University Press, Odense.

Riegel, K. (1979) *Foundations of Dialectical Psychology*, Academic Press, New York, NY.

Rietveld, H. (1994) 'Living the Dream', in *Rave Off: Politics and Deviance in Contemporary Youth Culture* (ed. S. Redehead), Aldershot, Avebury, ch. 4.

Robertson, J.F. (1995) 'Grandparenting in an era of rapid change', in *Handbook of Aging and the Family* (eds R. Blieszner and V.H. Bedford), Greenwood Press, Westport, CT, 243–260.

Robinson, G. (1996) 'Cross-cultural perspectives on menopause', *Journal of Nervous and Mental Diseases*, 184 (8), 453–458.

Rogers, C.R. (1961) *On Becoming a Person*, Houghton Mifflin, Boston, MA.

Roos, N.P. and B. Havens (1991) 'Predictors of successful aging: A twelve-year study of Manitoba elderly', *American Journal of Public Health*, 81 (1), 63–68.

Rossi, G. (1997) 'The nestlings: Why young adults stay at home longer: The Italian case', *Journal of Family Issues*, 18, 627–644.

Rotter, J. (1966) 'Generalized expectancies for internal versus external control of reinforcement', *Psychological Monographs*, 80, 1–28.

Rowe, J.W. and R.L. Kahn (1997) 'Successful aging', *The Gerontological Society of America*, 37 (4), 433–440.

Ruth, J.E. and P. Coleman (1997) 'Personality and aging: Coping and management of the self in later life', in H*andbook of the Psychology of Aging* (eds J.E. Birren and K.W. Schaie), 4th edition, Academic Press, New York, NY, 308–322.

Rutter, M. (1987) 'Psychososcial resilience and protective mechanisms', *American Journal of Orthopsychiatry*, 57, 316–331.

— (1996) 'Psychological adversity: risk, resilience and recovery', in *Conflict and Development in Adolescence* (eds L. Verhofstadt-Denève, I. Kienhorst and C. Braet), DSWO Press, Leiden, 21–34.

— (2000) 'Environmental influences on child psychopathology: Some challenges and some solutions', paper presented at the Millennium Conference on Current Knowledge on Childhood and Youth: Challenges and dilemmas, 11 February, University of Stockholm.

Salahu-Din, S. (1996) 'A comparison of coping strategies of African American and Caucasian widows', *Omega*, 2, 103–120.

Salmela-Aro, K. and J.E. Nurmi (1996) 'Uncertainty and confidence in interpersonal projects: Consequences for social relationships and well-being', *Journal of Social and Personal Relationships*, 13 (1), 109–122.

Salthouse, T.A. and T.J. Maurer (1997) 'Aging, job performance, and career development', in *Handbook of the Psychology of Aging* (eds J.E. Birren and K.W. Schaie), Academic Press, New York, NY, 353–364.

Sander, E. (1993) 'Die Situation des Alleinerziehens aus der Sicht betroffener Mütter – Vergleich einer Fragebogen- und Interviewstudie', *Psychologie in Erziehung und Unterricht*, 40 (4), 241–248.

Sander, E. and S. Draschoff (2000) 'Evaluation of an interactive learning program for trigonometry tasks', paper presented at the XXVII International Conference of Psychology, 23–28 July, Stockholm.

Schaie, K.W. (1996) *Intellectual Development in Adulthood: The Seattle Longitudinal Study*, Cambridge University Press, New York, NY.

Scheibel, A.B. (1997) 'Structural and functional changes in the aging brain', in *Handbook of the Psychology of Aging* (eds J.E. Birren and K.W. Schaie), Academic Press, New York, NY, 4th edition, 105–128.

Schrumpf, E. (2000) 'Slave eller selvstendig? Om barnearbeid og barndom før og nå', *Barn*, 18 (2), 7–19.

Schuchts, R.A. and S.L. Witkin (1989) 'Assessing marital change during the transition to parenthood', *Social Casework: The Journal of Contemporary Social Work*, 70 (2), 67–75.

Scraton, S.J. (1986) 'Images of femininity and the teaching of girls' physical education', in *Physical Education, Sport, and Schooling* (ed. J. Evans), Falmer Press, London.

Seavey, A.A., P.A. Katz and S.R. Zalk (1975) 'Baby X: The effect of gender labels on adult responses to infants', *Sex Roles*, 1, 103–109.

Seeman, T.E. (1994) 'Successful aging: Reconceptualizing the aging process from a more positive perspective', in *Facts and Research in Gerontology: Epidemiology and Aging* (eds B.J. Vellas, J.L. Albarede and P.J. Garry), Serdi, Paris, 61–73.

Seeman, T.E., J.B. Unger, G. McAvay and C.F. Mendes de Leon (1999) 'Self-efficacy beliefs and perceived declines in functional ability: MacArthur studies of successful aging', *The Journals of Gerontology, Psychological and Social Sciences*, 54B (4), 214–222.

Seltzer, M.M. and C.D. Ryff (1994) 'Parenting across the life-span: The normative and non-normative cases', in *Life-span Development and Behavior* (eds D.L. Featherman, R.M. Lerner and M. Perlmutter), Lawrence Erlbaum Associates, Hillsdale, NJ, 1–40.

Sharp, D. and G. Lowe (1989) 'Adolescents and alcohol – a review of the recent British research', *Journal of Adolescence*, 12, 295–307.

Shaw, S.M. (1994) 'Gender, leisure and constraint: Towards a framework for the analysis of women's leisure', *Journal of Leisure Research*, 26 (1), 8–22.

Shaw, S.M., D.A. Kleiber and L.L. Caldwell (1995) 'Leisure and identity formation in male and female adolescents: A preliminary examination', *Journal of Leisure Research*, 27 (3), 245–263.

Shek, D.T.L. (1996) 'Midlife crisis in Chinese men and women', *Journal of Psychology*, 130 (1), 109–119.

Shimamura, A.P., J.M. Berry, J.A. Mangels, C.L. Rusting and P.J. Jurica (1995) 'Memory and cognitive abilities in university professors – evidence for successful aging', *Psychological Science*, 6 (5), 271–277.

Shucksmith, J and L.B. Hendry (1998) *Health Issues and Young People: Growing Up and Speaking Out*, Routledge, London.

Silbereisen, R.K., S. Walper and H.T. Albrecht (1990) 'Family income loss and economic hardship: Antecedents of adolescents' problem behavior', *New Directions in Child Development*, 46, 27–47.

Singer, D. and M. Hunter (1999) 'The experience of premature menopause: A thematic discourse analysis', *Journal of Reproductive and Infant Psychology*, 17 (1), 63–81.

Skinner, B.F. (1938) *The Behavior of Organisms*, Appleton, New York, NY.

— (1957) *Verbal Behavior*, Appleton, New York, NY.

— (1983) 'Intellectual self-management in old age', *American Psychologist*, 38, 239–244.

Skinner, M.L., G.H. Elder Jr and R.D. Conger (1992) 'Linking economic hardship to adolescent aggression', *Journal of Youth and Adolescence*, 21, 259–276.

Smith, J. and P.B. Baltes (1999) 'Life-span perspectives on development', in *Developmental Psychology* (eds M.H. Bornstein and M.E. Lamb), 4th edition, Lawrence Erlbaum Associates, Hillsdale, NJ, 47–72.

Solivetti, L.M. (1994) 'Family, marriage and divorce in a Hausa community: A sociological model', *Africa*, 64 (2), 252–271.

South, S.J. and K.M. Lloyd (1995) 'Spousal alternatives and marital dissolution', *American Sociological Review*, 60, 21–35.

Spencer, J.P., B. Vereijken, F.J. Diedrich and E. Thelen (2000) 'Posture and the emergence of manual skills', *Developmental Science*, 3 (2), 216–233.

Spielberger, C.D. (1966) *Anxiety and Behaviour*, Academic Press, London.

Stacey, M., R. Dearden, R. Pill and D. Robinson (1970) *Hospitals, Children and their Families: The Report of a Pilot Study*, Routledge and Kegan Paul, London.

Stattin, H. and M. Kerr (2000) 'Parental monitoring: A reinterpretation', *Child Development*, 71, 1070–1083.

Stattin, H. and D. Magnusson (1990) *Paths Through Life, Volume 2: Pubertal Maturation in Female Development*, Lawrence Erlbaum Associates, Hillsdale, NJ.

Staudinger, U.M. (1999) 'Older and wiser? Integrating results on the relationship between age and wisdom-related performance', *International Journal of Behavioral Development*, 23 (3), 641–664.

— (2000) 'Wisdom and the art of life', paper presented at the XXVII International Congress of Psychology, Stockholm, 23–28 July.

Staudinger, U.M. and P.B. Baltes (1996) 'The psychology of wisdom', *Psychologische Rundschau*, 47 (2), 57–77.

Staudinger, U.M. and A. Freund (1998) 'Krank und "arm" im hohen Alter und trotzdem guten Mutes?' *Zeitschrift für Klinische Psychologie*, 27, 78–85.

Stephen, J., E. Fraser and J.E. Marcia (1992) 'Moratorium-achievement (Mama) cycles in lifespan identity development: Value orientations and reasoning system correlates', *Journal of Adolescence*, 15, 283–300.

Stevens, N. (1995) 'Gender and adaptation to widowhood in later life', *Ageing and Society*, 15, 37–58.

Stewart, A.J. and J.M. Ostrove (1998) 'Women's personality in middle age: Gender, history, and midcourse corrections', *American Psychologist*, 53 (11), 1185–1194.

Stroebe, W. and M.S. (1993) 'Determinants of adjustment to bereavement in younger widows and widowers', in *Handbook of Bereavement* (eds M.S. Stroebe, W. Stroebe and R.O. Hansson), Cambridge University Press, Cambridge, 208–226.

Sutton-Smith, B. and R.E. Heron (1971) *Child's Play*, Wiley, New York, NY.

Swaab, D.F. (1991) 'Brain aging and Alzheimer's disease: "Wear and tear" versus "use it or lose it"', *Neurobiology of Aging*, 12 (4), 352–355.

Swanson, J.L. (1992) 'Vocational behavior, 1989–1991: Life-span career development and reciprocal interaction of work and nonwork', *Journal of Vocational Behavior*, 41, 101–161.

Takeuchi, D.T., D.R. Williams and R.K. Adair (1991) 'Economic stress in the family and children's emotional and behavioral problems', *Journal of Marriage and the Family*, 53, 1031–1041.

Thelen, E. (1983) 'Learning to walk is still an "old" problem: A reply to Zelazo', *Journal of Motor Behavior*, 15, (2), 131–161.

— (1984) 'Learning to walk: Ecological demands and phylogenetic constraints', in *Advances in Infancy Research*, vol. 3, (eds L.P. Lipsitt and C. Rovee-Collier), Ablex, Norwood, NJ.

Thelen, E. and D.M. Fisher (1982) 'Newborn stepping: An explanation for a "disappearing reflex"', *Developmental Psychology*, 18, 760–775.

Thelen, E., D.M. Fisher, R. Ridley-Johnson and N.J. Griffin (1982) 'The effects of body build and arousal on newborn infant stepping', *Developmental Psychology*, 15, 447–453.

Thelen, E. and L.B. Smith (1998) *A Dynamic Systems Approach to the Development of Cognition and Action*, 3rd edition, MIT Press, Cambridge, MA.

Theodossiou, I. (1998) 'The effects of low-pay and unemployment on psychological well-being: a logistic regression approach', *Journal of Health Economics*, 17 (1), 85–104.

Thomas, J.L. (1994) 'Older men as fathers and grandfathers', in *Older Men's Lives* (ed. E.H. Thompson Jr), Sage, Newbury Park, CA, 197–217.

Thompson, L.W., D. Gallagher-Thompson, A. Futterman, M.J. Gilewski and J. Peterson (1998) 'The effects of late-life spousal bereavement over a thirty-month interval', in *Essential Papers on the Psychology of Aging* (eds

M.P. Lawton and T.A. Salthouse), New York University Press, New York, NY, 722–738.

Thornton, A., L. Young-DeMarco and F. Goldscheider (1993) 'Leaving the parental nest: The experience of a young white cohort in the 1980s', *Journal of Marriage and the Family*, 55, 216–229.

Thornton, S. (1995) *Club Cultures: Music, Media and Subcultural Capital*, Polity, London.

— (1997) 'The social logic of subcultural capital', in *The Subcultures Reader* (eds K. Gelder and S. Thornton), Routledge, London.

Thorsen, K. (1998) *Kjønn, Livsløp og Alderdom*, Fagbokforlaget, Bergen.

Tikoo, M. (1996) 'An explanatory study of differences in developmental concerns of middle-aged men and women in India', *Psychological Reports*, 78 (3), 883–887.

Timberlake, E.M. and S.S. Chipungu (1992) 'Grandmotherhood: Contemporary meaning among African American middle-class grand-mothers', *Social Work*, 37 (3), 216–222.

Toledo de Paula, A.G., K.R. Pinto de Castro, P.M. Prestes dos Reis, C.M.E. Berthoud and A. Leônidas de Oliveira (2000) '"Adultescence": Is this the new meaning of adulthood in our contemporary social context? – A Brazilian study', poster presented at the XXVII International Congress of Psychology, Stockholm, 23–28 July.

Trent, K. and S.J. South (1989) 'Structural determinants of the divorce rate: A cross-societal analysis', *Journal of Marriage and the Family*, 51, 391–404.

Trost, K., H. Stattin and M. Kerr (2000) 'The importance of communication in parenting', poster presentation at the XXVII International Conference of Psychology, 23–28 July, Stockholm.

Tschann, J.M., J.R. Johnston and J.S. Wallerstein (1989) 'Resources, stressors, and attachment as predictors of adult adjustment after divorce: A longitudinal study', *Journal of Marriage and the Family*, 51 (4), 1033–1046.

UNICEF (2000a) *The State of the World's Children 2001*, Oxford University Press, Oxford.

— (2000b) *A League Table of Child Poverty in Rich Nations*, Florence.

Uotinen, V. (1998) 'Age identification: A comparison between Finnish and North-American cultures', *International Journal of Aging and Human Development*, 46 (2), 109–124.

Vaillant, G.E. (1994) '"Successful aging" and psychological well-being: Evidence from a 45-year study', in *Older Men's Lives* (ed. E.H. Thompson Jr), Sage, New York, NY, 22–41.

Vaknin, S. (2000) 'The blessings of the informal economy', *Central Europe Review*, 2 (40), http://www.ce-review.org/00/40/vaknin40.html, down-loaded 16 January 2001.

Valsiner, J. (1997) *Culture and the Development of Children's Action: A Theory of Human Development*, 2nd edition, Wiley, New York, NY.

Valsiner, J, and R.B. Cairns (1992) 'Theoretical perspectives on conflict and development', in *Conflict in Child and Adolescent Development* (eds C.U. Shantz and W.W. Hartrup), Cambridge University Press, Cambridge, 15–35.

Van den Boom, D.C. and J.B. Hoeksma (1994) 'The effect of infant irritability on mother–infant interaction – a growth-curve analysis', *Developmental Psychology*, 30 (4), 581–590.

Van der Meer, A.L.H. (1997a) 'Keeping the arm in the limelight: Advanced visual control of arm movements in neonates', *European Journal of Paediatric Neurology*, 4, 103–108.
— (1997b) 'Nyfødte vet hva de gjør', in *Noen Deler Viten* (eds N.E. Tveter and T. Kvenild), NTNU, Trondheim, 86–88.
Van der Meer, A.L.H., F.R. van der Weel and D.N. Lee (1995) 'The functional significance of arm movements in neonates', *Science*, 267, 693–695.
— (1996) 'Lifting weights in neonates: Developing visual control of reaching', *Scandinavian Journal of Psychology*, 37, 424–436.
Van der Molen, M.W. and K.R. Ridderinkhof (1998) 'The growing and aging brain: Life-span changes in brain and cognitive functioning', in *Life-span Developmental Psychology* (eds A. Demetriou, W. Doise and C. van Lieshout), Wiley, Chichester, 35–99.
Veevers, J.E. (1991) 'Traumas versus stress: A paradigm of positive versus negative divorce outcomes', *Journal of Divorce and Remarriage*, 15 (1/2), 99–126.
Vereijken, B. and K. Adolph (1997) 'Transitions in the development of loco-motion, in non-linear developmental processes', *Proceedings from the Colloquium, Amsterdam, 29–31 January* (eds G. Savelsbergh, H. van der Maas and P. van Geert), Royal Netherlands Academy of Arts and Science, Amsterdam.
Vereijken, B. and E. Thelen (1997) 'Training infant treadmill stepping: The role of individual pattern stability', *Developmental Psychology*, 30 (2), 89–102.
Voran, M.J. (1991) 'Grandmother social support to adolescent mothers: cor-relates of support and adolescents' satisfaction', unpublished dissertation, University of Virginia, VA.
Vygotsky, L.S. (1930) 'Tool and symbol in children's development', in *L.S. Vygotsky: Mind in Society* (eds M. Cole, V. John-Steiner, S. Scribner and E. Souberman), Harvard University Press, Cambridge, MA.
Walsh, S. and P.R. Jackson (1995) 'Partner support and gender: Contexts for coping with job loss', *Journal of Occupational and Organizational Psychology*, 68, 253–268.
Watkins, D. *et al.* (1998) 'Cultural dimensions, gender, and the nature of self-concept: A fourteen country study', *International Journal of Psychology*, 33 (1), 17–31.
Watson, J.A. (1997) 'Grandmothering across the lifespan', *Journal of Gerontological Social Work*, 28 (4), 45–62.
Watson, J.A. and S.A. Koblinsky (1997) 'Strengths and needs of working class African-American and Anglo-American grandparents', *International Journal of Aging and Human Development*, 44 (2), 149–165.
Watson, W.J., L. Watson, W. Wetzel, E. Bader and Y. Talbot (1995) 'Transition to parenthood: What about fathers?' *Canadian Family Physician*, 41, 807–812.
Weiner, B. (1972) *Theories of Motivation*, University of Chicago Press, Chicago, IL.
Welford, A.T. (1968) *Fundamentals of Skill*, Methuen, London.
Werner, E.E. (1990) 'Protective factors and individual resilience', in *Handbook of Early Intervention* (eds S.J. Meisels, and J.P. Shonkoff), Cambridge University Press, Boston, MA, 97–116.
Werner, E.E. and R.S. Smith (1982) *Vulnerable but Invincible*, McGraw Hill, New York, NY (Reprint Adams, Bannister, Cox, 1989).

— (1992) *Overcoming the Odds: High Risk Children from Birth to Adulthood*, Cornell University Press, Ithaca, NY, and London.

Whitbourne, S.K., J.R. Sneed and K.M. Skultety (2001, forthcoming) 'Identity processes in adulthood: Theoretical and methodological challenges', *Identity: An International Journal of Theory and Research*.

Wichstrøm, L. (1999) 'The emergence of gender difference in depressed mood during adolescence: The role of intensified gender socialization', *Developmental Psychology*, 35 (1), 232–245.

Wilbur, J.E., A. Miller and A. Montgomery (1995) 'The influence of demographic characteristics, menopausal status, and symptoms on women's attitudes towards menopause', *Women & Health*, 23 (3), 19–39.

Willis, P.E. (1977) *Learning to Labour*, Saxon House, Farnborough.

Wolvén, L.E. (1990) *Jakten på det goda livet – om konsten att fånga välfärd och livskvalitet*, Rabén & Sjögren, Stockholm.

Woodroffe, C, M. Glickman, M. Barker and C. Power (1993) *Children, Teenagers and Health: The Key Data*, Open University Press, Buckingham.

Wortman, C.B., R.C. Silver and R.C. Kessler (1993) 'The meaning of loss and adjustment to bereavement', in *Handbook of Bereavement: Theory, Research and Intervention* (eds M.S. Stroebe, W. Stroebe and R.O. Hansson), Cambridge University Press, Cambridge, 349–365.

Wyn, J. and R. White (1998) 'Young people, social problems and youth studies', *Journal of Youth Studies*, 1 (1), 23–39.

Zinnecker, J. (1990) 'Vom Strassenkind zum verhäuslichten Kind. Kindheitsgeschichte im Prozess der Zivilisation', in *Stadtgesellschaft und Kindheit im Prozess der Zivilisation* (ed. I. Behnke), Leske und Budrich, Opladen, 142–162.

Zinnecker, J. (1991) 'Untersuchungen zum Wandel von Jugend in Europa', in *Osteuropäische Jugend im Wandel* (eds W. Melzer, W. Heitmeyer, L. Liegle and J. Zinnecker), Juventa Verlag, Weinheim, 121–136.

Zisook, S., S.R. Shuchter, P. Sledge and M. Mulvihill (1993) 'Aging and bereavement', *Journal of Geriatric Psychiatry and Neurology*, 6, 137–143.

Zuckerman, A. (1979) *Sensation-seeking: Beyond the Optimal Level of Arousal*, Wiley, New York, NY.

Index of names

Note: page numbers in italics refer to authors appearing as '*et al.*' on the corresponding page.

I ndex of subjects